ELVIS LI

The Business of Being Elvis

By Pamela Thomas-Williams
Interview transcribing by Cindy Rose
Proofing and Editorial Assistance by Kay Robinson

Cover Design by Jason Cozy, Website Design by Jen Petrillo;
Webmaster: William Feltes

**Front cover photos are Martin Fontaine in The Elvis Story
production provided with permission by LCQ Productions.
Back cover photos are of Ryan Pelton,
Brandon Bennett, and Garry Wesley**

*Elvis Presley, Elvis Presley Enterprises, and Graceland
are registered trademarks*

Books by Pamela, Ltd.
www.pamelaltd.com
P.O.Box 2091
La Crosse, WI 54602-2091

ELVIS LIVES
The Business of Being Elvis

First printing July 2003   First edition   July 2003

Library of Congress Catalogue Number: 2002096806
SAN: 697-0729
SAN: 697-0737
ISBN: 0-9703882-2-5

All photos were provided with permission from the entertainers, managers, agents, or were obtained at various venues, contests, and shows, which are the personal property of Books By Pamela, Ltd. The quantity, quality, and size of the photographs is determined by the materials provided.

Printed in the United States of America

Dedicated to my family with love

Richard G. Williams; my husband, my strength, my friend, my love, best photographer and Elvis fan
My mother, Betty Thomas, also a great Elvis fan.

To my father, Dale, and my sister, Kim who are no longer with us on this earth. I hope that you are both still sharing your musical talents in heaven.

My precious nephews Nicholas and Christopher West, and my niece Brittany West

To all my friends that have put up with me throughout this long project, thank-you for your much appreciated moral support.

Special thanks to: William ("The Great Oz") Feltes, my friend and computer doctor who literally kept the project going (Cheryl too). Cindy Rose, Bruce ("Mushy") Mashak, Kay Robinson, Ingrid Brindley, Claudia Schwaegerl and "Jimmy," The Gayles, Dennis Roesler (Debbie), Gary Arentz, Little Linda, Patty Craig & Diane Gitzlaff—"The lawyer girls," Suzie Rogan-Menozi, Mary Messer, Jeff Moen, Lois Moen, Kris Harring, Don Cross, Rhona Lindsay-Payne, Walter Kuehnl—"The Molly's Gang," Kym Lewandowski, Sharon Roesler, Liz Walton, Jessica Baken, Troy Drake, Kyle Prentice (Deb), and Mary Greener.

To Elvis Aaron Presley, The King of Rock and Roll

"Only those who can see the Invisible, can do the Impossible."

—Anonymous

About the Author

A graduate in journalism from Marquette University, Pamela Thomas-Williams has been employed as a copywriter for a variety of advertising agencies, including her own. A winner of several advertising and achievement awards, she has also been listed in several editions of **Marquis Who's Who**, including **Who's Who of American Women, Who's Who of American Writers, Who's Who in America,** and most recently, **Who's Who in the World 2003.** She has written numerous articles for a variety of publications.

Pamela is the author of **The Bride's Guide, the Complete Guide to Planning Your Wedding**, now in its 7th edition with nearly 200,000 copies sold; the Spanish translation of that book titled **Guia Nupcial**; **Wedding Showers for Couples**; and **From My Pallet of Winter, Let Me Paint You Spring**, a poetry book.

Though Pamela's long-range plans still include a novel or two, the idea of writing about the people who follow the biggest icon in the world, Elvis Presley, was just too interesting to pass up. She never dreamed that her father, a self-taught, talented musician and entertainer who was also a huge Elvis fan, would have such an influence on her.

"The music was just always there, around the house, everywhere. My mother liked to sing and so did my sister. I couldn't carry a note with a co-signer. Nearly everyday I ask myself; who would believe that I would ever be writing a book about Elvis entertainers? At least I can honestly say I understand why, for a variety of reasons, so many people were inspired by Elvis Presley."

Table of Contents

Disclaimer

ELVIS LIVES—The Business of Being Elvis, is written with the intent of giving the reader an idea of what goes on in a world full of people that continue to follow, respect, and pay tribute to Elvis Presley. It is not an encyclopedia, anthology, or biography. The information obtained for this book was derived primarily by individual interviews, public information, and Internet access.

The author and publisher shall have neither liability nor responsibility to any person or entity with respect to any loss or damage caused, or alleged to be caused, directly or indirectly, by the information contained within this book.

The Business of Being Elvis is a huge business. It was not possible to talk to every single person. Many people were just too difficult to reach. In fact, given another year to work on this book, there would be much more information in this book. Maybe there is room for a sequel. It is important that the reader, as well as those who were interviewed and published herein, realize that accuracy, fairness, and interest relative to the subject matter was the criteria for the content.

Introduction

The critics are already out there. I'm not one of them.

"So," you ask, "What's the point?"

In the 25 years since the passing of Elvis Aaron Presley, the world he left behind has changed considerably. At the same time, try to understand the continued, and growing, popularity of the King of Rock 'n' Roll. Could this be the reason that it is claimed there may be 35,000 Elvis impersonators in the world?

According to *Forbes 2002*, Presley is ranked the number one deceased celebrity in earnings. Sales of "all things Elvis" totaled $37 million in fiscal year 2002, $4 million of which came from a British dance remix of his 1968 song **"A Little Less Conversation."** As of this moment, that song is still hitting number one on the charts all over Europe. Second on the list is Charles Schultz, creator of "Peanuts"; third is John Lennon; fourth is Dale Earnhardt, the race car driver, and the newest addition—at number five—is George Harrison.

That is the point.

Then there is the question: Is Elvis Presley alive?

According to the book written and published in 2001 by Dr. Donald W. Hinton **The Truth About Elvis Aaron Presley–In His Own Words,** Elvis Presley is now known as Jesse Garon Presley, the twin brother of Elvis who died at birth. Elvis is indeed alive. The book is filled with letters, gifts, and other convincing information passed on to Dr. Hinton from Elvis (Jesse). There is even a photo of Elvis at the age of sixty-six in a wheelchair holding his son Benjamin Stone. Dr. Hinton, a psychiatrist currently treating Elvis for chronic arthritis, is very convincing. On February 8th, 2002, radio hosts Frankie and Jean, with "Chucker" of **WRQT 95.7 The Rock** in La Crosse, Wisconsin, interviewed Dr. Hinton on **The Morning Sickness Show.** Dr. Hinton tells a compelling story about how Elvis faked his death and will be coming out of seclusion any day now.

Frankie: *"O.K., He's using the name Jesse. So, what I'm to understand, he faked his death…he did not actually die on the throne. He faked his own death to get away from the media?"*

Dr. Hinton: "That's correct and the Colonel (Parker) planned all of this.... Basically this is the year that he is going to come forward (2002) in letting the world know that this is true. Otherwise, I would never be speaking about this. I would have taken this to my grave."

Frankie: "How does he plan on doing this?"

Dr. Hinton: "Well, that is something you have to understand that I'm such a small part of this. This is obviously a huge thing that involves a lot of people and a lot of planning. And he is going to do it his way. There's certainly things I cannot speak about yet, but this is the year that's important to him (2001/2002). And he's talked about doing a DNA test. He has talked about things that he will still have to do to prove that he is who he really says he is."

Chucker: "...and I've also talked to many (Elvis) impersonators who are very angry about this, that they are saying that you are not correct. Totally not cool."

Dr. Hinton: "Well, you have to choose who to believe. You know I am a professional physician and I would not be risking my entire reputation on something that was not true. This is the truth and these people...I respect their opinion and everybody's shock at hearing this. I am not a fake. Jesse is not a fake. And as a psychiatrist, Jesse is not a person who is crazy or delusional. He is truly Elvis Presley. It's been proven to me by the people that are with him. The people that are with him go all the way to Washington, D.C. This man is protected more than the President of the United States."

Frankie: "The angry Elvis impersonators. Why do you think they are so angry?"

Dr. Hinton: "Well, I'm certainly not going to try to speak for anybody, but I can tell you one thing that Jesse has told me. He said he really wants his true fans to know the truth, but he said 'Doc, this is going to be a war because there are a lot of powerful people out there making a lot of money off me and they don't want me coming forward and telling the truth and, in fact, there are people who wished that he would hurry up and die so the truth can never be revealed.' So there is a lot going on right now."

Frankie: "What does Elvis think about all of the other Elvis?"

Dr. Hinton: "Well I think, in general, he is very happy. And it's just a lot of people obviously, as you have said, that he's one of the biggest stars there ever were. People admire him. To my knowledge, he has never impersonated himself or done anything like that, but I think he enjoys them (the impersonators) very much."

Douglas Roy not only impersonated Elvis while he was still alive, but in May, 1976, he was invited by Elvis to sing on stage with him in Lake Tahoe. It is generally known that Elvis enjoyed both seeing and meeting his impersonators.

Rick Saucedo began his career as an Elvis impersonator in 1972. He still continues to perform a very professional tribute to Elvis, due in part, because he was able to study Elvis while he was still alive.

Rob Garrett, known as the 'Elvis Aficionado,' is the only Elvis Tribute Artist (ETA) to see Elvis Presley perform 23 times live in concert. Rob is also the owner of **Rock and Roll Entertainment,** a booking agency based in Las Vegas, Nevada.

In 1977, following Elvis' death, Ronnie McDowell, a young performer, was so influenced by Elvis that he wrote and recorded a song called *The King Is Gone*. Let me tell you, that will bring tears to your eyes. It not only hit number one on the charts, it also helped put Ronnie on the map as a songwriter and performer.

In the early 80s, Phil Lynott wrote and recorded *The King's Call*. Then came *Black Velvet* by Alana Myles. All these were emotionally charged songs with poetic lyrics attempting to describe how they felt about their loss of The King.

In the beginning, there were mostly impersonators and only a few of these were considered tribute artists. Some of the veteran ETAs will tell you that Ronnie McDowell has the voice most like Elvis yet it has also been said that ETA Doug Church is "the voice of Elvis." Ronnie, however, does not dress like Elvis whereas Doug does.

Well-known recording artist Andy Childs does a very unique **Tribute to Elvis** in his show at *Elvis Presley's Memphis* on Beale Street. I would actually call it a tribute to rock and roll as Childs interfaces many songs and historical dialogue leading up to the invention of rock and roll. Of course Elvis Presley, and those who wrote his music, were instrumental in shaping the early foundation of this music. Childs does a wonderful job of performing Elvis' music while providing valuable and interesting insight into the background as well.

The chapters in this book, followed by the interviews with the ETAs, will allow you to see just how much dedication and commitment is required in the **Business of Being Elvis.** It was amazing for me to discover the amount of time, and money, it takes to re-create someone like

Elvis Presley. From the diversity in the 749 songs that Elvis recorded to the hundreds of costumes that Elvis wore, the total Elvis package is difficult to achieve. In addition to the physical and financial efforts of being Elvis, the ETA must have a personality that is kind and sincere, not to mention generous. Generous does not mean giving away material things, but donating time and performing at charitable benefits. The ETA must always recognize and appreciate the Elvis fans, including their own. The fans in the ETA world are tremendously generous and, at times, forgiving.

You will also learn that the veteran ETAs are very critical of anyone who wears the obvious 'Elvis impersonator' description. Their interviews should not be misunderstood as skepticism, but rather viewed as their sincerity out of respect for Elvis Presley. I admire their courage to voice an opinion.

Unfortunately, mention must also be made of the Elvis impersonators out there that just plain shouldn't be out there. They are the epitome of jokes and ridicule. Most of you know who you are. You are sincere because you love Elvis. Do you really? The worst of the lot are actually those that just don't get it—the ones that are consumed, possessed, or believe they ARE Elvis. **"Get a Life!"**

I hope you all will discover some new ETAs, as well as learn a bit more about your favorites. To the Elvis fan that is still not convinced, perhaps you will become more open-minded. Hopefully, you will at least seize the opportunity to take in some of their shows. I promise you will find yourself becoming emotionally charged. Maybe, just maybe, you will learn a little more about Elvis Presley, the person. If you really know your Elvisology, then you will indeed know the value of a tribute artist. Most ETAs have read Peter Guralnick's books a dozen times, listened to Elvis music in every version, and watched every Elvis movie, concert, and bootleg there is to find. If you believe you really are an expert, offer to be a judge at one of the hundreds of contests worldwide.

In compiling this book, we were only refused a few interviews. Some were perhaps apprehensive about the quality of the content, and rightfully so, but some were just plain rude or too busy: rude because I believe the portrayal of Elvis has orbited beyond an inflated ego; busy because they were…well, busy. As it turned out, this book became a better book without them. I feel we have the cream of the crop. *The Business of*

Being Elvis has elevated itself from that of impersonation to the level of professionalism worthy of a tribute artist. I apologize to those of you who could not be reached or found. We did our best working around everyone's busy tour schedules and time differentials. I would like to take this opportunity to thank everyone for sharing your stories, especially those of you who extended the extra effort to help us in many different ways. In the spirit of Elvis, God bless you all.

Martin Luther King said
"I Have a Dream"

Elvis Aaron Presley sang
"If I Can Dream"

What is Class?

Class never runs scared. It is sure-footed and confident in the knowledge that you can meet life head on and handle whatever comes along.

Jacob had it. Esau didn't. Symbolically, we can look to Jacob's wrestling match with the angel. Those who have class have wrestled with their own personal "angel" and won a victory that marks them thereafter.

Class never makes excuses. It takes its lumps and learns from past mistakes.

Class is considerate of others. It knows that good manners is nothing more than a series of petty sacrifices.

Class bespeaks an aristocracy that has nothing to do with ancestors or money. The most affluent blue-blood can be totally without class while the descendant of a Welsh miner may ooze class from every pore.

Class never tries to build itself up by tearing others down. Class is ALREADY up and need not strive to look better by making others look worse.

Class can "walk with kings and keep its virtue and talk with crowds and keep the common touch." Everyone is comfortable with the person who has class—because he is comfortable with himself.

If you have class you don't need much of anything else. If you don't have it, no matter what else you have—it doesn't make much difference.

CHAPTER 1

PRODUCING THE ELVIS ENTERTAINER

One of the most promoted assets on an Elvis Tribute Artist's (ETA) resume is emphasizing performing with the people who knew and/or performed with Elvis Presley. There are those ETAs at the top of the list who have also produced shows and recorded music with the well-known Elvis artists.

Some of the most popular performers include **DJ Fontana, Scotty Moore, Charlie Hodge, The Stamps Quartet, The Sweet Inspirations and The Jordanaires.**

DJ Fontana, Elvis' drummer for many years who also recently released his own book **The Beat Behind the King**, provided the following comment: *"I work with a lot of the guys (ETAs) and most are really good, as well as sincere in what they are doing. They would not do anything to deface Elvis' image, as most of the ETAs are big Elvis fans themselves. As for the fans that follow the ETAs, it is getting bigger. A lot of Elvis fans never got the chance to see Elvis in person so the ETA gives those fans a little of what it would have been like to see Elvis in person."*

While it is rather expensive to hire Elvis' artists, it is definitely a drawing card to promoting an ETA venue. Although I did not personally seek out a price quote, those who have hired these legendary performers say that the price ranges from a few thousand dollars to several thousands of dollars, plus expenses of course.

Last year in Memphis, Ray Walker of **The Jordanaires** joined Garry and Elaine Wesley's rehearsal at **Alfred's** on Beale Street. Garry is an Elvis Tribute Artist, while Elaine performs a mean rendition of Patsy Cline and back-up vocals with their band. Walker provides the famous base voice in **The Jordanaires** quartet.

Walker joined in on stage offering a fabulous re-creation of the actual Elvis recordings. He also very candidly provided the audience with a sense of humor so synonymous with Elvis Presley; *"I'm sixty-eight and a half years old and still enjoying Elvis, still getting paid, and still jogging,"* he quipped.

And Wesley piped up, *"You know, he's not kidding about the jogging. One time he asked me to run with him, and told me he'd be calling me real early in the morning. He sure did. We ran, or I should say he ran and, dead tired, I felt like the dog on a leash being dragged along."*

The Sweet Inspirations put together a come-back group in 1994 and have performed all over the world at Elvis Tribute shows, festivals, and ETA venues. They provide not only great vocals, but as the name suggests, sweet inspirations and memories of Elvis Presley.

There are also many of the folks that knew Elvis Presley, the person. Marion Cocke, Elvis' nurse; Sonny West, Elvis' bodyguard; Dick Grob, head of security for Elvis; Jim Mydlach, assistant to Colonel Parker (Elvis' manager); Ed Bonja, Elvis' official photographer; and of course, Al Dvorin, who was made famous by the classic announcement **"Elvis Has Left the Building."**

Donna Presley-Early, Elvis' first cousin and author, as well as a few other more distant relatives, host many ETA events and charitable functions.

They all make personal appearances in the name of Elvis Presley. They all get paid for their personal link to Elvis. They draw people to the events and promote the ETAs. This is all a part of the **Business of Being Elvis** in the process of keeping the memory of Elvis alive. The fans love it. The fans, after all, buy the tickets, buy the memorabilia, pursue the autographs, and 'grease the wheel.'

Then there's the infamous **Flying Elvis**, an Elvis look-alike skydiving troupe from Las Vegas. They were created from the movie **Honeymoon in Las Vegas** starring Nicholas Cage, Sarah Jessica Parker, and James Caan. My husband and I were extras in the movie to provide people for the crowd scenes upon being contacted by **Castle Rock Productions**. In exchange for their fees, a donation is made to charitable organizations in the Las Vegas area. Promoter Ronny Craig inquired about their fee to drop in (literally) at an event he was hosting in the Midwest and it was only a mere $12,000. Needless to say, it wasn't an option with this particular budget.

The most popular for-hire backup band that performs with many of the ETAs is the Chicago based **ExSpence Account Showband**. Charlie

Parks and Steve Fifer, currently the only original members, started the band in 1971. They played backup for Johnny Spence, one of the first original Elvis impersonators in the Chicago area. Around 1973, when they quit working with Johnny Spence, the band changed their name to **The ExSpence Account Showband,** clever play on words. Charlie has been a musician for 57 years in all, over 30 of those years as a professional. Charlie Parks, with sons Mike and Jason, Steve Fifer, Joe Zannelli, and Tom Madden comprise the band. Trish Sawilchik, who has a powerful voice, adds additional back-up vocals for the band. Charlie Piper is a replacement member on occasion. The band offers additional percussion if requested by a client.

My interview with Charlie Parks gave me the opportunity to learn so much about their band and the business of Elvis Tribute Artists. Charlie really deserves a book of his own. He is full of truths, candid thoughts, love for all of his children, and pride in his role as a musician. We talked at length about all of these things, but love of his children tops the list. He deeply appreciates the uniqueness in each of his four children.

What is the role of the **ExSpence Account Showband** when they perform with ETAs at contests?

"Our job is to make sure that the Elvis entertainers look their best. The judges at these contests look at how they dress, their style, the era they are performing. All I care about is...do they know the words? Can they sing the words? Do they have good timing? We have worked with many of these guys that are so scared. We give them a chord to get them in the right place, and they'll start singing somewhere else. We just go with them on it. Usually the guy will re-group and we will have already changed the key for him. We cover for him. People who come to these contests don't realize the mistakes that are covered by a band. The one thing we never tolerate is an ETA who thinks he is going to perform when he is drunk. They don't realize how bad that is. It hasn't happened very often though, but when it does we get him off the stage and we never perform with him again. The other thing we don't allow is for an ETA to sing a song that he is not scheduled to sing, which is usually because another ETA is already scheduled to sing the same song."

The band booked about a hundred dates in 2002, but could have booked far more than that.

The members all work full-time jobs so performances have to be juggled and booked accordingly. They need their jobs primarily for the extended benefits. They continue to perform because they love music and love Elvis.

"We certainly don't perform just for the money. Bands don't get paid much when you consider the amount of time they invest versus one singer. The ETA is one person without equipment, does a show and leaves. We have seven or more of us with equipment, plus the travel time to haul it, move it, set it up, then tear it down again. An ETA makes four to five times what we make individually in the band."

With the invention of Karaoke and track music that costs very little, why do so many ETAs and contest organizers continue to hire bands?

"Bottom line on that is that a band puts life into a performer and his show. It also gives the ETA a more star-like quality."

Though Charlie Parks is probably one of the few musicians in this business who never had the opportunity to see Elvis perform live, he is probably the only one that attended the same Humes High School in Memphis just a couple of years after Elvis graduated. In fact, the same football coach still worked there. If only those walls could talk!

"That coach hated musicians, he hated long hair, and he probably didn't like Elvis. It was much like the story of when Red West defended Elvis against a couple of football players in the Humes High School bathroom one time. I was in a band then, but I also was heavily involved in athletics—a jock if you will. Our band played for a lot of dances and school functions. Who would have ever thought that Elvis would become a focal point in my musical career?"

There are many ETAs in the business that have the benefit of performing with a band of their own. In order to be successful, the ETA must have the financial resources and sufficient work to keep a band busy enough to remain loyal. The bands are unique, of course, because they are strictly performing Elvis' songs. Generally, the ETAs with bands produce venues or concerts where they have the opportunity to charge an admission fee.

The invention of Karaoke revolutionized the music industry by virtually giving anyone the opportunity to perform in front of a live audience whether or not one could sing, read music, or even know the words to the songs. It doesn't matter. And, rather than transporting a band in a bus, one can simply pack a track CD in your pocket. When you read the ETA interviews, you will discover that many of the younger entertainers got their start working with Karaoke, while those who have been in the music business for a while worked only with live bands.

There are numerous people in the business of producing the high quality, digital tracks. One of the original, and most well known, is a company called **King Tracks**. As the name implies, they specialize in Elvis music. There are also companies such as **Music Maestro,** which offers a comprehensive list of song titles that include a variety of recording artists, and **Golden Voice,** which offers a more selective list of just Elvis music.

Ralph Foster, owner of **King Tracks**, started recording music back in the 1980s. It is his love of Elvis that inspired him to begin his career as a musician. Through Ralph's friendship with **The Jordanaires**, he was hired to produce an album for them in 1992. From them he learned that there were many Elvis impersonators looking for good, quality reproductions of Elvis' songs. Ralph utilized his musical and technical recording skills to produce the best tracks in the business. Since then, **King Tracks** has recorded over 300 Elvis songs. They are currently producing some of Elvis' concert tapes, including *Aloha From Hawaii*. Teri, Ralph's wife and partner, commented, *We're still going strong and the popularity of Elvis continues to be even stronger.*

There are a variety of professional seamstresses and tailors, including someone's mother, who can be hired to make an Elvis costume. There is Will Reeb who, because he was one of the first Elvis impersonators in the business, was sort of forced to get into the costume-making business. J.J. Wiggins, of Jim and Jane Wiggins, was the most admired husband and wife costume making team. When Jane passed away, Jim continued on in the business at the age of 70, lending him the title of being the oldest. **Jumpsuits Fit For A King,** just as the name suggests, is yet another Elvis wardrobe producing company promoted via the Internet. These are just a few of the sources that are available to the ETAs.

When it comes to the legacy of Elvis, however, it is **B & K Enterprises (Costumes),** which, for a variety of reasons, offers the closest thing to authenticity. First of all, they are the only ones in the world who have the original patterns that belonged to Elvis Presley, and the only ones with permission from the original designers to reproduce the wardrobe. Secondly, although there is no formal arrangement with **Elvis Presley Enterprises**, when **Graceland** receives inquiries regarding costuming, the calls are referred to **B & K Enterprises**. In the **Business of Being Elvis,** that speaks for itself. **B & K** has also earned a reputation for quality workmanship, as well as, for being more expensive.

Bill Belew, who designed all of Elvis' costumes beginning in 1968 with the famous **'68 Comeback Special** leather to the **Aloha From Hawaii** jumpsuit just prior to Elvis' death in 1977, and Gene Doucette, the legendary celebrity tailor known for his intricate embroidery and bead work on some of Elvis' jumpsuits, are a part of the team at **B & K Enterprises**. Owners Butch and Kim Polston, who started the business in 1980 out of a basement, is yet another example of a husband-wife team working successfully together. Butch, an Elvis fan all of his life, still leaves a humble impression with those who have met him. The Polstons probably never dreamed their enterprise would become a full-time business that continues to expand its customer base. The **B & K Enterprise** résumé is chalk full of movie credits, celebrities, and ETAs with international recognition.

Elvis costumes range in price from about $800 to over $4000, and often take several months to receive. It is obvious that the Elvis jump-suits are ornate and labor intensive. **The Dragon** jumpsuit is about 80 hours of time to pattern and cut, plus 10 hours to sew, another 10 hours for stones, and maybe another 10 hours for the belt. **The Aloha Liberty Eagle** jumpsuit is about nine hours to cut and sew, 50 plus hours to stud the garment and make the cape, with another 10 hours for the belt. With **B & K Enterprises** it is important to note that the grade-A fabric and specialty rhinestones they use come from a variety of European manufacturers, which is a major indicator of their commit-ment to authenticity and quality.

According to several of the **B & K** customers, it is assumed that an ETA donning a **B & K** suit seems to get a little more respect among the other ETAs in the circuit. I don't know if it is true, but the extra ounce of confidence sure can't hurt. **B & K Enterprises** also offers a complete line of other Elvis wardrobe accessories including belts, capes, glasses, wigs, and boots.

We know that there are a countless number of Elvis Tribute Artist fans out there, but what we haven't determined yet is just how many scarves, tainted with sweat, have been draped around the neck of an enraptured female.

Jerry Brian, aka the **"Scarf Lady,"** is a seamstress from Melbourne, Kentucky. She doesn't have the answer, but she can tell you from her experience that it must be a lot!

"In just 2002 alone, with 30 clients (ETAs), I made 12,000 scarves. It's interesting to me that the women don't care about the color of a scarf is, so long as they get one. The guys, on the other hand, are very particular. I have a list...this one doesn't like yellow; this one doesn't like black, this one likes a special blue. They are all made with either a satin or shiny (called the 'light one') polyester weave. I buy my fabric by the bolt from a wholesaler in New York. They send me samples and it works out really well."

When Jerry's husband passed away five years ago, she decided it was time to pull out all of her Elvis memorabilia from the closets. She realized she had collected more than she realized and it became apparent that some remodeling would have to be done to the house in order to properly display Elvis.

*"Elvis is everywhere. He's on the walls, he's on the ceiling...I even have a **Blue Suede Shoe** rug."*

Jerry, a young and retired 60-year-old Elvis fan, doesn't let the grass grow beneath her feet. She has three sewing machines. There's one in the house and two in her shop allowing her to have several scarf projects going on at the same time. She travels to at least two ETA contests each month and she goes to Memphis every year for ten days to attend the **Images of the King Contest** and other events. The money earned from making scarves helps to pay her expenses for the annual trip to Memphis during the anniversary week of Elvis' death. She doesn't make much profit; so for Jerry, it really is a labor of love.

"I know some of these guys don't have much money. The cost of fabric keeps going up and I felt bad when I had to raise the cost of a scarf an additional nickel this year. I always take my sewing machine to Memphis because it seems there's usually a need for it. One example is the time there was a knock on my hotel door from a person looking for some emergency sewing work. It turned out that an ETA had ripped his suit, so I promptly fixed it.

Later, I learned it was for Ryan Pelton and then when he discovered that it was me that repaired it, Ryan said; 'Jerry, I should have known it was you.'"

I tried to calculate the total cost for an ETA to enter the **Business of Being Elvis** and, even for the tackiest of impersonators, I realized that the personal rewards must outweigh the expense. Their investment is on-going: there is always the need for new sound tracks, the desire for one more special jumpsuit, the inventory of scarves and/or teddy bears to distribute, the dream of producing a CD or a concert and, not to mention, achieving the ultimate goal of earning recognition and the reputation for being the best ETA one can be.

Unfortunately, very few ETAs accomplish all of their goals, but it is a sure bet that the ETAs all get a tremendous amount of satisfaction out of performing their tribute to the King. It is the only way they know to express their love of Elvis.

CHAPTER 2

THE CONTESTS

In October of 2002, **Elvis Presley Enterprises (EPE),** the business arm of the multi-million dollar Presley estate, sent letters to various contest and festival organizers stating that they would no longer associate with those using Elvis Impersonators. In other words, you better not allow any Elvis entertainers, Tribute Artists, look-alikes, or clones that might even remotely resemble the King?

What? Did we get that right? An Elvis Festival without Elvi? (That is plural for more than one Elvis.) An Elvis contest without contestants? Elvis fans without an ETA fan club to join? Memphis without Elvis entertainers performing everywhere? How are they going to stop all of the Elvis impersonators in the world?

After a wave of protest letters from fans and organizers, **Graceland** reversed its decision to sever support of festivals featuring those that impersonate Elvis. Money does talk. Someone must have reminded them that **Graceland** is the most visited tourist attraction in the United States next to the White House in Washington D.C.

Let us not forget the hundreds of thousands of dollars that the Elvis Tribute Arts, including impersonators if you will, raise for various charities in the name of Elvis Presley. Isn't that what we truly remember most about Elvis—his generosity, anonymous donations, and concern for making the world a better place?

It remains unclear as to whether or not the organizers, promoters, and such can use the name Elvis to describe their event. I am wondering what it would sound like when the Master of Ceremonies says "I would like to introduce to you Impersonator of the King #1, #2, #3, and so on." Or if the M.C. makes a mistake and accidentally says the word **"Elvis,"** will someone have to be sure to "bleep" it out as if it were a curse word?

There are many varieties of these contests, festivals, extravaganzas, fairs, conventions, or whatever you choose to call them, all over the world. The Europeans seem to be exempt from the threat of legal reprisals, at least from the standpoint that they have more free reign in the use of the name and likeness of Elvis. The good news is, for now anyway, EPE has accepted the idea that *"ELVIS LIVES"* and the *Business of Being Elvis* will continue.

IMAGES OF THE KING

The most recognized Elvis contest in the world is *The Images of the King* held in Memphis each year throughout the week of August 16th as a tribute on the anniversary of Elvis' death. Originally known as *The Images of Elvis*, E.O "Doc" Franklin and his wife Jackie started the contest in 1981. It was formally established in 1987 upon the tenth anniversary of Elvis' death with the purpose of keeping the memory of Elvis alive. "Doc" was Elvis' former veterinarian and still maintains a private clinic in the Memphis area.

Although there have been numerous controversies surrounding the contests, this one seems to ignite the most debate. Some say it is too political and connected to Doc's old southern roots. Some believe the judging isn't fair. Some say it is just about making money. Others say it is Doc's influence and background with the Presley family that keeps the contest safe from any legal ramifications. Regardless of the count-less opinions, *Images of the King Contest*, often referred to as the *Superbowl* of Elvis impersonators, is still considered to be "the contest" to win. Most of the winners of this contest have, in fact, developed successful careers in the Elvis business. The contests, whether the con-testants want to admit it or not, generate a huge amount of exposure. They create new fans and open new windows of opportunity for the ETA.

The Images of the King Contest is beneficial because it is held in the heart of Memphis. Many fans plan their vacations around it. They tour **Graceland**, participate in the candlelight vigil, attend many other fantastic Elvis tribute shows, and take in all of the food and excitement of the infamous Beale Street.

In mid-2002, Nance Fox, owner of the **Elvis Entertainers Network (EEN)** and Ronnie Craig, an Elvis entertainer and, most often, the Master of Ceremonies at numerous ETA venues, purchased a percentage share of ownership in **The Images of the King Contest.** Gauging from all of the interviews gathered for this book, an overwhelming majority of the ETAs are very excited about this partnership, merger, or possible future buy-out. The ETAs feel it is a much-needed change. I am told there was a time when many of the guys even boycotted the contest. It could be that some of their comments are a result of jealousy or resentment because they didn't win, but never-the-less they cling to the hope that **The Image's** new blood will also bring new ideas and a higher standard of fairness to the contest.

According to the interview aired in mid-2002 of Jackie Franklin with Joanna Johnson, owner of **Ladyluckmusic.com's** radio program, Jackie feels that the partnership is needed because of the overwhelming workload.

"Right now Ronny Craig and Nance Fox are partnering with us in this. I plan on letting them handle more and more of the load. As much fun as it is, it really is a lot of work year round. They're in the entertainment business and you know it would seem right for them to be handling more of it. Doc and I will always be involved, and we will always have a hand in it, and we will always be at the contests and we'll always be representing **The Images**, *but I'm not averse to letting someone else handle the work."*

Every contest has a panel of judges and a method of judging. Apparently, every contest in the world is judged differently. A majority of the contests' rules do not allow the contestant to see the final score sheets. One of the purposes for the ETA to be able to see his score sheet is to allow him to learn what his weak points are and the areas that he must work harder to improve on. The other complaint is whether or not the judges are qualified to judge. It is important that a judge knows a lot about Elvisology and can remain unbiased by the pressure of the fans that follow each ETA. These are the major issues surrounding the validity of the contests.

Almost Elvis, a documentary film produced by John Paget, follows several Elvis impersonators on their journey to becoming the next "World Champion Elvis Impersonator" during the **Images of the King Contest**. John Paget's production, available on video or DVD, is an excellent exposé utilizing actual film footage and interviews of the ETAs to portray the deep level of commitment and dedication that is required to win. They all have the desire to fulfill their dream of becoming the next best thing to being "the King" himself.

Paget also points out, through the interview with Doc Franklin, that the controversy surrounding Robert Washington, an African-American Elvis entertainer, still exists. Washington has competed in the finals for many years without a win. He is extremely talented and a huge Elvis fan. Many of those that know Washington say it is discrimination and prejudice that keeps him out of first place. If the accusations are true, you would have to ask how Mori Yasumasa, a Japanese Elvis impersonator who does not speak any English other than his Elvis songs, could win first place in 1992? Some say that was just smart business because the Japanese market represents huge Elvis fans and profitability. Perhaps **The Images of the King** is looking to expand the contest in Japan. After all, many great ETAs from the United States have toured Japan and continue to perform Japanese venues there with great success.

The Images of the King also endorses approximately ten satellite contests, or so called regional contests, that allow an ETA to pre-qualify for the finals in Memphis. Each contestant is required to pay an entry fee of $50, as well as support all of their own transportation costs, lodging, and other expenses. The prize is a mere $1000, a gift certificate from **B & K Costumes**, and the hope of a financially rewarding future in the **Business of Being Elvis.** The contest is a week-long event that is held at the **Holiday Inn Select Hotel** near the Memphis airport. With approximately 100 contestants narrowing to 20 finalists by the weekend, the contest can be exhausting. The performances take place in the ballroom which seats about 1200 and is always sold out. The VIP admission charge for the entire week is $150 per person. Food and beverages are sold in the ballroom, as are program booklets, roses, ETA photos, CDs, and other promotional items. There are also vendors selling Elvis souvenirs.

During the week, there is karaoke in the lobby of the hotel offered to anyone who desires to sing without entering the contest. Track music is utilized for the preliminaries, but **The ExSpence Account Showband** performs back-up music for the finals. Ronny Craig, a well-known performer in the entertainment business, is the Master of Ceremonies.

The 2002 winners were: first – Brandon Bennett of Ponchatoula, LA; second – Mario of London, England; and third – William Stiles of Memphis, TN.

A few of the ETAs put on their own contests which not only gives them an opportunity to produce their own shows, but also helps to promote other ETAs. One of the most respected contests, and pre-qualifier to Memphis, is **Ronny Craig's Elvis Explosion** held in La Crosse, Wisconsin. The respect surrounding Ronny Craig stems from his own career as an ETA and from the relationships he has developed with numerous Elvis entertainers over the years. If I heard it once, I heard it a hundred times from so many of the ETAs that have worked with Ronny Craig; "*I do the contests for Ronny because I like Ronny.*" For these obvious reasons, it is my opinion that the new partnership with **The Images of the King** could provide a perfect team with which to bring the contests to a bigger and better level.

COLLINGWOOD

One of the largest Elvis festivals/contests is held each year in late July.

Imagine a small Canadian town with a population of 16,000 wrapped around Lake Huron where the lakeshore is dotted with million dollar homes and cottages. The Blue Mountain area enhances the backdrop. Collingwood is proud of its seven private ski hills and numerous golf courses. The downtown main street is about six blocks long and lined with unique shops nestled between an old brick clock tower, city hall and some banks. It is peaceful.

Each storefront window is tastefully decorated with Elvis Presley mementos and photos while the streetlights with speakers sound out the music of the King. There is the aura that something big is about to happen here in Collingwood, Ontario, Canada.

While thousands of the religious flocked to pay respect to Pope John Paul II in Toronto there will soon be nearly 80,000 people gathering to see the return of Elvis. There are over 100 Elvis Tribute Artists scheduled to perform during the three-day event known as the **Collingwood Elvis Festival,** sanctioned by both **Graceland** and **Elvis**

Presley Enterprises. It costs approximately $300,000 to produce, but it is expected to generate 9 million dollars in addition to the tourism interest it creates. The entire town embraces the festival, and Elvis, in a big way.

According to Collingwood locals, however, the festival experienced some tough beginnings and some painful growing pains. There was one year that they were short about $1500 and considered not having the festival at all. There were many meetings with the local politicians, residents, and businesses. They eventually came up with a plan to raise the seed money and the festival has continued to grow every year since. Then, there was the year that the *Flying Elvis* parachuters were hired to drop into Collingwood and the local residents weren't aware of the event. It created quite a stir on Highway 26 as people stopped their vehicles to watch seven-costumed Elvis jumping from an airplane like a surprise invasion of a UFO filled with Martians that look like Elvis clones.

Now in its eighth year, the festival obviously does more things right than wrong. It is now recognized as the largest Elvis Tribute Festival according to both **Graceland** and **Elvis Presley Enterprises**. The festival office now operates year round with full- and part-time staff and is blessed with the help of hundreds of volunteers. It has also gained the support of numerous sponsors including **Molson Canadian Light Beer.**

The Elvis Tribute Artists will perform each day at 13 local pubs/restaurants/businesses who have bought into the venue division while competing in the international contest in the downtown arena. There are also many other Elvis entertainers who turn out to watch their competition, connect with promoters and agents, or just to celebrate Elvis Presley.

On Thursday, the day before the festival, signs are posted to halt all parking in the downtown main street by 6 p.m. Immediately following, the streets are blocked off and an army of people begin setting up the main stage adjacent to the arena. Retail and food venders begin to set up shop underneath their individually marked white tents.

Friday morning arrives and people are already lined up at the Festival Information booth to pick up tickets, packets and event schedules. The Elvis begin to appear everywhere. The fans have donned their favorite Elvis attire and are armed with cameras and pens for autographs.

Welcome to the **Collingwood Elvis Festival**.

A variety of entertainers begin to perform on the main stage as the fans meet "Friends of Elvis" Marian Cocke, D.J. Fontana, and **The Sweet Inspirations**. The fans will also hear special performances from ETAs Ray Guillemette Jr., Matt King, Leo Days, and Brandon Bennett. As the evening begins, the Elvis Tribute Artists offer the audience their best of Elvis. One ETA, Reggie Randolph, feels lucky. He has landed a slot at 10:30 p.m. to sing for 30 minutes as somewhat of a headliner for **The Martels**, a featured band. It is a surprise break for Reggie who knows that this is a perfect opportunity to attract the early attention of the judges and, hopefully, new fans. He's dressed in the western attire as Elvis was in the movie **Love Me Tender** and sings the vocals **Loving You**, followed by a medley of Elvis favorites from the 60s and 70s. There isn't room to squeeze one more fan into the street and the crowd is taken by storm…especially the dedicated female fans.

The street concert continues with the performances of numerous other talented ETAs and the "street party" goes on into the wee hours of the morning. At midnight, the crowd shifts a bit as many leave to participate in a candlelight vigil ceremony that could be described as a re-creation of the one held at **Graceland** in Memphis.

Saturday morning comes early and begins with the Elvis Tribute Artist parade. There are more than 100 antique and classic cars each chauffeuring an Elvis Tribute Artist or two. It is truly one of the most exciting events. What a creative and fun idea!

The afternoon is consumed with the free participating venues and the competition officially begins. Free shuttle buses are provided to transport the fans and the ETAs to the various locations. Most of the venues also set up huge tents outside of their property in order to accommodate all of the people. It's time to sit back, relax, and enjoy listening to the performers. Some of the fans also purchase tickets to the contest semi-finals and grand finals held at the arena downtown. They are conducted under strict contest rules and judged by a panel of six men and women known for their background of Elvis, music, and credibility. The ETAs now get the opportunity to compete using a live band. The festival has hired **The ExSpence Account Showband**, a band internationally recognized for its talent and knowledge of Elvis Presley's music. The six judges have a very difficult job in light of their required knowledge of Elvis Presley's music including each era of costume.

The Grand Competition finals do not begin until 8 p.m., but by 6:30 the fans that were fortunate to get tickets begin to line the entire street downtown for blocks waiting for the doors to open. There are 20 ETAs chosen to compete in the final draft of the Professional Division and in the Non-professional Division. There is also the 16-and-under Youth Division. The winner in 2001 was Lance Dobinson, 16 years old and highly respected as a wonderful role model for young people. Some members of the Canadian Mounted Police brought him to my attention. It was great to hear about someone utilizing their talent in such a positive way at such a young and impressionable age. In the Professional Division, it is a tough competition to say the least. The 2002 placements were: first – Robin Kelly; second – David Lee (Rosenberry); third – Roy Evans; fourth – Reggie Randolph; fifth – Johnny Loos; sixth – Mark Leen; seventh – Shane Jeffery. Only three ETAs officially place, but the top seven are recognized.

The judges also give out an award for the fan of the year. The 2002 Fan Of The Year Award went to Sandra and Brian Skilton. They are also the proud parents of five-year old Aaron. Not only is Aaron the youngest Elvis performer that I have ever seen, he can also sing over twenty-five Elvis songs from memory. Though his voice has certainly not matured yet, he sings with every bit of passion that Elvis did. He is extremely shy...until he puts on one of his era Elvis costumes and hits the stage. Aaron also enjoys writing his name (he's pretty good at it) on his photos for the fans.

Sunday morning offers a wonderful gospel service in the arena. Pastor Zavitz conducts the service with special guests **The Sweet Inspirations**, Darrin Hagel, Danny Squires, Eric Erickson, and Jim Penny. This is another very special touch to the festival.

In between all of the various happenings, we were able to take some time to talk with the local folks and businesses. Our favorite stop became **Molly Bloom's Irish Pub & Grill** right down from the main street. Owner Kevin Cross and his father, Don, were very helpful and friendly. Don also gave us (my husband Richard) a first class tour of Lake Huron in his boat. What a terrific experience even though we didn't catch any fish. **Molly Bloom's** does not participate in the venue segment of the festival for some understandable reasons. Their theme is obviously Irish with some blues-type bands and they have a very strong regular clientele base, some of whom prefer to sort of just leave Elvis alone. Let's face it—we all need a little break from Elvis once in awhile and besides, the air conditioning was a nice reprieve.

It is nearly impossible to list all of the events, the great food and creative retail vendors. It is not my intention to exclude anyone. Now it is Monday morning. I have gathered all of my interviews, information, and terrific souvenirs. It is time to face the 17-hour drive back to Wisconsin. I would like to thank you all in Collingwood for your hospitality, especially to Don Wilcox and Rosemarie for their assistance.

PEOPLE'S CHOICE AWARD AND PERFORMERS' SHOWCASE

If the **Images of the King Contest** is one of the oldest and most recognized, then the annual **People's Choice Award Contest** and the **People's Performer's Showcase** are the contests most considered to be an honor and privilege to win. The contests, held in Montreal, Canada, are produced by Joanna Johnson of **LadyLuckMusic.com**. Both events bring only 10 ETAs to the stage to perform and compete during the separate two-day events. An ETA comes to these competitions via invitation only. The judges **are** the audience and consist of 500 or more in attendance. Each receives a ballot with only the name of the ETA on it. The rules are simple: no local ETA can compete and, if the goal is to win, the ETA must entertain the audience.

"They (ETAs) all end up to be winners really. It's amazing to me that each year there is literally two votes' difference between each guy. There are two different winners, two different guys. The winners receive trophies and plaques, but they all receive digital audio CDs of their performance. All of the ETA's expenses are paid, except for their transportation to get here, they are all promoted equally and there is no entry fee. There is no cash reward, only recognition. I am very selective about who I invite. If they think they are Elvis, well, I'm sorry, there was only one. I find the audience knows and senses this. If the ETA pours his heart out and pays tribute to his idol...come on, you can't not appreciate that. Never mind that they've got a good voice, *they're cute. There is something that attracts the audience to each one of them…wonderful personality, smile, a scarf…anything that reinforces the fan base. That's what I look for,"* explained Joanna Johnson.

Joanna uses professional track music rather than a live band to back up the ETAs. She feels that the expense of a live band can be better utilized somewhere else, such as quality lighting, sound equipment and other things to enhance the star-like quality of the ETA. She also believes that track music provides a better sense of fairness to the competition.

"Montreal is so wonderful. It also attracts a huge international base of Elvis fans and tourists. The audience gets very involved in our contests because they enjoy being entertained and for the simple fact that Elvis is so universal all over the world. If an ETA that performed at our contest tells you there were 6000 people in the audience, that's because of all the noise and excitement. Our audiences really get involved," Joanna added proudly.

LadyLuckMusic.com is a company that produces its own radio show on ECAR 125 Montreal, contests, venues, and—as the name depicts—the internationally known web site for Elvis Tribute Artists. It began in 1980 as **Lady Luck Music,** the band with Joanna featured on the keyboards and fellow band member Jimmy on the guitar until the band eventually rounded out with four to five members. They have been performing for 27 years now and are very well known throughout Montreal. The duo began as in-house musicians for radio stations producing jingles, eventually doing scores and soundtracks for movies *"We recorded several 45s or plastics as they were called…. In fact, I think we pressed the last one before CDs started,"* Joanna added.

In about 1990, Joanna, together with her husband and Jimmy and his wife, took a vacation to Las Vegas. As Joanna has been a big Elvis fan all of her life, the foursome took in some Elvis impersonator shows. This was long before Joanna knew who John Stuart (**Legends in Concert)** was. She was so overwhelmed that she decided to return to Montreal with the idea of putting a contest together.

"When we got back, I put a contest together in a small bar that served food. It had a variety of customers from country to rock music. The first year we had ten enter, the second year we had twenty, and it stayed that way for ten years. National television CBC picked up on it and hired us to

produce an Elvis Show with ten performers. It was like a history of Elvis 50s up to Trilogy...beautiful story...outdoors."

In June 2000, the radio show was launched.

"Although the site had been up awhile, we were searching for the 'voice of Elvis.' So we asked people on the site to send in their recordings, which was our contest. In the search we found **The Voice of Elvis, Doug Church,** through the Elvis Entertainers Network. I couldn't believe it. Jimmy did every kind of technical test possible to prove that really was the voice of Doug Church and not Elvis Presley. The song was **It's Not You.** I was totally blown away. We already had twenty ETAs picked to play. We did our show, did our first interview...international contest with Doug Church. Tried lots of things in production and the show just grew and grew. We never imagined. We just loved it. The guys kept sending me stuff so we created a profile page that now has 350 pages. We added Cortney Amador and Carol Hunter as writers. The love of Elvis, Elvis Tribute Artists, and the fans that follow will never diminish, we see new faces every day," Joanna summarized.

ISLE OF CAPRI CASINO

The newest and most exciting Elvis impersonator contest is sponsored by the **Isle of Capri Casinos**. They own 13 individual **Isle of Capri** properties throughout the United States. Each casino holds a preliminary contest and their winner goes on to become a finalist at the **Isle of Capri Casino** in Lula, Mississippi. The grand prize for the winner of **The $50,000 Tribute To The King Contest** is, well, $50,000. The preliminaries each pay out up to $5000 to the finalists as well. This is where the **Business of Being Elvis** really gets competitive. The best ETAs in the world want to win the money, honor, and **money**!

Each contestant is required to send a video (under ten minutes) of themselves, photo, and biography to be considered for acceptance. Each of the preliminaries has their own set of rules, a panel of judges of their choosing, and is organized by the entertainment director of each separate property.

In the final competition, each contestant was allowed only eight minutes to perform. The 2003 winner, Garry Wesley, sang **Hurt,**

Suspicious Minds, and **Can't Help Falling In Love**—the concert version with a dynamic ending. Ironic enough for Wesley who was a finalist last year, this was also the very first contest he has ever entered. Wesley was somewhat singled out because of a bit of controversy started by one of the other contestants. This, in turn, stirred up some debate amongst the ETAs about whether or not it would be fair to allow Wesley to compete. First of all, Wesley lives in Biloxi, therefore he's considered to be a local ETA. Secondly, he was also the first ETA scheduled to perform in the finals. Thirdly, Wesley was accused of bringing his own band for backup. All of these issues were not founded, yet it does point out how fiercely competitive the contests can become. Every ETA has a following, numbers are drawn out of a hat as to the order in which the ETA will perform, and, regardless of who the band is (though it was not Garry Wesley's), an ETA who is used to performing only with karaoke tracks will be at a disadvantage. This year, Elvis Tribute Artist Gary Elvis Britt, who also competed in 2002, was the only contestant to go over the eight-minute time limit. Although he was not disqualified for that, the judges did stop his performance upon reaching the eight minutes.

According to Linda Ivy, Entertainment Director for the **Isle of Capri Casino** in Lula, Mississippi: *"We had five judges that were selected from a variety of southern states. They were all from the Elvis generation, grew up with it and were Elvis fans. In fact, I didn't even meet the judges until the day of the competition. It was standing room only in our 1400 seat showroom. The audience was excited. It was really a wonderful event. There was no charge for admission."*

Now in its second year, Linda Ivy had not received word yet about the casino's plans for the contest next year. She and many of the ETAs are hopeful that the contest will continue. The ETAs also hope that each of the preliminaries will become uniform in their rules and regulations for the contest. It is just something that would help to standardize the contests, while helping the ETA to prepare for a specific contest. The 2003 finalists are: second – Matt Joyce; third – John Ieyoub; fourth – Kraig Parker; fifth – Greg Ring; sixth – Irv Cass; seventh – Eddie Miles; eight – Gary Elvis Britt; and ninth – Fred Jenkins.

POTOWATAMI CASINO

The **Potowatami Casino** in Milwaukee, Wisconsin is the "newest kid on the block" in the contest arena. Kurt Brown, Entertainment Director for the casino, researched the Internet for information about contests and how to find Elvis impersonators. Kurt is also a big Elvis fan and former impersonator of a variety of artists such as Neil Diamond, Willy Nelson, Louis Armstrong, Garth Brooks, Elton John, Buddy Holly, Tom Jones, and Elvis. He decided that he wanted to put together a contest with a **Honeymoon in Las Vegas** movie twist to it. The idea would be to have the preliminaries for the contest conducted in the middle of the casino where all of the patrons could watch. The Elvis impersonators would arrive at the casino dressed in costume and mingle while they were waiting to perform. It would create an atmosphere much like it was in the movie with the appearance that there are Elvi everywhere.

"*I wanted to bring a national, Las Vegas type of production to the contest as well,*" Kurt said. "*We brought in ETA Garry Wesley and his band with back-up singers, drummer* **DJ Fontana**, *and* **The Jordanaires** *to perform for the finals in the Northern Lights Theatre in the casino. All of the contestants were very nice, very polite. With the trials and tribulations of our first contests, the guys communicated with us really well about things we needed to change along the way, which kept it all running very smoothly. The guests really had fun with the whole idea.*"

There were about 25 contestants with three days of preliminaries and one day and night of the finals. There were four finalists picked each day of the preliminaries, of which the first place winner is paid $5000 each day. Second place is $1000; Third place is $500 and fourth place is $100. Jesse Aron placed first on two different days and Ryan Pelton placed first on two different days. On the fourth day, Ryan removed himself from the finals saying: "*I think it is time that I step down and give someone else the opportunity.*" Isn't that just like Ryan to do something like that? They also had the opportunity to perform along with **DJ Fontana** and **The Jordanaires.** The screening process required the ETA to submit an Elvis-type photo and an audio recording. Many of the applicants responded through the casino's website at www.paysbig.com—some with their own video trailers.

Ballots that are handed out to the entire audience of 500 or more in attendance at each show over the four days is the system used in the judging. There is no charge for the tickets to this event, and they are distributed through a promotion with a local radio station in Milwaukee. This is the only contest that uses this method, but from what I witnessed, it appears to be quite fair. The audience watched each ETA closely, getting very involved because they know that their participation really matters. All of the guests sitting next to me were excitedly chatting about their opinions of this ETA or that ETA.

There was one ETA who was disqualified from the contest and literally escorted out of the building by security. Milwaukee's own Tom Green, whose mother died of breast cancer five years ago, during the competition made this statement to the audience: *"Today is Elvis' birthday, and in the spirit of Elvis and his generosity I will donate my winnings to the Susan Komen Breast Cancer Foundation."* According to the **Milwaukee Journal Sentinel** Friday, January 10, 2003 edition, Green was then asked to leave the building because casino officials thought he was attempting to publicize his disqualification, therefore disrupting the contest.

"I am reasonably sure we will be doing the contest again next year. We're looking into making some changes based on suggestions, probably pay out a little more money...the show and the contest was very successful and the guests had so much fun with it. I had a great time too, but it sure was exhausting. If I hadn't been quite so tired, I would have liked to sing along with everyone and hang out. After a week of folks kidding me about being a former Elvis impersonator myself, it was fun to see the audience reaction when I sang **Can't Help Falling In Love**, *the 1969* **Blue Hawaii** *version at the end of the finals. And* **The Jordanaires** *are incredible to sing with."*

Chapter 3

Road to Stardom

The most difficult and risky part of the Elvis business for an ETA, or any entertainer for that matter, is management. Understanding a profit and loss statement is one element; the other is the ability to procure a reputable and trustworthy manager/agent. A majority of the ETAs believe that there are a lot of "wanna be" people out there offering empty promises for the sole purpose of financial gain.

We all realize that even Elvis Presley's manager Colonel Tom Parker, a renowned con artist, made Elvis and mostly himself a significant amount of money. Parker also grossly took advantage of Elvis' naiveté and generosity. Many Elvis fans continue to blame Parker and Dr. Nickopolas for Elvis' eventual death. There remains that gnawing question of whether or not Elvis would have become the icon he is today without them. Even now, to answer that is like handling a double-edged sword.

At the **Collingwood Elvis Festival** 2002, I bumped into a depressed and desolate ETA who had just been dumped by his manager. All the way from Nova Scotia, Canada, ETA Raymond Clyke had checked into his motel just the day before with his manager and an inventory of his own CDs to sell. When he awoke the next morning, he discovered that his manager had abandoned him. Clyke was left with only his clothes, his CDs, a wounded spirit and utter shock. The optimism he once held on to, hoping for a win in the contest that he had placed in a few years ago, had diminished. Penniless, Clyke's only chance left was to hawk his CDs in order to raise the money needed to pay the hotel, food and some sort of transportation to get him back home.

Upon hearing of his plight, several people gathered to brainstorm ways to help out. By a miracle that only Elvis himself could have provided, local residents Emma and Keith (last name withheld at their request) came to Raymond Clyke's rescue. They provided him with their personal vehicle to use, expense money and an airplane ticket home. They also offered encouragement to the talented Clyke by arranging meetings with several of their friends in the music industry.

There is also the story of ETA Ryan Pelton who, in a moment of excitement upon winning **Dick Clark's Impersonator Contest** in 1999, the first contest he had ever entered (upon a dare from his mother), signed a contract with an agent that appeared to be credible. By the time Pelton discovered that certain things were not being handled properly by the agent, the situation required the expense of a lawyer to terminate the relationship. Though Pelton is very happy with his current agent, Dan Lentino, he is quick to advise other ETAs new to the business *"to be careful in choosing who will represent and market you."* Pelton is also the 2001 winner of the *Images of the King Contest*.

I am grateful to have had the opportunity to interview a few of the best managers/agents in the business. There are numerous agencies out there, so it just wasn't possible to talk to all of them. It is important to note, however, that I was refused interviews with a few of the agencies. Let us move forward to some of the positive forces in the business of managing and promoting Elvis entertainers.

Nance Fox

Just a few short years ago, the name Nance Fox probably didn't mean much to most of the people in the ETA world. Since then, Nance continues to climb the ladder of recognition for her contributions to the **Business of Being Elvis.** In an obvious male-dominated industry full of politics and backbiting, Nance holds tight to every rung.

Raised in a military family, Nance traveled extensively and attended 18 different schools. She holds a Bachelor of Science Degree in chemistry and worked in the medical technology field for about 18 years. In 1985, Nance decided to enter a new profession in real estate. Somewhere in the middle of these two professions, she married her second husband, a veterinarian. In assessing Nance's background, you begin to realize that she probably has acquired the best training in the world for this business.

In 1997, Nance met Elvis impersonator Johnny Thompson, who was just starting out from a transition as a stripper in the Chicago area where Nance resided. She always enjoyed Elvis' music, but confesses that she was not an "Elvis nut."

"Johnny was very green, but he had a great Elvis look. He was also starting to get a fair amount of work and needed some help in managing the booking end. So in 1998, I became his manager."

Johnny Thompson is the founder of the **Elvis Entertainers Network (EEN)** from which he developed a page on his website called the **Professional Elvis Impersonators Association (PEIA).** The purpose of the **PEIA** is to provide a vehicle for communication and professionalism to all Elvis impersonators. The **EEN** extension promotes a vehicle for the Elvis impersonators who are hired to perform all over the country. As Nance became involved in the management end, she began generating more work for Johnny, while also creating an elevated interest in Elvis fans wanting to hire an Elvis impersonator. In July of 1999, Johnny decided to venture to Las Vegas, so Nance purchased the **Elvis Entertainers Network** from Johnny for $5,000. At the time, Nance was homebound caring for her husband who later passed away in September of 1999. When he died, Nance made a huge decision to, according to Nance, *"do the Elvis thing full-time."*

Nance's journey into the ETA business hit a few roadblocks along the way. A circle of cliques weaved a web of negative entanglements, and at times controlled this society of Elvis impersonators.

"I had just lost my husband…Johnny left…I had guys to book and I was receiving so many inquiries. My website was deliberately sabotaged and crashed, which in turn initiated rumors that I was out of business. Luckily my son came to my rescue on that one. I had one competitor call all of my vendors who told them my Elvis impersonators weren't any good, that I didn't have permission to use the name Elvis and I was going to be sued."

While dealing with all of the bad luck, Nance became even more determined to utilize her organization, the **EEN,** to elevate the Elvis impersonators to a higher level of professionalism by developing ethical standards for the industry. She had witnessed too much negativity at contests with the Elvis impersonators not speaking to one another, or even associating with one another.

"I think when I started out in this business, I think people looked at me as an Elvis fan…just playing. Once it started growing, then they thought I'd

fall flat on my face. I've come to the conclusion that I'm not going to fight with them. It takes too much away from the positive side. The tendency of this business is to let the negative pull you in."

Irv Cass, who would often say to Nance, *"You can do it...keep on!"* was the first ETA to sign on with Nance at **EEN.** Irv, Vice-President of Public Relations, along with Jerome Marion, Vice-President of Technical Direction, Doug Church, Vice-President and Musical Director, and Ronny Craig, Marketing Director, are close advisors to the **EEN** organization. They are all well versed in the entertainment industry and have a strong ETA background. They all continue to work together to implement the criteria required to join the **EEN.** The **EEN** requires a video, photos and biography from each applicant for review. More recently, it was decided that an interview with a staff member be added as a requirement. Recently, Nance Fox and Ronny Craig also became partners in the **Images of the King Contest.**

"I have 56 promo packages right now to review. We've had over 500 apply in the last four years. We currently have 65 members, so that shows you the ratio. When the reviewing process is completed, we send each ETA a letter in the form of a critique. Some make it; some don't and some make it after a second or third application. Some don't handle the rejection very well and send me nasty letters, which is O.K....because we don't want members with that kind of an attitude anyway. There are no stars in this business. Bottom line is that they are all impersonators. We all must work at improving the image."

Nance Fox is full of enthusiasm and she shared with me many great ideas that she is going to work on in the near future. I'm not going to let you in on those right now, but it is her effort and, therefore, her right to benefit from trudging in the trenches of this incredible **Business of Being Elvis.**

Dan Lentino

Reserved, inconspicuous, devoted family man and musician extraordinaire are the words that come to mind when describing Dan Lentino. Dan, owner of **Dan Lentino Management, Ambassador Talent Services (ATS)** and **East West Entertainment,** talent, booking and management agencies, is also one of the more respected people in the Elvis entertainment business. If an ETA catches the eye of Dan, he is almost sure to become a rising star.

It all began when Dan, at the age of eight and his brother, at the age of ten, teamed up with another set of brothers to form a band called **The Fabulous Ambassadors.** The roster of entertainers that the band worked with is proof alone of their talent. **Johnny Cash** and **June Carter, Waylon Jennings, Kiss, Ted Nugent, Def Leopard, Blood, Sweat and Tears, Chuck Berry, Chubby Checkers, Bob Hope** and **Johnny Carson** make up just a portion of their name-dropping list. His group, with Dan on lead vocal, had a record on the charts in 1983 that even had airplay in Europe.

"About nine years ago, I semi-retired from performing. I think my own background in performing and having degrees in business, music, and voice is what gave me the advantage over many other people in this business because instead of being only able to watch the entertainers from the audience's perspective, I was able to be on the stage watching from the entertainers' perspective. I was able to see the faces of the audience. I was able to see what worked and what didn't work...first hand...night after night."

Dan believes that timing and fate play a major role in the entertainment industry as well. For example, in 1972, Dan had a show band that performed 50s and 60s music. One day while cruising the neighborhood **Boys Club Carnival,** he spotted the then-15 year-old Rick Saucedo, who is now considered to be not only the premier Elvis Tribute Artist, but one of the longest running tribute performers.

"Rick was only a sophomore in high school when I first met him. He could only sing a couple of Elvis songs, but he looked so much like Elvis that we brought him into our band and developed him. We had Rick learn more Elvis songs and Elvis moves, then we added more costumes and by 1977, we made him the most publicized and sought after Elvis Tribute Artist in the Midwest. Then, of course, Elvis Presley died."

The Elvis fans wanted more than anything to keep the memory of Elvis alive. Every facility that they performed in brought long lines of people wanting to see Rick Saucedo as Elvis. There were many sell-out shows. It was evolving into something incredible. About the same time, Dan Lentino learned that auditions were called for a new play on

Broadway at the renowned **Palace Theatre** in New York called **Elvis, The Legend Lives.**

"We brought Rick out to the audition. Originally, the producers wanted three separate artists to portray Elvis through the different eras. When they saw Rick, they decided he was the only choice for all eras of Elvis' career. With **The Jordanaires**, **DJ Fontana** *and the prestige of the world renown Palace Theater, this Broadway play was just the thing to bring credibility and to take being an Elvis Tribute Artist to a respected level. We toured the U.S. and Canada with that same show for two years and then brought it to Las Vegas. I just became naturally involved in the business side of the show and gained recognition for my association with a Broadway production, and for building one of the most popular ETAs ever...to a level beyond any other. The business people associated with the show in New York at this time were some of the shrewdest and toughest businessmen anywhere so I learned very early that in order to survive we needed to be sharper than they were and that if I showed impeccable integrity I would succeed in earning the respect of good and bad alike. By living on the road with* **The Jordanaires** *and* **DJ Fontana,** *I learned a lot about the real Elvis, how he developed and what made him the greatest entertainer of all time. I also made many contacts that would ultimately help pave the road for the future."*

Then in 1984, a producer affiliated with the **Star Palace Theatre** in Merryville, Indiana, contacted Dan about putting together an Elvis Birthday Tribute. Convinced this was very marketable and honorable, they soon partnered. Even though Dan and Rick Saucedo had already parted ways, Dan still brought in Rick, along with several other well-known ETAs from the Chicago area, for the first show.

"As Rick was now an independent, I needed to find another entertainer that had that special quality I was looking for. I call it 'the gift'...simply the ability to become Elvis on stage for a few seconds per song or several times throughout the performance. For business purposes, I needed what we call 'a hook.' Then I remembered a young performer I had met at one of Rick's shows that eventually gave the name of Trent Carlini. Trent lived in Italy at the time, but was visiting his father in Chicago who had just purchased a business there. His father approached me about letting his son sing on stage." As Dan further described this scene to me, I could just picture **The Godfather** style of conversation with the heavy Italian accent that followed.

"His father said; 'My name is Lorenzo Trentacarlini. My son, Roberto
Trent Carlini, he sings. Could you let him sing with your band?' I found out
that he could sing a couple of songs that weren't Elvis tunes, so I put this
very good looking, young blond-haired-kid up on stage. He literally set the
stage on fire. The girls went crazy...screaming for more...Rick was very
jealous. When the break came, I found out that Rick Saucedo was so mad
about the girls' reaction to Trent that he punched a hole in the wall of his
dressing room."

By the time the two of them began working together, Trent had
already moved to Florida. He wanted to perform in the United States,
but he really wanted to, just once, perform an Elvis show. In order to
convince Dan that he had the ability to do a really good show as an
ETA, he recorded the Elvis song **C.C.Rider** with his band and sent a
copy of it to Dan. The tape had been mixed with Trent singing, then
Elvis singing, then Trent, and so on. Dan was very impressed with the
quality of Trent's voice.

"I said to Trent, if you will let me call you **The Italian Elvis,** I will put
you in this big Elvis show. Trent replied, 'You can call me whatever you
want as long as it's just one show.' This was the 'hook' I wanted...**The
Italian Elvis.** Trent literally sewed together his own jumpsuit and put the
studs on, and bought a pair of brand new boots. Trent charges out and slips
on the stage. The whole audience catches a big gulp in their throat, while
Trent sincerely explained to them that he 'was so thankful for this opportunity to be here and be able to sing some Elvis Presley songs' that the audience
just ate it up and my phone began to literally ring off the wall. That is when
I decided it was my fate to bring on and develop another ETA after Rick
Saucedo."

Remember that comment about timing and fate?

"Even though Trent had decided to be on his own a few years later, I
convinced him to do the **First Worldwide Impersonator Contest** in
Montreal, Canada for a prize of $10,000 cash. He had gotten real comfort-
able with the idea of performing in Las Vegas. He didn't want to go anywhere else and didn't want to grow. I had gotten him several movie auditions, but Trent didn't want to be part of 'a cattle call' as he referred to it.
So what happened is, by getting Trent involved in that contest, I ended up
meeting a talented ETA by the name of Shawn Klush. Shawn and I met
over breakfast and got to know each other a little bit. When I saw Shawn's

performance on stage and the reaction he got from the audience, I thought to myself, boy he has got the gift. Other than Trent, and Rick in his earlier days, Shawn was the only other ETA that had that appeal. I asked Trent if he knew why and Trent agreed it was because Shawn was the only natural one, the others were all very plastic. Shawn's Elvis goes way beyond mere impersonation. Even Elvis' own friends and musicians lose themselves during Shawn's performance."

Dan started guiding Shawn Klush along, working with him full-time along with **Legends in Concert** and hooking him up with many major events and tours. Down the road, Dan received a call from ETA Irv Cass about Ryan Pelton. Irv said: *"Dan, you gotta see this guy."*

"I gave Ryan a call and we talked for some time. He sent me a video, but I was not that impressed. Then when I learned it was only his first performance and after getting to know him, I realized that he had the desire and dedication it takes to become very good in this business. I decided that I would like to work with him. I sent him recordings, videos, and other tools that I think are necessary for the ETA to use and learn from. Ryan works extremely hard to improve himself and has truly become an excellent entertainer. He is a gentleman in the true sense of the word and is destined for great things even beyond the world of the ETA."

Ryan Pelton is now doing commercials and modeling and is currently working with the **Legends in Concert** production. It is Dan Lentino who arranged the audition for Ryan with John Stuart of **Legends.**

"John Stuart respects my opinion, without a doubt. John calls me constantly, but there are very few people that I have sent to audition with John. His shows are based on what he thinks an Elvis entertainer is, and that is much different than what I look for. John is the key person in his organization. There is no question that he has changed the corporate structure of **Legends**. *It became a public company and, as the public company started to experience financial troubles, a new group of investors were brought in. These individuals and even some of the cast members may not realize it yet, but there is only one person in that company that is trained and experienced in the entertainment business. That is still John Stuart. The rest of the people are strictly money people. The company is diluted with politics, but John is still 'The Master' in the business of impersonating and entertainment. If you ever have the pleasure of knowing him personally you'll know he is truly a man of integrity."*

How does Dan Lentino find his talent?

"They sort of find me. I pay very little attention to the contests. Only if there is somebody involved that I might want to take a look at. Generally speaking, I stay far away from the contests. I am not actively looking for new clients but my ears and eyes are constantly on the ETA scene. Once again 'The Gift' is the key and I am actually debating at this moment whether or not to help develop a new kid on the scene. He's only 18 years old, but the gift is very strong in him. He just needs someone to help bring it out and develop it."

Clearly, Dan's ability at succeeding in the **Business of Being Elvis** surpasses his customary nod to "timing and fate" as the key players. Although Dan may not actively pursue his talented ETAs—remember, they find him—his unique ability to recognize raw talent and ability speaks volumes about Dan. Dan may recognize "the gift" but it is ultimately Dan who wraps it.

In summary, I would like to add that Dan's contacts in the business continues to be powerful. Dan is well respected and well loved even by the people who actually lived and worked with the real Elvis. He recently worked with a promoter out of Utah to bring ETAs Garry Wesley and Travis LeDoyt together for a major concert in Chile, South America. In fact, it was so successful that Dan is scheduled to bring the venue back as soon as the details are worked out. Dan continues to co-produce **The Elvis Birthday Tribute Tour** now in its 17th year and will also bring the tour to Switzerland the summer of 2003. He continues to be the entertainment coordinator for **The Chicago White Sox** and several large venues throughout the country.

Help Wanted : Elvis Impersonator to Perform. Pay negotiable.

ELVIS-A-RAMA MUSEUM

In Las Vegas, Nevada, Elvis is everywhere. There is Chris Davidson, owner of the **Elvis-A-Rama Museum**. He generally has four impersonators who represent different eras of Elvis' career performing shows throughout the day at the museum. I am told the pay is not very good at $1200 a week, compared to a production show where an ETA can make as much as $3500 per week.

ELVIS WEDDINGS

The biggest opportunity in securing an Elvis job in Las Vegas is the business of "I do." I attended an Elvis wedding ceremony at the **Elvis Chapel** featuring Michael Conti as Elvis. After a brief exchange of vows officiated by owner Oscar Marino and Michael singing a couple of Elvis love tunes, Michael provided his own set of vows. To the groom: *"Repeat after me. I promise I will always love you tender and never leave you in a heartbreak hotel. I'll never have a suspicious mind. I'll always be your hunk-a-hunk of burning love."* To the bride: *"Repeat after me. I promise I'll always love you tender and never return you to sender. I'll never step on your blue suede shoes and I'll always be your loving teddy bear."*

At the end of the vows, Michael crooned **Can't Help Falling In Love** then proudly posed for pictures with the newlyweds. The newly pronounced husband and wife, Mr. and Mrs. Terry Nash, went off to the bridal suite at the **Golden Nugget Casino**...staying in room 666. Elvis offered such a special mist of nostalgia that there didn't even seem to be the slightest thought about being superstitious.

The **Elvis Chapel,** located in downtown Las Vegas, has been in business about five years with the average wedding cost of $250. *"We enjoy doing weddings, especially Elvis weddings. Our weddings are like productions hiring only the top Elvi here. We do approximately 2400 weddings each year with Elvis weddings averaging 1700 per year,"* Oscar Marino said.

There are many wedding chapels to choose from...and many Elvi to choose from.

Legends in Concert
John Stuart

Many of the ETAs believe that John Stuart is sort of a god in the industry. Maybe he is. Everyone in the impersonator industry also seems to have a different opinion about him personally. The fact remains: he is the real meal deal. John Stuart, truly a visionary, is the original creator and producer of the well-known **Legends In Concert**.

Legends in Concert at the **Imperial Palace** in Las Vegas, is the longest running independent production show. Stuart has taken **The Legends** show all over the world. The theatrical production relies on nearly 200 impersonators representing approximately 75 different celebrities, dead or alive, as the subject of its tribute acts. **Legends** is now a publicly traded company owned by **On Stage Entertainment, Inc.** Though there are numerous competitors in this business, only Spring Time Productions stages such shows on a continuous basis and in more than one location. Spring Time runs the **American Superstars Show**, produced by Donny Moore, at the **Stratosphere Casino** in Las Vegas. **Superstars** currently hosts Darren Lee as Elvis. Patrick Graham is the Elvis at the Las Vegas **Legends**, but because Stuart rotates the impersonators, often requiring them to travel to other **Legends** locations, it is difficult to say who is currently performing the Elvis act. His performers also work six nights a week. John Stuart travels extensively in order to ensure the production and its staff maintains the quality he expects.

Regardless of the corporate structure now in place with **The Legends In Concert**, John Stuart is still considered to be the only entity bearing real entertainment experience. In the process of creating **Legends**, Stuart endured many hardships. He even received a serious threat one time that was directed toward him and his family. The threat involved a demand for a portion of the profits of his production or else…. Stuart, a pioneer in the entertainment business, also weathered many financial difficulties along the way. Described as a workaholic by those around him, Stuart is committed to producing the best shows with the best talent in the world.

Most of the ETAs only get to dream of an opportunity to work with **Legends In Concert**. Those ETAs who have auditioned for John Stuart are often stunned by his directness and honesty. He is very critical of the impersonators, partly because he knows exactly what he is looking for and what he expects in his performers for **The Legends** type of show, but also because it is simply Stuart's demeanor. Some of the ETAs that have worked with Stuart describe him as being extremely knowledgeable in the business, but without a "bedside manner" or of "lacking in people skills."

Legends Alive-Progressive Concerts
John Kondis

John Kondis, a native of Toronto, Ontario, Canada, began his career in the entertainment business as a drummer and vocalist. Performing the music of the mid-60s and 70s with a traveling group called **The Inspirations of Canada**, the band became well known throughout Canada. With a desire to change direction professionally, Kondis accepted an offer with the Canadian **Holiday Inn Motel** franchise as their Entertainment Director. It was in this position where Kondis developed the idea of becoming an independent talent agent. When Kondis proposed his idea to his employer, **Holiday Inn** decided to enter into an agreement with Kondis. He secured a five-year exclusive contract to hire talent for all of **Holiday Inn's** 48 properties in Canada. With his first client now on board, Kondis formed his new company the **Progressive Concert Productions, Inc.** The **Progressive Concert and Convention Services** is a multi-faceted entertainment company dealing with every aspect of the entertainment field. They procure talent for concerts, conventions, hotels, theatres, and more.

In 1987, **Progressive** produced *Legends: A Tribute to the Superstars*, the original major impersonator show in Canada. Now called *Legends Alive*, this totally live stage production show toured all across Canada and into the United States. The Canadian cast of *Legends*, with the exception of an American Elvis, ETA Garry Wesley and an American Neil Diamond, began as the **Legends Dinner Theatre** in Toronto. *Legends* currently has 30 acts to choose from, giving the show its continued variety and freshness.

"*We play to a lot of the same audience, but every time they see it, it is different. We keep giving them a good product; we constantly change the theme around and make it more visually attractive. The Legends show...I can't see an end to it because people want to reminisce...it's nostalgia. You never run out of acts. This week Shania Twain is the hottest act, but next week it may be someone else. Elvis, however, is always hot. We always close our show with Elvis. We use a lot of video in our show to create different and exciting illusions with each act. It is an expensive production...our cast always signs autographs, allows photos, sells their merchandise...interact with the audience after the show.*"

The concept, obviously, is very successful. **Legends Alive** is a 2-1/2 hour show selling out to audiences of 5000 to 7500 and up to 20,000 at the **Saddle Dome** in Calgary where the National Hockey League plays. Admission to the production is twenty dollars American or thirty dollars Canadian.

"We work hard to secure the best performers and tribute artists. Some of the acts I've been to or worked with are better than some of the originals. I've got a Kenny Rogers that even Kenny Rogers made a comment 'I wish I could sing like this guy.' I think it's flattering. It should be flattering to turning out their name...and if they're paying tribute, there shouldn't be a law against that. It is difficult to find a good Elvis. Many of them have such egos. We absolutely can't have that because it rubs off on the other cast members. We don't want these guys that wake up and think they ARE Elvis. We try to get guys that are even-keeled. They do this for a living, knowing they are blessed to be working and making a living doing impressions. The economy is rough, especially in this business. It's so watered down, but good ones always seem to survive...come to the top. Our show has the best out there. This year, by the looks of things, will be one of our better years...more work from the States is coming. Two years ago we were in the Midwest...did so well it was extended to Florida. We are returning in November (2003) doing 20 cities in the United States."

John Kondis, once a partner with John Stuart (**Legends in Concert**) in Toronto for about a year, does not go unnoticed by Stuart. *"We have a worldwide registered trademark for* **Legends Alive***, yet we occasionally receive correspondence from* **Legends in Concert***. Our attorneys respond to their attorneys...nothing they can do. I personally like John Stuart. He is a nice guy. It is unfortunate that John is surrounded by people who don't have any idea what they are doing (in the entertainment business). But, John Stuart himself? I don't have any complaints about John. Some people think he is ruthless. I think he is just a good businessman. I don't know where he gets all of his energy, which is the bottom line of his successes. John will always prevail."*

The whole industry is competitive. **Elvis Presley Enterprises** continues to hint at its desire to collect additional licensing fees. The issues of Internet copyrights, burning (copying originally recorded) CDs, using celebrity names and look-a-likes, especially for profit, remains uncertain.

"*We have a show called* **The Roy Orbison Story**. *Sam Orbison, the sibling of Roy is in the show. We can go anywhere we want with the show because Sam is in it. But if he leaves the show, and we have already been warned by Barbara Orbison, this show will not be able to perform under that name again. But in Canada, they can't stop you because it is called a 'right to work' law here. We also have union and non-union mixture here. At one time it was union only, but now they've relaxed that rule here. We work together. But in order to go to the United States, we all have to be union because of immigration reasons.*"

John Kondis enjoys working with ETA Garry Wesley as Elvis in the **Legends Alive** show. He is very excited about Garry's recent win at the **$50,000 Tribute to the King contest** at the **Isle of Capri Casino** in Lula, Mississippi. He said, "*We intend to utilize this in our promotion of the show.*" In summary, Kondis added: "*When the phone stops ringing, that's when I'll stop promoting.*"

"The Elvis Story"

Steve Preston

Craig and Sam Newell

Chris MacDonald

Irv Cass

Ryan Pelton

The Scarf Lady — Jerry Brian

Aaron Skilton

Keith Henderson

Robert Washington

Mark Leen

Picture: © Dominick Walsh
Photography Ireland

Johnny
Thompson

Mark Leen

Ronny Craig

ELVIS with the JORDANAIRES

Elvis with The Jordanaires

THE JORDANAIRES

The Jordanaires

Jay Allan

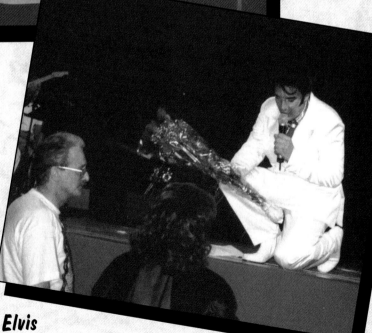

Kjell Elvis

𝄢

Michael
Dean

Darren
Lee

Rated # 1 Elvis Tribute Artist in the World
Memphis, TN 1997
www.darren-lee.com

Paul Fracassi

Nance Fox with (l. to r.)
Doug Church, Ronny Craig,
Irv Cass

Brandon Bennett

Leo Days

Richard Williams with
son-look-alike Leo Days

Richard Messier

Kraig Parker

Author Pamela Thomas-Williams with Martin Fontaine

Martin Fontaine from The Elvis Story

David Lee

Curt Lechner

Steve Chuke

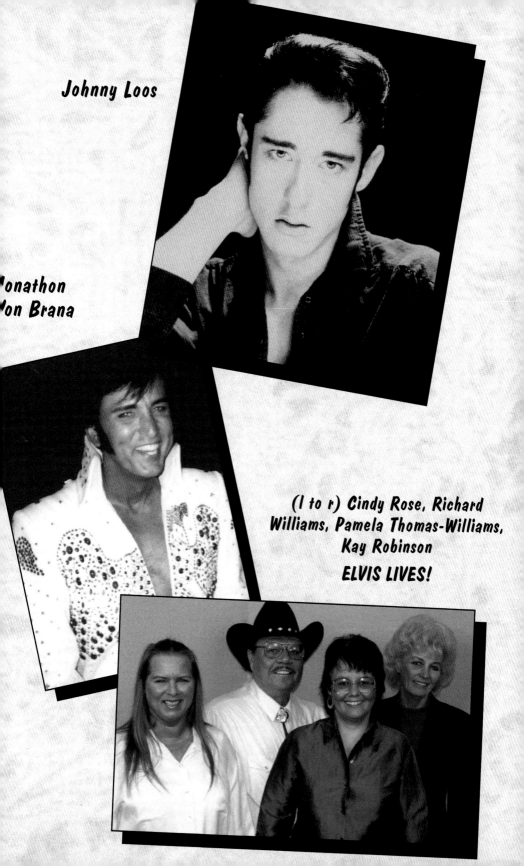

Johnny Loos

Jonathon Von Brana

(l to r) Cindy Rose, Richard Williams, Pamela Thomas-Williams, Kay Robinson
ELVIS LIVES!

Garry Wesley and wife Elaine

Doug Church

Rick Marino

Eric Erickson

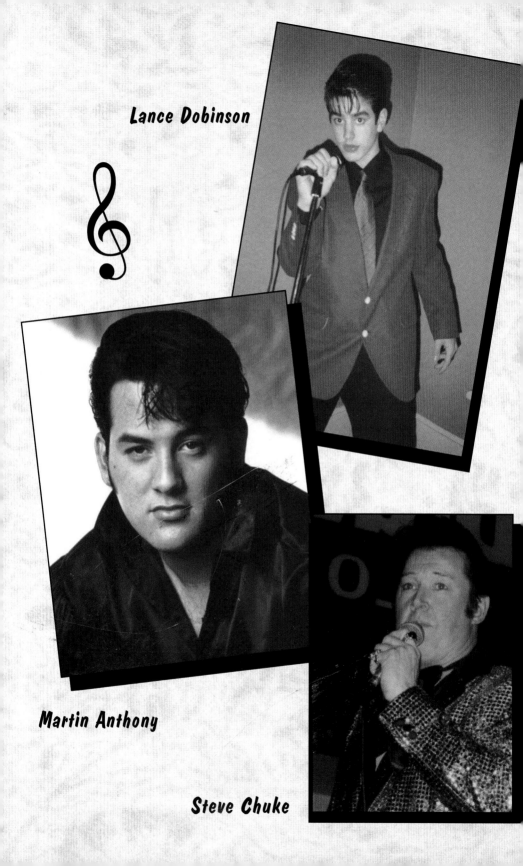

Lance Dobinson

Martin Anthony

Steve Chuke

Adam Ashcroft

Jailhouse Rock
from The
Elvis Story

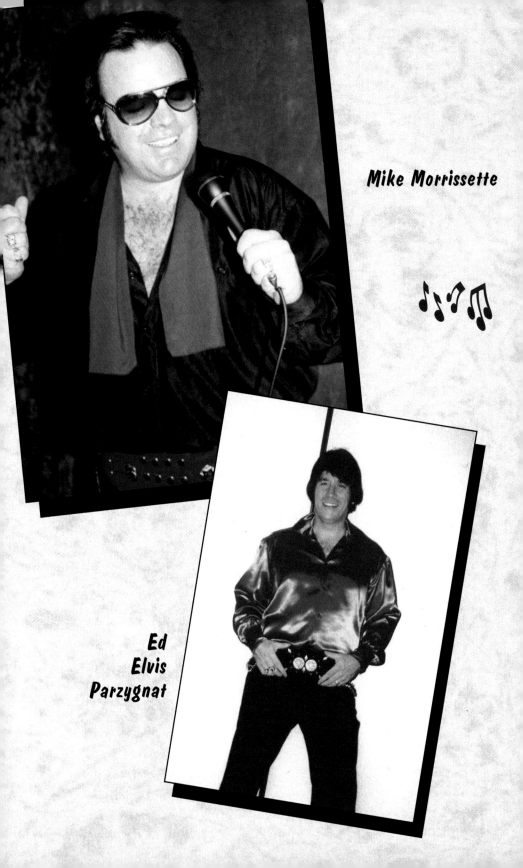

Mike Morrissette

Ed
Elvis
Parzygnat

Jack Smink

Travis Morris

Nance Fox and Ronny Craig

Joe Tirrito

Eddie Miles

David "Jesse" Moore

oore
Grove Rd.

Stephen Freeman

Martin Anthony

Rick Lenzi

Jerome Marion

Todd C.
Martin

Bob West

Kavan
Creamer

Michael Conti

Todd C. Martin

Butch Dicus

Paul Casey

Trent Carlini

(l to r)
Ronny Craig,
Doug Church and
Jerome Marion

Shawn Klush

Everette
"Howie"
Atherton

Tony Grova

Rob Garrett

Jim Barone

Paul Halverstadt

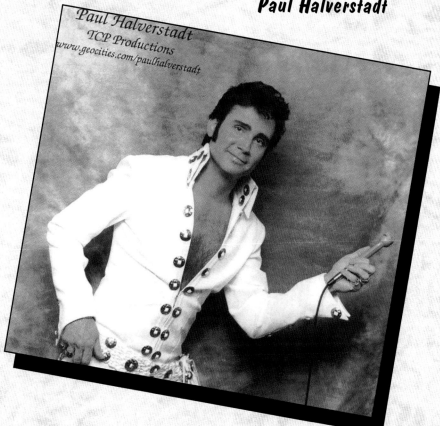

Paul Halverstadt
TCP Productions
www.geocities.com/paulhalverstadt

Ray Guillemette, Jr.

Robin Kelly

Matt King

Scene from
The Elvis Story

Leo Days

Everette
"Howie"
Atherton

Michael Dean

Jesse Aron

Jim Barone

Lance Dobinson

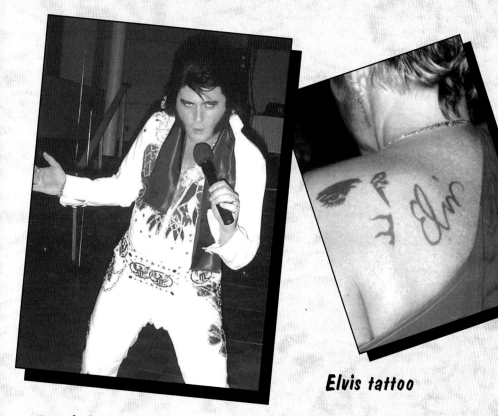

Elvis tattoo

Butch Dicus

Doug Church

Paul Casey

Stephen
Freeman

Robert Washington

Kjell Elvis

Irv Cass

Garry Wesley

Jack Smink

Jonathon Von Brana

Ray Guillemette, Jr.

Johnny Thompson

Johnny Loos

Tony Grova

Robert
Washington

Keith
Henderson

Steve Preston

Johnny Loos

Robin Kelly

Eddie
Miles

Mike Morrissette

Sam Newell

The Elvis Story

Jerome Marion

Curt Lechner

Jack Smink
with fan
"Mushy"

Aaron Skilton

Todd C. Martin

Jay Allan

Steve Preston

Johnny Loos

Picture :© Domnick Walsh Tralee Ireland '03

Mark Leen with the
xSpence Account
howband in Ireland

Aaron Skilton

Matt King

Bob West

CHAPTER 4

"THE ELVIS STORY," STARRING MARTIN FONTAINE

Martin Fontaine is the star of **The Elvis Story** and plays the lead role as Elvis Presley.

It is a show that is much more than a musical revue, yet different from a Broadway production. It is a show that creates the illusion of Elvis while telling the story of Elvis through his music. In conjunction with **LCQ Productions** and **Park Place Entertainment,** the show was brought to the **Grand Biloxi Casino** in February 2001 and in 2002.

The bizarre twist to it all is that Fontaine looks nothing like Elvis Presley in real life. Nor does he want to. He is a redheaded French Canadian performer with a heavy French accent who hails from Quebec City, Canada.

In September of 1998, vice-president of **Elvis Presley Enterprises** and brother-in-law of Priscilla Beaulieu Presley, Gary Hovey came to see the show.

"It is the closest show to reality," he said.

In fact, it is currently the only show endorsed by **Elvis Presley Enterprises. The Elvis Story** premiered in 1995 at Quebec City's **Le Capitóle Theatre** and has been produced in the U.S. for the last two years performing to sell-out audiences. The show was originally performed in French (except for the singing) and translated into complete English for the American debut. Tickets sales indicate that over 900,000 people have seen the show and over 96% of those surveyed said they would see it again or at least recommend the show to others regardless of the distance required to travel to see the show.

To appreciate **The Elvis Story**, you don't have to be an Elvis Presley fan. But if you are, you will recognize that not a single detail has been overlooked. Fontaine has read nearly every book that has been written about Elvis Presley, from his life and biography to those researching hundreds of photos of Elvis depicting every musical phase. Fontaine's Elvis expertise is one of the reasons he is the art director for the production as well.

The most unusual aspect of Fontaine performing **The Elvis Story** is that he portrays all of the Elvis parts himself. In fact, he does 16 complete costume changes in 90 minutes, including at least five or six wig, sideburn, and eyelash changes of various styles and color. The wigs are natural looking and, at a cost of $2,000 or more, they should be. Fontaine accomplishes his quick changes with the assistance of one very talented makeup artist and two costume change people. He is so detailed about his costumes that he even insists on the correct jewelry, shoes, and socks for the era and the specific song he is performing in order to be exactly as Elvis Presley was when Elvis performed it.

As the various eras unfold in **The Elvis Story**, so does the stage. Each prop is carefully replicated and coordinated. The stage is complimented with additional movie screens that provide the backup documentary dialogue complete with narration and enhanced with actual Elvis archived photos. The backdrop is delicately done to blend with each set change to keep the audience focused without a moments' distraction from Elvis. The audience soon begins to really believe in the illusion as they are gradually drawn into the perfect persona of Elvis Presley. Some of them begin to smile affectionately, while others weep to emotional levels as high as the day that Elvis Presley died.

All of the songs are performed live and sung by Martin himself, which is another incredible aspect of his extreme talent. A four- to five-piece band surrounds Martin with six backup singers and six dancers, bringing the total to 25 individuals who complete the production staff. An estimated $250,000 is invested in the production and props alone. The curtain lifts and the story begins with a replica of **Graceland** complete with the musical note-emblazoned gates—gates that actually open to the winding driveway to the place Elvis called home. The scene becomes very lifelike with the high vaulted ceilings of the beautiful **Grand Biloxi Theatre** that seats over 1700 people. There is complete silence in the audience as the mourners on stage gather at the gates to hang flowers and signs to signify that Elvis will live forever.

The story then moves to a young 18-year old Elvis at **Sun Records** in Memphis in 1954 singing **That's Alright Mama,** to his infamous haircut and induction into the Army. Full-scale production numbers follow and restage some of the most triumphant moments in Elvis' life. Some of the highlights include: the totally re-created dance number from **Jailhouse Rock** complete with the double-decked jail cells, sliding cell doors, and the clanging of billy clubs by the uniformed guards. Fontaine, clad in the reminiscent striped prisoner garb, slides down the pole dancing with fellow prisoners, just as Elvis originally choreographed himself in the movie. There is also Elvis' famous 1968 **Comeback Special** featured on NBC television. In this number, Fontaine appears on an empty stage with only his backup band, surrounded by an intimate audience while wearing the signature black leather outfit. Then, of course, there is Elvis' 1969 mega-show in Las Vegas right up to the 1973 outstanding performance of **Aloha From Hawaii** via satellite, and seen by one billion viewers around the world featuring the famous white jumpsuit, flowing cape, and Hawaiian lei.

Throughout the story, Fontaine weaves an emotional web with a medley of Elvis' movie songs. The story ends in 1977, when an older, ailing Elvis begins to forget some of the lyrics and is escorted off the stage towards the end of a concert, unable to continue. The encore, however, features Elvis restored to health in a paradox of sad, but happy ending rendition of **My Way**.

Who is Martin Fontaine the person? He is a handsome, 38-year old actor, composer, songwriter, singer and accomplished musician on several instruments. He is also the father of two beautiful, young daughters with companion and soul mate Marie-Claude LaPointe, who is a backup singer and musician in the show. I would like to further note that as we continue into the interview with Fontaine, his comments and responses, which carry a strong French dialect, are quoted and not paraphrased.

It should also be emphasized that his accent is not noticeable at all when he's performing as Elvis.

Beginning at an early age, Fontaine surrounded himself with music. By the age of 16, he had mastered the basics of almost every musical instrument he touched. He also began to focus his skills on ballet, jazz and acting while enrolled in a private college. Fontaine always had a band and performed in numerous performances including a Broadway musical in Paris called **Starmania** during a three month break from **The Elvis Story**.

In 1995, when the producers of **The Elvis Story** began conducting auditions for the lead role of Elvis Presley, Fontaine was determined to walk away with the part. He impressed the creative producer so much that the immediate reaction was— *"But he doesn't look at all like Elvis Presley, what are we going to do with his looks?"*

Not only did Fontaine secure the part, he ultimately changed the direction of the entire production. The producers intended to cast more than one person for the lead because it just didn't seem possible that one person could handle the multiple parts that would be required to tell **The Elvis Story**. After Fontaine's rendition of **Love Me Tender** and **My Way**, it was clear to the producers that Fontaine could mesmerize the audience with his interpretation of Elvis' music. Thank goodness for the magic of costuming and a professional make-up artist in transforming Fontaine into the illusion of Elvis Presley.

"I believe that when they were looking for someone to personify Elvis in the show, soul is what they wanted. That is what they were looking for. And look at me! What do you think they found? They found soul," Fontaine recalled. *"When I met Mr. Jack Soden, president of* **Elvis Presley Enterprises,** *the most amazing thing to me was he said to me: 'It is your talent that is so great, not only as Elvis, but your talent, Martin. Don't forget that.'"* Then, with a smile on his face, Fontaine added, *"The other guy, Mr. Morgan, said 'You should get an award for the hair.'"*

Why does Martin Fontaine focus his abilities on Elvis Presley?

"I get inspired by his spirit and his love that never dies," he said. *"There is also the tremendous challenge to perform as an actor, a singer portraying such a great entertainer such as Elvis Presley."*

Remember that Fontaine does not look at all like Elvis in real life and he is very pleased about that. With so many impersonators out there that enjoy looking like and being like Elvis Presley, why would Fontaine want to miss out on the public recognition?

"Because the magic only operates when I'm on stage. You know you can sense when something is clicking. So I think it is my acting skills, my vocal skills, my music skills. I choose to do this. I could have chosen to do something else, to do my own compositions, shows, or Broadway instead of Elvis.

I can do whatever I want and I decided to put all of my skills into this. I chose to put everything I could to make art with this. That is the main differ-ence between a lot of people. Everything you do must be like art you see and hear. It has to be polished, you know. Seeking perfection because you are talking about...like making a movie," said Fontaine.

Specifically, why Elvis Presley the person, the performer?

Martin added, *"I think I just wanted to straighten things out. You know, using all my abilities and as an Elvis lover.... I think he is my best friend now. He's looking upon me. I think he is somewhere saying like 'Martin, go ahead....' And I think I am doing something that people like to see or to feel or experience.... Because I think this is my job on this earth now.... For now, for the period of time, to try to portray what Elvis was about."*

As if his total dedication as a performer is not enough, add to that the challenge of his responsibility as the art director.

"I watch every detail....I think I have to amaze myself....I really have to enjoy what I do, believe in what I do...to always be more," he said.

The casting for the show is also difficult.

"It is very hard. You can make it. And as long as you have the same vision of what we want. But it is also wonderful to have the control. For example, the set. You won't believe me, but one day they wanted to change the set and everything. So I made a demo with Legos—you know, like the Legos building blocks. To scale and everything was perfect. I said, let's put the gates there and the lighting with little flashlights and all," Fontaine said, as he referred to the specific set of **Graceland**

Fontaine also feels extremely privileged to be part of such a won-derful show.

"I get to travel with my family. That's very important to keep that bal-ance. I keep both feet on the ground all the time. This is work for me. This is my job, which I love and which I want to do the best way possible. I need my family. I need my balance. It is hard to do sometimes. But I am privi-leged that my producers allow me to do so and they treat me real well," he explains.

How does Fontaine's family adjust to the scheduling? They travel with a nanny who takes care of and tutors the children during the daily rehearsals and evening performances. She speaks both French and English. The Fontaine children are too young to know much English yet. But during the times and days when they are not performing (two nights off) Fontaine and Marie-Claude LaPointe are very devoted parents creating an environment as normal as possible. While performing at the **Grand Biloxi Casino,** they live in a suite complete with cooking facilities. They also maintain a home in Canada that, like most people, Fontaine is anxious to return to in order to catch up on the yearly maintenance and upkeep of the property. He generally only has two or so months off a year.

"*My wife thinks I should be doing something besides Elvis. She thinks I am hiding behind the guy. That's what she thinks. Because she thinks I could do so much more. I could write more songs and I could be Martin. I keep telling her I gotta do this because I do a good job and people like what I do. It is my job for now. When I am tired of it, I will decide. If you ask her, that is what she will say. She thinks I am hiding behind the character…and it's a bit true. It is also a show that works, it's a show that makes money, it's a show that attracts people,*" Fontaine added very confidently.

Though Fontaine has never been in an Elvis impersonator contest, he once judged a convention/contest in Montreal, Canada. Fontaine's explanation for his disapproval of Elvis contests provides an interesting glimpse into Fontaine, the entertainer.

"*It was a huge competition, like an Elvis Festival. There was like 10 to 12 Elvis entertainers. Some of the best in the world. There was Doug Church, Shawn Klush, Mike Albert, Trent Carlini and others. It was billed as something like 'All The Best.'* **The Jordanaires** *were there as judges too. They had like a $10,000 first prize. They had a full band that was terrible. But I think it was all arranged…like a big promotion. You know, an occasion to see a show, to bring in a lot of people, to make money. People paid money to come to see the competition. To see a show. I am curious about the contests because I hear negative things about them. I don't understand why people can't just do shows, instead of the competition for Elvis impersonators, themselves? I don't believe it is for the audience; it's for them—they want to win the money. They want to win. They want to be the best…the best what? I say, get your life! You should want to make music, sing songs, and get in from the audience. That's the thrill. That's respectable. But to be the best? You are the best, but who cares? I don't think it should be treated as a sport. It's entertainment. It doesn't matter if you sing with tracks or with a band or go out there and tell jokes. Contests…it is not a contest. They are* not horses. Who decides who is the best? Who are the judges and what are the criteria. You have like two or three winners. Some of them make money and some of them don't. The organizers make the money. That is the way I feel about Elvis. Leave him alone. Let us do what we do, and for the guys that do this for the good reasons, which are for the public, for the beauty of it, for the challenge, for the love, and for the music. If it is for the money, the way you look, to get women, or to get fame and power? You have people out there who don't know how to sing or move like Elvis. They don't know music. They just want to do this. I'm not building a house because I don't know how to do it. Elvis was a singer, an entertainer. He was natural. He didn't copy anybody, but he was inspired by a lot of things, like everybody. We have the right to be inspired. They think they have everything by providing...just looking like Elvis. That is the saddest part of all. You have to have a life. Some of them don't know who they are anymore. Look at me for God's sake. I am Martin with an accent, with my looks, and my abilities, and my limits. I know who I am. I know what I can do," Fontaine summarized.

The future for Martin Fontaine is certain for the next three years with his contract. Then what? He wants to be in Las Vegas, Paris, London, or Japan. When I spoke with Fontaine several months after this interview, he confirmed that he would be touring in Japan. It would be great if Fontaine could land in Las Vegas so that so many more people could see his show. Las Vegas is best, not only because it is considered the capital of Elvis entertainment, but also because it has the most global effect, bringing tourists from all over the world.

"It is also my hope that Lisa Marie Presley will someday see **The Elvis Story**," added Fontaine.

And with this the year that Elvis Aaron Presley, aka Jesse, his deceased twin brother, is rumored to be alive and coming back, here is what Martin had to say:

"Is it interesting to me? No. Could he have staged it? Yes. But why? He was such a good entertainer. That was his entire life. He loved being Elvis Presley. He dedicated his whole life to his fans, to the stage, and to his music. He loved being recognized. Why would a man like that stay in a place secret? But also I think that one of the key things about Elvis Presley being Elvis Presley is the fact that he had a twin brother that died at birth. That's what drove him all these years. That guilt. Why me? Why was I the one to survive? And he had to live the life of two persons instead of only one," said Fontaine.

"Now the end is near, and so I face the final curtain." In the grand finale of **The Elvis Story**, Fontaine closes with the perfect ending by singing Elvis' version of **My Way.** The entire cast then returns to the stage. They hold hands and take a bow to a standing ovation.

Fontaine moves forward to the front of the stage and politely says, *"Thank you for coming. My name is Martin Fontaine."*

As the curtain falls and Martin returns to a quiet dressing room, the narrator announces ***"Elvis Has Left The Building."***

CHAPTER 5

THE PEOPLE
BEHIND THE SCENES

Much has been said about the impersonators and tribute artists, especially Elvis. The following people work just as hard, if not harder, behind the scenes in the impersonation industry.

BEA FOGELMAN

Bea Fogelman is the author of three wonderful entertainment and celebrity impersonator books, including **Who's Not Who, Showtime** and **Copycats**. I fully enjoyed readying **Copycats**. It is evident that Fogelman knows her way around Las Vegas and the biggest names in the entertainment business. A legend in her own right, she was part of Las Vegas when it was still a small town. Fogelman was able to see some of the very first production shows, as well as watch some of the first impersonators perform. She is the owner and founder of **The Entertainment Network**, a booking agency for impersonators.

"I started **The Entertainment Network** in 1996 while my daughter, Sherie Rae Parker, was performing as Bette Midler and Janis Joplin steadily since 1983 in the cast of **Legends in Concert**. Several of her friends were not performing and she wanted me to locate work for them by promoting them to the agents and producers I had met through writing my book **Copycats**. When **Legends in Concert** began, there were other producers and agents who booked events using celebrity impersonators, but John Stuart was the first one to produce a showroom spectacular using dead celebrities; Marilyn Monroe, Elvis, Buddy Holly and Janis Joplin to begin with. Stuart, a former actor and successful artist in his own right, knew that they had to be authentic, believable look-alike, sound-alike move-alike duplicates of the stars they *emulated. When the curtain came down that first opening show, John knew he had a successful show…and the audience loved seeing the stars they loved come back into their lives again. The celebrity impersonator industry **had** to grow because of audience demand. With the growth of the industry, clients and venues learned that their audiences wanted more variety of talent in their shows and events…and soon actors, comedians, sports figures, TV personalities and political people began walking around conventions, appearing on television, becoming voice-actors and stand-ins for film."*

The Entertainment Network receives from seven to as many as twelve requests a day from agents and producers who seek talent for their events and shows worldwide. In respect to requests for just Elvis impersonators, Bea said, *"I have nine full pages of Elvi on my talent lists…all sizes, looks, nationalities and voices. Recently, I received a request for eight different Elvis impersonators for a commercial and one to be a midget. I had to send a casting call out for that one and the agents cooperated to locate them. The industry has changed and expanded, however, I personally enjoy watching a show where the Elvis, Neil Diamond, Bette Midler, Marilyn, Nat King Cole, Madonna, and other **actors**, who are celebrity impersonators…who look, sing and perform **exactly** like the original stars they emulate. That is what sets the greatest from the mediocre and the amateur. What I don't like is seeing a television actor, known for his/her name, impersonating a star or personality in a film or whatever, when an actor who actually is a profession celebrity impersonator would be better in the role. This indicates to me that the celebrity impersonator industry is still not recognized as a professional entity…yet."*

Through her company, Fogelman also publishes a newsletter called **Beg & Brag**. It was originally called **Copycats** and was mailed out to the 100 or so people on her list.

*"When Richard Screen, a technical internet writer and Billy Joel impersonator, arrived from England to America, he liked what **The Network** was doing and began placing the newsletter on my book website www.BeaFogelman.com. It became a source of exposing contact information (e-mail addresses) so they could be reached by the agents and producers for their events. At the same time, the artists could tell everyone (now there are 1700+ on the list) what they are doing and where they are appearing. **Begging** for work and letting everyone know who they are and what they are doing in their professional and personal lives. **That's Bragging!"***

Bea Fogelman is also involved with the **International Guild of Celebrity Impersonators and Tribute Artists (IGCITA).** She was recognized for her contributions to the industry with a **Cloney Award** from **IGCITA** in 2002 *For the Network and Generous Support of the Guild.*

FIL JESSEE

"The ability to earn money in the skill of performing, producing and working in any allied field of the performing arts is not in itself the definition of a professional. What separates the professional from the amateur is the recognition of the association, organization, guild or society that designates him as an "artist" in his field.

Membership in such a group of peers produces a bond of friendship, pride, and accomplishment. Recognition by such a community designates the performer and/or the allied members a professional artist. Without it, he is an amateur."

Bea Fogelman, author
Showtime 2001

In 1999, Fil Jessee and his wife, Valera, established the **International Guild of Celebrity Impersonators and Tribute Artists, Inc.** The **IGCITA** is the world's first and currently, the only professional, registered organization for professional look-alikes, impersonators, and tribute artists of celebrities. Jessee, talent agent and producer, has over 30 years of experience in the casting industry.

According to the **IGCITA** website (www.IGCITA.org) their primary mission is *"to provide for members an on-going, dynamic and adaptable program of assistance offering improved network, opportunities, enhanced recognition of professional achievement, collective power to influence the talent market, and the realization of common goals."*

The site also provides information about the organization, their code of ethics, membership applications and qualifications.

By 2000, the **Guild** distributed its first brochure and initiated a quarterly newsletter called **Cue Tips.** In 2001, the **Guild** hosted its first convention and implemented the **Cloney Awards** ceremony. Ms. Elyse Del Francia, a California based talent agent, organized the **Celebrity Impersonator Convention (CIC)** that is held in Las Vegas. Later, the scheduling of the **CIC** was changed to coincide with the **Cloney Awards**. This prestigious award and ceremony has now become the *Grammy* of the impersonator world. Due to the results of a survey by attendees of previous conventions, the Board of Directors of the **Guild** decided to not officially participate in the **Celebrity Impersonator Convention** in 2003. Instead, it will host its own annual convention in Las Vegas, Nevada, and probably in other cities in years to come. However, the Guild-sponsored event, with the exception of the annual **IGCTA** Board of Directors meeting and other business sessions of primary interest to members only, will be open to the entire celebrity impersonation industry. The convention will include the **Cloney** Awards, and talent showcases, a professional show by celebrity impersonators and the addition of a trade show.

2002 **Cloney** Awards are: Michael Lee Clayton as Robin Williams for **BEST COMEDIC IMPERSONATION**, Sherie Rae Parker as Bette Midler for **BEST MUSICAL STAR IMPERSONATION**, Janie Minick as Elizabeth Taylor for **MOST OUTSTANDING IMPERSONATION OF A FEMALE FILM LEGEND**, Ralph Chelli as Clark Gable for **MOST OUTSTANDING IMPERSONATION OF A MALE FILM LEGEND**, Melody Knighton as Lucille Ball for **BEST IMPERSONATION OF A FEMALE BROADCAST MEDIA LEGEND**, Al Mager as George Burns for **BEST IMPERSONATION OF A MALE BROADCAST MEDIA LEGEND**, Sherie Rae Parker as Bette Midler for **MOST OUTSTANDING PORTRAYAL OF A CONTEMPORARY STAR**, Wil Collins as Liberace for **BEST IMPERSONATION OF A MALE BROADCAST LEGEND**, Judith Gindy for **BEST HISTORICAL IMPERSONATION**, Hollie Vest for publishing the book *Made You Look* —**BEST SUPPORTING ENHANCEMENT OF CELEBRITY IMPERSONATION**, Corporate Express for featuring Greg Chelew as David Letterman for **BEST USE OF AN IMPERSONATOR IN A PROMOTIONAL CAMPAIGN**, Brent Mendendall as President George W. Bush for **BEST USE OF A CELEBRITY IMPERSONATOR IN A HISTORICAL REEN-**

ACTMENT, Stacey Allemeier as Britney Spears for **DIRECTOR'S OUTSTANDING RISING STAR,** and Bea Fogelman for the network and generous support of the guild for **MOST OUTSTANDING INDUSTRY AMBASSADOR.**

There is no doubt that the **IGCITA** is an organization worthy of membership and participation if you are affiliated with the impersonator industry. I didn't see any Elvis impersonator winners, but I know that Darren Lee is a member. Let's get on board! I will make brief mention here that there is also the **Professional Elvis Impersonator Association (PEIA)** directed by ETA Johnny Thompson.

E-IMPERSONATORS.COM

The newest kid on the block is **E-impersonators.com**. The site went online sometime in late 2002 and provides a database of Elvis Tribute Artists, a listing of vendors for ETAs, monthly articles and biographies of ETAs.

A gentleman going by the name of Big T is the primary author for the site. Though he claims not to be an Elvis impersonator, he has been entertaining people for over 30 years as **Big T's Karaoke Show.** An Elvis fan since he was a child, he teamed up with classmate and friend Kevin, to create this site. Big T has been told he has the ability to sound very close to Elvis when he sings Karaoke.

According to the **E-impersonators.com** site, this question was posed to them: Why Elvis impersonators rather than Elvis Tribute Artists? Though the site quickly agrees that the impersonators should be referred to as Tribute Artists, the response was: "*Marketing. We researched the use of the term Elvis Tribute Artists compared to Elvis Impersonators on an Internet search engine. In a 30- day period, there were over 7600 searches for Elvis Impersonators, but only 497 searches for Elvis Tribute Artists. (That's more than 15 to 1.) The public is looking for E-impersonators, therefore we are E-impersonators.com.*"

SUITE 101.COM

According to their website, Suite.101 is an online publishing community of writers, readers, and educators who have come together to share their passion. It is comprised of 487 writers (contributing editors) who publish over 700 articles each month, adding to the existing archive of 25,453 articles and offering 20,068 links. The site offers an unlimited amount of information with hundreds of topics to choose from.

The sites of particular interest to me are the Elvis Tribute Artists column written by Melody Sanders and the Elvis Presley column written by June Moore. They have also teamed up to write the book **Walk A Mile In Their Shoes** that includes several interviews they have collected with the ETAs. Sanders provides insight into controversial issues that surround the **Business of Being Elvis,** as well as fun and enlightening interviews with the ETAs she met in her various travels. A native of Canada, she began her journey in the ETA world as the president of the International Fan Club for Darren Lee. Lee is the 1997 World Champion of the **Images of the King Contest** in Memphis.

CHAPTER 6

THE FANS

"There are no qualifications...not sex, race, criminal background or even talent...but the fans will sift things out."

–Nance Fox

The Elvis Presley fan clubs and ETA fan clubs exist in numbers that defy easy calculations with official **EPE**-sanctioned clubs alone totaling 700. According to various Internet resources, over 10,000 fan clubs exist worldwide. Every ETA and Elvis impersonator has a fan club with its own personalized name and president. Official **EPE** fan clubs are required to comply with strict guidelines including meeting times, club newsletters, and both positive and respectful news about Elvis Presley. The ETA fans clubs are primarily designed to follow the career path of the club's favorite ETA. Each club has a website boasting of the best ETA and his accomplishments.

Meikel Jungner from Sweden is a tremendous Elvis Presley fan, but he is also a huge ETA fan. He maintains the website, ETribute—Elvis tribute artists and sound-alikes. Meikel's Web publishes reviews of every ETA he hears about. He offers his complete dedication to the Elvis business as a hobby and not for any monetary purpose. Born in 1977, Meikel never had the opportunity to see Elvis perform live.

"Elvis was, and is, very popular in Sweden. My mother and father had a cassette tape with Elvis. I listened to it a couple of times when I was very young. I didn't think much about music then. Around 1994, I started to become more and more interested in music. Unlike most kids my age, I followed in the footsteps of my parents when it comes to music style. I started to listen to a lot of music from the 50s, 60s and 70s. In 1995, Elvis would have been 60 years old; there was a lot of Elvis music on the radio and TV. I started to really enjoy his music...not just his songs, but his voice. It was dif-

ferent from all other artists. I became a member of the Swedish Elvis Fan Club. Then, when I first heard of tribute artists and impersonators, I saw that I had a chance of being able to experience Elvis' music with living artists. I think I first saw an ETA on Swedish TV...it was actually three different artists: Jorgen "Hubbas" Anderson, Stefan Wikstrom, and a guy named Tord, I believe."

Meikel collects as many records, CDs and videos as his budget will allow. He listens to Elvis and Elvis sound-alikes everyday while searching the Internet for the buzz of any new ETAs.

"There are many very good tribute artists. Some are great in sounding like Elvis, some are great look-alikes and some have really practiced the moves Elvis had on stage. There are only a few that are really good in all of these areas, and many more that are great in one of these areas," according to Meikel.

David Sumpter from England also provides a not-for-profit website strictly for ETAs. An Internet engineer by trade, Sumpter is motivated by his passion for Elvis in the construction of his interesting site. In addition to listing ETAs from all over the globe, David's site includes the capacity to search for an ETA by name, country, or state in the United States. He also provides book reviews, an updated Elvis quiz and a message board. With his knack for the net, Sumpter regularly updates his Web site with new features. According to David, *"We will soon be putting up ETA photos arranged in a random order in which the ETA fan can choose the most interesting."*

"What delights me about running my site **www.elvisisinthebrowser.com** *is the diverse range of people from all over the globe who bring their own particular talents to bear in offering tribute to the King. I just love talking to all of these folks in the common language of Elvis Presley. I must admit that I was shocked about how powerful an ETA's performance could be when I saw my first one—Liberty Mounten at Cheltenham Town Hall, England, 1994. Elvis was no longer a great memory and a stack of records, but a vibrant legacy."*

On the lighter side of the ETA fan world is Wisconsin native Bill Bibo. He is an architect by trade and maintains **www.biboland.com** plus hosts the link, **Hall of Kings**.

"I was, honestly, never really an Elvis fan...In fact if I sang, it would be the audience that leaves the building, not Elvis. I was always more fascinated

with Elvis culture. I love Elvis kitsch. Then, about seven or eight years ago, a good friend of mine gave me a copy of the CD **Graciasland** by Elvis impersonator El Vez. I was blown away. He is one of the best there is. He doesn't sound anything like Elvis but he took Elvis songs and made them his own. He is quite an entertainer. So I wrote to him and he sent me an autographed photo. I still have it on my desk at work. From then on, it was all downhill as my wife says. I started looking for Elvi, writing to them and getting autographed photos."

About four years ago, Bill registered the name of his site and went online. It started out as a place to post his collection, which at the time only included 25 autographs. Four months after the site went up, **www.biboland.com** was chosen by **USA TODAY** as the Hot Site of the Day and his Web popularity continues to soar. Kim Kamando spotlighted Bill's Web site on her tech radio program. Bill was interviewed on **CNET** radio in San Francisco. He was additionally contacted by a German journalist in her search for information for her documentary on European Elvi.

"Now, the Elvi write to me asking to be on my site. I have modest success now with about 250 hits a week. It really picks up in January and August, obviously. Through all of this I have become an Elvis fan. I have met some interesting people…like Miss Cybelvis Monroe. She is one of the funniest acts you've ever seen. She is a professional Marilyn Monroe impersonator who also does Elvis, or should I say Marilyn doing Elvis. My favorite Elvi are the ones that don't take it too seriously. Face it; they shouldn't pretend to be Elvis even off stage. Give it a rest!"

Bill has many funny and interesting stories about the Elvi world, so stay tuned. He is almost finished writing his children's novel.

"It's about two boys and a robot working in an orbiting fast food restaurant. I'm going to call it **Hamburger Madness**."

The largest European collector of Elvis Presley memorabilia is Andylon Lensen from the Netherlands. She owns the **International Elvis Shop** in Holland and most recently opened a second shop in the United States. She is known by insiders of the Elvis world as a big private collector of unreleased studio material, such as out-takes and live shows, known as soundboards, and 8mm and 16mm films. Andylon is also the owner of her company, **Elvis Collectors Gold**. Andylon became a collector forty years ago at the age of eight: "I became an Elvis fan and fanatic too. I then became the youngest member of The Dutch and Belgium Elvis Fan Club."

She grew up with the 50s and 60s music, singing Dutch songs with her entire family on stage and on radio programs. Andylon's mother would write original songs and accompany her five children with the accordion or guitar. When Andylon was thirteen years old, her mother became ill and later divorced Andylon's father. This changed her entire life. Andylon buried herself in Elvis' music.

"I became a hermit in my own little Elvis world, which consoled me in the many ups and downs in life. I went to see many Elvis movies and began buying 78 rpm records of Elvis with my own money that I was earning. One day, I just realized I had collected so many Elvis items…even many duplicates, so I had this idea to open up a shop."

For the last few years, Andlyon used the Internet to purchase unusual objects for herself as well. She also collects memorabilia from 50s and 60s rock 'n' roll artists including Chuck Berry, Eddie Cochran, Jerry Lee Lewis, Roy Orbison, Bobby Darin, Timi Yuro, Brook Benton, Gene Vincent, Johnny Burnette and his Trio. She sells collectables of these artists and others in her shop. Her all-time favorite is the U.S. female singer, Timi Yuro, the original singer of the song **Hurt**. In 1961, Timi's **Hurt** climbed to number one on the pop charts in both the United States and the United Kingdom. Andylon composed the music for the lyrics of three songs written by Timi plus she additionally arranged a great deal of music and songs for other European artists. Then, as everyone knows, Elvis made **Hurt** his own hit song in the 1970s.

"When Elvis died, I had a booking agency for national and international artists, including a modeling agency. When I heard the news at 7 o'clock in the morning, I collapsed. I bought all the newspapers from around the world. It took me a long time to get over it. I then devoted myself to becoming a songwriter. I wrote the music, lyrics, arrangements and produced over 300 songs."

Andylon is also involved with book authors, films, documentaries and DVDs about Elvis due to her large collection of unpublished, rare and never-before seen photographs. She is currently promoting her own book to be released in May, 2003, **Elvis Rockin' Through The Years. Vol. 1.** Be sure to log on to her website for more details and

while you're there, listen to the beautiful jazzy piece she wrote called
Candle Burn.

Andylon is a very humble and extremely hard-working person, often working 16 hours a day. I know because I have talked with her often at 3 o'clock in the morning Dutch time. For the most informative information about Elvis Presley, she recommends the websites **Elvis World Japan, Solid Gold** and **www.ElvisNews.com**.

In regards to the ETAs, fans, and Elvis industry today, *"Some of these Elvis fans are behaving in an anti-social way without morals...this wasn't happening when Elvis was alive. The fans weren't competitive. You have more of a family feeling with people helping each other. Now, it's all about how to make money or rip-off Elvis fans with high prices. It's really sad and I miss the old days sometimes."*

Paul Dowling, owner of **WorldWideElvis**, collects and sells hard-to-find Elvis vinyl records. His specialty is BMG CDs and vinyl from all over the world including some DVDs, VCDs and books. **WorldWideElvis** does not sell Elvis bootlegs or memorabilia.

"I discovered Elvis in the early 60s when I was in high school. I went to see **Follow That Dream** *with a friend of mine and ended up falling in love with Elvis' music. I didn't have any money then to buy his records, but we had a radio show—in Baltimore where I lived at the time—that aired a program called* **The Elvis Hour** *every night. I would tape every show. From that show, I found out about the magazine* **Elvis Monthly** *and I promptly subscribed to it. I had no idea this was to be the start of an addictive hobby as well as a full-time job."*

Elvis vinyl collecting, especially at an addictive level, costs money. It was tough for Paul to buy Elvis vinyl records without a job. At first, he borrowed money from his mother and sister and then he started selling some of the duplicate records from his collection. Ultimately, he began compiling a small mailing list by contacting readers of the various Elvis magazines. Then, one day, Paul decided to take the biggest gamble of his life. He borrowed $20,000 to buy a mailing list with 500,000 names and printed his first catalogue.

"Well, believe it or not, these catalogues were arriving in people's homes the week of Elvis' death. It was very difficult for me as I went into such a shock after Elvis' passing. I went to the post office and I must have had 10,000 orders! I was totally stunned as we were all (Elvis fans) with what

had happened…losing our idol…a friend whom we had never met but still felt close to. But, now I had to deal with these orders and with the 1000 a day that continued to come in for the next three months or more. That's another story, however that is why I developed my website **WorldWideElvis** *in 1977."*

In an interview with Andylon Lensen (early 2002) posted on her website www.epgold.com, Andylon asked Paul about the future of his business and his thoughts about some of the fanatic Elvis fans… *"nut-cases…morons…? They have crucified everyone like Ernst Jorgenson, you, Joe Tunzi, Gerry Rijff, Geller… and even me."*

"I am currently working on a CD project, however, there may be a problem at BMG in the United States may be putting a freeze on anyone outside of the main label doing anything this year because they want to be the only outlet selling Elvis during this 25th Anniversary. I am hoping to find out more soon. It will be posted on my website. Those fans? I guess its like…why do people sometimes read the **Inquirer** *or the* **Star**? *We all go to Willem's site for the message board for unknown reasons or maybe because we like to read the crazy things people write. Seriously, I only go to this mes-sage board when someone tells me that there may be some absurd story on me and I guess I just like to have a good laugh. I probably only visit the site once a month as I have better things to do."*

When I asked Paul if he had any interest in the ETAs, he high-lighted his favorite and told why:*"Yes, Doug Church is the best. His CDs sell better for me than Elvis' in some cases!"*

James J. Curtin, known as ETA Jim "E" Curtin, is one of the lead-ing authorities on Elvis Presley and one of the largest collectors of Elvis memorabilia in the world today. He was also a personal friend of Elvis Presley from 1970 until his untimely death in 1977. Jim is also the owner of **The Elvis Empire** and the **James J. Curtin Archives**, both registered names. Curtin claims to have over 25,000 photos of Elvis and over 10,000 collectables of Elvis, some 5,000 records of Elvis from all over the world, 10,000 feet of unreleased concert footage on Super 8mm film and 3 original stage-worn jumpsuits that previously belonged to Elvis. Elvis personally gave Curtin one of the jumpsuits and Vernon Presley gave him one other suit. Curtin began his collection in 1961 and it is now housed in a 12-room building requiring 24-hour security in Philadelphia. Curtin's collection is now more than a full-time job and he would now like to slow down from his hobby. His **entire** collection is for sale for the mere asking price of **$5 million dollars!** He will sell the three jumpsuits for $1 million and the photos for $2 million. He believes he has over 100,000 hours and $1 million dollars invested in his time-consuming collection.

Curtin has written many books about Elvis, including photo calendars, and magazine articles, and provides expert commentary regarding the *Business of Being Elvis.* He always enjoys talking about his love and respect for Elvis.

In 1973, Curtin designed and ordered a custom-made Gibson J-200 guitar from the Gibson Guitar Corp. in Kalamazoo, Michigan for Elvis. He wanted Elvis to know how much he admired him. The guitar was black in color with the crowns and Elvis' name in Mother-of-Pearl. The guitar cost him over $2000 and took a little over a year to make. Curtin also ordered a special guitar case made with a brass plate for the personalized inscription: *"To the world's greatest singer, performer and entertainer. From your buddy, Jim Curtin."*

On Monday, August 26, 1974, he purchased two plane tickets to Las Vegas, Nevada, from Philadelphia, Pennsylvania. One ticket was for Curtin, the other for the guitar. He presented the guitar to Elvis at the Hilton Hotel in Elvis' private suite following his midnight show on August 31, 1974. I encourage you to check out his Internet sites to read the entire story of Curtin and the guitar he gave to Elvis.

Curtin is considered to be one of the first ETAs to perform, beginning his career in 1975. Though he enjoyed performing as a small child for his family and friends, he didn't initially have any thoughts about singing professionally.

"I stumbled into it unintentionally, in a sense. I never thought it was going to turn into a professional business. I thought it was going to be a flash-in-the-pan kind of thing. The Elvis craze is big and then Elvis dies...and there's this big demand for Elvis impersonators...I hate that word 'impersonator.' It's grown so big since then. It's like everything else. There are good professionals in this line of work and there are also amateurs. Unfortunately, because of all of the people that have jumped on the bandwagon since Elvis died, it has become a mockery. You've got all these guys walking around trying to impersonate Elvis Presley that don't even have the qualifications. As far as I'm concerned, there are 1500 that have come out

of the woodwork. Only 1 percent of them do Elvis justice. I think the rest of them are wasting their time."

Curtin feels that he was fortunate in the Elvis business. He was gifted with a natural voice and a natural look. He didn't have any training to sing like Elvis, he just sang as Jim "E" Curtin and he sounded like Elvis. According to Curtin, he shook Elvis' hand 32 times, hugged him 5 times, and saw him perform more times than he can count. He hung out at **Graceland** with Elvis' friends and family. Curtin would write every story he heard about Elvis on any piece of paper, napkin, or brown paper bag that he could find. Curtin has hundreds and hundreds of stories regarding Elvis. He says he has about 2500 more unpublished stories with the notes piled up in two huge trunks. You can be certain that Curtin will be releasing more books with his former manager and editorial assistant, Renata Ginder.

*"I would go to **Graceland** about three or four times a year...hanging out at the gates, meeting his aunts and uncles. Elvis' Uncle Vester and I became pretty good friends. One day, Uncle Vester let me guard the gates while he went to check the grounds. He told me if anybody came to the gate and blows their horn, I should just push this button and let them in. Sonny West pulled up and blew his horn, so I pushed the button and opened the gates for him...but I pushed the button to close the gates too soon and the gates took all of the chrome off of Sonny's brand new car. He got out of the car fuming mad. We all laugh about it now. Sonny is a really great guy."*

Curtin wants to write more books. He believes there is more money in publishing now than in performing. He also wants to help other Elvis performers in the business.

"I have performed over 500 concerts. I'm in my fifties now. It's always good to get out when you're on top, so to speak. The music industry has changed drastically with the invention of the Karaoke. I wouldn't dare perform with Karaoke. If I can't use a live band, I won't perform. A good Elvis impersonator should not even attempt to get up on stage with a Karaoke machine. It is so fake and amateurish. An ETA should have a live band behind him at all times to generate that same sound and excitement of a live performance like Elvis did. The clubs won't hire live bands anymore when they can get a DJ to spin records or do the Karaoke thing for a whole lot less money."

Curtin shares his expertise as a seasoned ETA on his Web site, the **ETA Hall of Fame**. His site features the world's best and well-known

ETAs and Curtin also promotes them to organizations, companies, and private individuals interested in hiring an ETA. Jim "E" Curtin is, by far, one of the more devoted associates to the industry of being Elvis and in his efforts to keep the memories of Elvis alive.

On that note: **Is Elvis Presley still alive?**

"Absolutely, 100 percent not. I know several of the people that went down and viewed his body. Elvis loved to perform and he loved his fans. There's no way he could sit back and not be up on that stage. I truly know the kind of appreciation Elvis had for his fans. I know how much he loved to sing. It's too bad that there are people out there just trying to make a buck on the whole thing."

THE MAN IN THE GLASS

WHEN you get what you want in your struggles for self
AND the world makes you KING for a day,
JUST go to the mirror and look at yourself
AND see what THAT man has to say.

FOR it isn't your father or mother or friends
WHOSE judgment you must pass,
The FELLOW whose verdict counts most in your life
IS the one staring back from the glass.

SOME people may think you're a straight shootin' chum
AND call you a wonderful guy.
BUT the man in the glass says you're only a bum
IF you can't look him straight in the eye.

HE's the fellow to please, never mind all the rest
For HE'S with you clear up to the end,
AND you've passed your most dangerous, difficult task
IF the man in the glass is your friend.

YOU may fool the whole world down the pathway of Life
And get pats on the back as you pass,
But your final reward will be heartaches and tears
IF YOU'VE CHEATED THE MAN IN THE GLASS.

– Author unknown

CHAPTER 7

ELVIS TRIBUTE ARTISTS
THE INTERVIEWS

Jay Allan
Martin Anthony
Jesse Aron
Adam Ashcroft
Everette "Howie" Atherton
Jim Barone
Brandon Bennett
Trent Carlini
Paul Casey
Irv Cass
Steve Chuke
Doug Church
Michael Conti
Ronny Craig
Kavan Creamer
Leo Days
Michael Dean
Butch Dicus
Lance Dobinson
Eric Erickson
Paul Fracassi – KidElvis
Stephen Freeman
Rob Garrett
Ray Guillemette Jr.
Tony Grova
Paul Halverstadt
Keith Henderson

Robin Kelly
Matt King
Shawn Klush
Kjell Elvis
Curt Lechner
Darren Lee
David Lee
Rick Lenzi
Mark Leen
Johnny Loos
Chris MacDonald
Rick Marino
Jerome Marion
Todd C. Martin
Richard Messier
Eddie Miles
David "Jesse" Moore
Travis Morris
Mike Morrissette
Craig Newell
Kraig Parker
Ed Elvis Parzygnat
Ryan Pelton
Steve Preston
Aaron Skilton
Jack Smink
Joe Tirrito
Johnny Thompson
Jonathon Von Brana
Robert Washington
Garry Wesley
Bob West

JAY ALLAN

It was 1992 and Jay Allan was a senior in high school with plans of becoming a police officer. He was told by many of his friends that he looked like a young Elvis. Jay grew up with music and, like his father— a drummer—he also developed the ability to play the drums. Always an Elvis fan, Jay naturally learned his music as well. He even had the fortune to meet D. J. Fontana, Elvis' personal drummer.

"I just wanted to keep the memory of Elvis alive. The girls in school would ask me to sing an Elvis song and the guys would ask me to do rap. I can do both, which is an interesting combination I guess."

Though Jay has concentrated on the 50s era of Elvis, which includes the GI Army routine, he recently started doing shows with the **'68 Comeback Special** wearing the infamous black leather. He performs at weddings, private shows, nightclubs and casinos. Some of the highlights of Jay's career include two MTV TV commercials, appearing on the VH1 TV show **Rock of Ages**, and CNN. He can also be seen in the movie **3000 Miles to Graceland** with Kurt Russell, Kevin Costner and other stars.

"This last year has been especially exciting for me. I've been on tour in New Hampshire, Kentucky, Tennessee and Maryland. I had the honor of being one of the Ladyluckmusic.com featured ETAs in Montreal, Canada, with an audience of over 1,000 people. RCA Records and BMG hired me to perform the hit British re-mix of the song 'A Little Less Conversation' at their release party," exclaimed Jay.

Knowing that Jay Allan is versatile in his musical talents, it is not surprising that he was selected to open for the **Hootie and The Blowfish** performance last year. Over the last five years, Jay has continued to write his own original music with his live band **Cat Daddies.** In fact, he currently has some label interests in Los Angeles with one single receiving airplay on stations in both New Jersey and New York. He's also produced a new CD titled **Lightning Does Strike Twice** and a promotional video. In the beginning of his career, Jay also did a few contests. Jay performed in Memphis during the Anniversary week of Elvis' death. He also performed at the **Collingwood Elvis Festival** in front of 35,000 people. He feels it has all been a great experience.

"Even if the original music end really took off, I would still continue to do Elvis. It helps me keep things in perspective. I just try to do a tribute to Elvis remembering that no one can be Elvis."

Jay's biggest fans and supporters are his parents. I would imagine that there are plenty of girls in his fan club also because—at least of this writing—he is still single!

If you get an opportunity to visit Bethlehem, Pennsylvania, you should have a good chance of catching Jay Allan on his way to a show in his personal limousine that he purchased a few years ago—or if you like football, you could end up sitting right next to him at a Philadelphia Eagles football game. He is a huge fan of the Eagles, but not as much as he is of Elvis.

MARTIN ANTHONY

For Martin Anthony, becoming an Elvis entertainer started January 4th, 1992. He was just 18 years old and had only recently discovered Karaoke. A fan of oldies music primarily, some friends convinced him to sing an Elvis tune. Their reaction was a pleasant surprise for Martin.

As luck would have it, there was a convention planned at the **Los Angeles Hilton** near his home. He made a major decision to perform for the convention and began to put his plan in place.

Martin started by learning four Elvis songs, reading books and watching videos. When he learned that his aunt could sew, he put her to the task of making a gold lamé jacket.

"It was just a gold jacket, not with the silver trim. I borrowed my grand-mother's shiny silver blouse and bought a gold tie," Martin said with a smile. *"I know it sounds funny,"* he continued, *"but I really didn't know any better."*

Martin, who had never performed with a band, decided to learn **My Happiness**, a song he discovered from a lost track at the time, accompanied with his guitar. As it turned out, Martin learned the song in the wrong key, but he did not realize his error until some time later. He was very nervous. He was so nervous, in fact, that when he was

told to be ready to perform at 12:00 o'clock on Saturday, he didn't realize until he arrived at about 10:30 in the morning that he was actually
scheduled to perform at midnight and not at noon. Martin sat there for
12 hours, incognito of course, watching all of the other Elvis impersonators who were wearing jumpsuits. As the night went on, the audience
began to get tired and starting leaving.

*"I wanted to back out for fear of getting booed off the stage and I thought
maybe I shouldn't do this guitar thing, but I said 'no' I've been waiting all
day for this. I think I felt like Elvis did the first time he went to Vegas,"* said
Martin.

When Martin opened with his rendition of **"My Happiness,"** the
audience started filtering back into the showroom. Needless to say,
Martin was overwhelmed with their response and enjoyed the thrill
and excitement that every performer loves to feel with his reception.

From his convention appearance, Martin went on to meet **D. J.
Fontana, Scotty Moore, The Jordanaires** and presented a few shows
in Las Vegas, Palm Springs,and Germany. Martin really began to take
performing seriously by learning more about Elvis Presley and his
music.

Reflecting back, however, he admits to being an Elvis fan at around
the 7th grade with original aspirations focused on an acting career and
not on Elvis. He even candidly admits that he put on an Elvis jumpsuit
Halloween style for an oldies showcase in the 10th grade at Pioneer
High School in about 1989. He also wore this "famous" jumpsuit on
his first professional job at a lawyer's house for seventy-five dollars.
Martin tolerated a lot of teasing during his early career until his experience in Germany. Martin's German reception opened his eyes to the
realization that people all over the world share the love for Elvis. It
was especially interesting to Martin because the only English words
most of the German fans knew were Elvis' lyrics.

From his German experience, Martin went on to work in several
commercials with James Earl Ray for **Atlantic Bell.** Appropriately for
Martin, **Atlantic Bell's** motto was "we're not just another impersonator."
A couple of years later, Martin received an offer to go to Nashville and
try his hand as a country singer. Although he has no regrets, his
Nashville adventure ended up being somewhat of a mistake for Martin.
After spending five years learning to sing country music, Martin realized

it just wasn't him. He was paid well, met countless celebrities, performed in places like **Dollywood** and also recorded some music.

When I met Martin Anthony, he was performing at the **Isle of Capri Casino's Tribute to the King Contest** in Marquette, Iowa. He said he didn't perform many contests in the beginning, but now has a different attitude towards contests.

His advice and comments to those who want to do contests: *"If you're going to the contests, you should enter them for the fun and experience, not necessarily to win."* This particular contest offers a $50,000 grand prize if the contestant makes it to the finals, but Martin was really in it for the fun and experience.

Currently, Martin is working hard to get back into performing as an Elvis Tribute Artist. He currently has a CD, **Martin Anthony,** that includes a splendid variety of Elvis greats. He views his tribute career as being very compatible with his goal of a potential acting career. He also attributes his focused attitude to meeting the love of his life, Araceli. By the time you read this, Martin Anthony Valdez will be happily married. Sorry girls!

"Follow your dreams, stay balanced by realizing you are NOT Elvis off the stage. Don't get caught up in it, have a plan A and plan B, and learn all you can about Elvis Presley, the person. If you study him and his music, you will realize that your job is to give the audience a re-recreation that for, at least a little while, will allow them to feel what Elvis was all about —like a great movie can do," Martin concluded.

JESSE ARON

Jesse Aron, although only in the Elvis business for about six years now, was fortunate to have the best teacher of all to learn about Elvis Presley—that is, next to Elvis Presley himself. Jesse's father was an Elvis impersonator for 30 years performing 13 of those years in the Chicago area. It also means that Jesse's father was one of the few individuals performing as Elvis while Elvis was still alive. Needless to say, little Jesse probably heard little but Elvis music growing up.

Perhaps that is why Jesse Aron is somewhat unique in the Elvis musical selections he performs.

"I like to sing the rare stuff like **Unchained Melody, Softly As I Leave You**, *and the songs from Elvis' movies. I do the requests and popular songs also, but I really like to sing the more rare ones. But,"* he admits, *"it's tough because Elvis just had so many good songs."*

There have been many exciting moments and performances in Jesse's career so far. According to Jesse, one of his memorable moments is his trip to Canada last year as one of the featured ETAs in **Lady Luck Music's** ETA Radio Showcase.

"It was really fun to meet up with the other ETAs, get carted around in a limo all week, and feel as babied as a big celebrity," Jesse said with a smile.

Joanna Johnson, owner of **Ladyluckmusic.com**, puts together a fantastic network for the ETAs. They all enjoy the honor, and the opportunity to work with her. Jesse is looking forward to returning to Canada in the future.

Jesse feels that one of his greatest fans is his costume maker, Shirley Salubring. And, in addition to his family, he also gives credit to his girlfriend's parents, Mike and Georgie, for their support. In fact, Jesse's first jumpsuit was a gift from Mike and Georgie. He also receives significant encouragement from his neighbors in Milton, Wisconsin, where he now resides.

"The fans, in general, are very loyal and appreciative," Jesse added. *"That makes it much easier to weed out all of the other stuff out there… because there's plenty of that too, unfortunately."*

The future for Jesse Aron includes doing some original material as well. He is currently working with a writer and hopes to try his hand at putting those lyrics to music. Jesse realizes that one can step out of the spotlight and be Elvis.

"I'm living out something I am having a lot of fun with. Performing as Elvis makes a lot of people happy and if I can bring back just even a little bit of the memory of what Elvis did, then that's cool…that's really cool," Jesse concluded.

In January, 2003, Jesse Aron took first place at the **Potowatami Casino's Tribute to the King Contest** in Milwaukee, Wisconsin. Following a week of preliminaries, Jess stole the hearts of the audience during the finals with his dynamic voice and an Elvis replica "Tiger" jumpsuit.

ADAM ASHCROFT

With a pronounced British accent, Adam Ashcroft is an Elvis entertainer and owner of the largest Elvis impersonator-booking agency in the United Kingdom. His agency is called **Pure Elvis.** Though Adam receives dozens of Elvis applications, he is extremely particular about who he hires. It is a difficult job at times because **Pure Elvis** covers all different types of shows all over the country and in various parts of Europe.

"I have untold numbers of Elvis impersonators who want to go on the books to have work from me. I scrutinize every one of them. They have to sound good and look good. Perhaps pick one out of forty or fifty who apply. So, we are a very choosing agency. I probably use five or so regularly because I know their shows are good and can be trusted as well," Adam said.

Growing up in England, it would seem that Adam would be an obvious Beatles fan, but it is his love of Elvis Presley's music that excites him the most. By traditional standards, Adam is a late bloomer to the Elvis world. He jumped into the entertainment business at the age of 27 and, with tremendous dedication, built a successful career during the last ten years. Adam's variety of show performances in France, Germany, and Holland clearly indicates from his success that the popularity of Elvis Presley is still quite high.

"I think Elvis' influence mainly comes from his music. Just his voice, his charisma, and that his appeal on the people in the last couple of years have really come to the front of music. Especially the youngsters... now they love Elvis!"

Adam can't explain how he is able to lose his accent when he sings. He feels the exposure to American television has had the greatest affect on Europeans, including Great Britain. According to Adam, Europeans watch a lot of American television from which, *"the teenagers even pick up the American slang words, like 'oh man' and such,"* he added.

Adam's presentations include a variety of shows from the classic Las Vegas style to a full re-creation production. He uses both backing tracks (or Karaoke as we call it) and live bands, the selection depending on the client's budget. The busiest part of his agency is performing for weddings. Europe is noted for its numerous medieval castles and it is quite vogue for couples to get married in the splendid architecture. Most castles also have large banquet halls making them ideal choices for wedding parties and other events.

"*I average a couple of weddings a week. I have also performed in bowling alleys all of the way up to major shows with audiences of 6,000 or so. A theatre show costs 10 pounds or $18.00 U.S. dollars.*"

Adam would love to come to America, but there's just one small obstacle. Between Adam's schedule and his wife handling all of the public relations-booking arrangements, they have a family of nine children. The children range in age from two years to 18 years of age. They have all expressed an interest in the music business, some with their own bands and playing instruments, to the girls who tend to move more towards dancing and acting.

"*It would be difficult to get a month off with the kids and all. I wouldn't change it for the world though and I feel fortunate to make a good living in a business that supports that.*"

Adam has been asked to do a show in Uganda, Africa, the summer of 2003. We'll have to follow this on his web site. If you're planning a wedding, don't forget to consider an alternative to the Las Vegas chapels. Imagine an enchanting and romantic adventure in an old English castle as the charm of an Elvis entertainer echoes **Love Me Tender**. Sounds exciting, doesn't it?

EVERETT "HOWIE" ATHERTON

Based out of the Minneapolis, Minnesota, area, Everett "Howie" Atherton is an Elvis Tribute Artist. He is also a Native American. Honored with the birth of his mother to the Chippewa Tribe, he is also blessed with many of the Native features similar to the natural traits of Elvis Presley. Adopted at a young age, Howie became mesmerized with Elvis the minute he saw his first Elvis movie, **Change Of Habit,** released in 1968.

"*I thought that guy was so cool. Seeing it in a movie theatre was so alive. He did a great performance, had great hair, and did some great music,*" according to Howie.

Howie believes he nearly drove his sister, Martha, crazy from the age of 11 on singing Elvis songs over and over—not to mention monopolizing the bathroom mirror. Martha, no doubt, had to become a huge fan of Elvis Presley, and "Howie."

About eight years ago, Atherton, the given Indian name he reclaimed for performing, was re-united with the rest of his siblings. Due to one sister's genealogy efforts and accessibility to the Catholic Charity organization's records, she was able to locate the entire family.

"It was extremely emotional, very wonderful. It was fun to share with them my love of performing Elvis."

Howie stays very busy. In addition to his performances as an Elvis Tribute Artist, he is also employed full-time with the Ford Motor Company. He would like to perform full-time, however, Howie recognizes his need for benefits, especially medical insurance. He is also a single father raising two young boys, 13 and 15 years old.

"I will wait for my children to get a little older as well. They are the most important things in my life. Family is important to me, now more than ever."

Howie performs at a variety of events, including weddings, private shows, and venues at Casinos. He recently performed in his second contest, held in La Crosse, Wisconsin and hosted by Ronny Craig.

"The contest is tough. These guys are really good. I am proud to be part of it and I try not to take the winning or losing very seriously. You can always be learning and sharing advice. It is good to venture out and see what's out there," he said.

Howie is a quiet man. He seems wonderfully content with his own thoughts and passion for Elvis Presley, the man and his music. Perhaps that is just another blessing that could be attributed to his Native American heritage—heritage that I believe keeps him balanced. You will appreciate Howie's recently released CD, **One Night With Elvis**, which transcends Elvis' voice and demeanor in a flavor all of its own.

JIM BARONE

Jim Barone resides in New Jersey, but his ancestors are from Italy. He is very proud of his heritage and living in America. Yet, even with his mixed eastern and Italian accents, Jim manages to eliminate his accent when he sings Elvis' songs. Jim did not participate in any formal training activities, but he did join a variety of drama, acting and singing electives in high school. Jim believes it was his high school experiences that helped him overcome his fear of the stage.

"I started out with tracks and Karaoke. Then one day, someone who liked Elvis as much as I did...and other music as well, heard me sing. He was a guitar player and he approached me about putting a band together. So we found another guitar player and a drummer and that's how it all got started. I went through a few bands back then. Now I just hire bands for certain venues."

Although Jim works mainly in the New Jersey area, he has traveled great distances to perform for charities. Jim likes participating in the contests, but he also realizes the controversies that sometimes go along with the competitions.

"A lot of the contests are very political. When I perform at contests, I really watch the audience's response to me. It seems that in nine out of ten contests, I will come out on top. I've done Memphis, but the best one was in Canada at the first **Branford Elvis Festival.** *I took first place there, but that is not why it is the best for me. I am mostly proud of the fact that I was judged to be the first in comparison with many Canadian contestants...performing in their own backyard, so to speak."*

Jim is a member of the **EEN**. He enjoys the network and believes that it is a good opportunity to keep in touch with what is going on in the ETA industry. Nance Fox, president of the **EEN**, recently booked a show for Jim in the New Jersey area.

"I hope one day to be able to get into my own songs and, eventually, producing and performing my own ultimate tribute to Elvis. I would love to do that...but it takes money to do a major venue or concert. I have a great wife and a big extended family that supports me like **The Godfather.** *My father is my sound man for my shows and my own godfather comes along to make sure I don't have to deal with any weird or obsessive fans. Fortunately, we don't get too much of that. But it just tells you how close we are."*

Jim is currently 30 years old and has no plan to retire at the age of 42 because he knows he is not Elvis. He's recorded an emotionally charged CD, **A Tribute To America,** that begins with a verbal dedication to the rescue workers and volunteers of **9/11**. Jim's CD includes a collection of patriotic and inspirational songs and he sings in the spirit of Elvis with hope for the world, especially for Americans.

BRANDON BENNETT

Brandon Bennett is the 2002 **Images of the King Contest** winner. Now 22 years of age, he began performing when he was only 15 years old. Brandon's success is more proof that the **Business of Being Elvis** is expanding to include younger performers. Brandon also took second place in August 2000 at **Images**, in which he became the youngest ETA to ever place and win. It was his first contest as well.

It could be just Brandon's luck that he has such an obvious, yet natural, resemblance to that of a young Elvis Presley. Before he even had a chance to discover Elvis on his own, people everywhere were telling him he looked like Elvis Presley. It must have been difficult for Brandon considering he didn't have much choice in the matter.

"My mom always told me she thought I looked like Elvis, but never thought much of it," Brandon said. *"From her influence of watching Elvis on television, I knew who he was and couldn't help being a fan,"* Brandon added.

Brandon's high school was having a 70s day at school so mom took to the task of making an Elvis jumpsuit for Brandon. He received a good response to his show and his classmates all wanted their pictures taken with Brandon Bennett as Elvis.

"I had fun with it and really didn't think that much about it," Brandon said with a boyish grin. *"The next thing I know, the drama teacher encouraged me to perform at a sock hop."*

He dressed up like Elvis and sang a couple of Elvis songs for the first time in public.

"I am shy, still very shy. My parents, and others, will tell anybody that when I go on stage it's like flipping a switch. I'm a totally different person," Brandon added.

Well, the drama teacher told the choir director about Brandon's talent and the choir director convinced Brandon to practice his vocals with the piano. Then, of course, Brandon joined the choir. Brandon's only regret regarding his choir experience was that he had not participated in choir for the whole four years of high school. Since then, Brandon recorded at least three CDs of his own and appeared on the **NBC Nightly News** and **The Ricki Lake Show**, where he won the **2002 Ricki Lake King of Kings Competition**.

"I'm even more of an Elvis fan now. I've got to say it's been a pretty neat ride," concluded Brandon.

Brandon receives a great deal of support from his family, friends, and, at the time of this interview, his girlfriend. He considers himself very lucky to be an ETA, a job that he really loves. He enjoys doing the contests, but following his big win in Memphis, I'm sure you'll be seeing Brandon perform in major venues all over the world.

TRENT CARLINI

There is no single word in the English language that accurately describes Trent Carlini. Trent was born seven years after his parents migrated to the United States from Italy. Even when Trent is not performing on stage, his presence in any room is quickly noticed. He is confident, polished, is natural in his looks and, maybe just a little bit, well aware of his appearance. Even without sideburns, sunglasses, or costumes, the aura of Elvis is clearly revealed in Trent's persona.

Trent has been entertaining since he was ten and his family returned to Italy. It is in Italy that he received his education and began his interest in music. By the time he returned to the United States in 1987, he was already well established as an artist in Europe. Following his move back to the United States, Trent began to perform at numerous clubs in Florida, his new home.

"You know, the intent of being or performing like Elvis was never there, not once in my whole career. I loved the guy, I loved his music, and I thought he was phenomenal. But I never thought it was humanly possible for one person to portray another person...until I came to Chicago," said Trent.

Trent grew up with Elvis' music, as well as other forms of music in Europe. Once in Chicago, he started performing a **Rock A Billy** show, which eventually led him to an Elvis Tribute show performed by Rick Saucedo. Trent was so overwhelmed and impressed by Saucedo's abili-

ty and talent that he developed a more focused appreciation of Elvis'
vocal techniques and the way Elvis enjoyed music on stage.

"*I started practicing and studying—more than just trying to be Elvis. I
never try to talk like him. It's just an appearance on stage, it's just an attitude, it's a way of being,*" Trent explained, as he described the difference
between an Elvis Tribute Artist versus an impersonator.

By 1990, Trent was receiving a lot of bookings. That same year,
Trent was chosen as the **Entertainer with the Most King-Like
Charisma** at an Elvis performance competition in Dallas, Texas. Trent
also received the attention of John Stuart, the producer of **Legends in
Concert**. In 1992, Stuart flew Trent to Las Vegas where Trent immediately began performing with the **Legends** at the **Imperial Palace**. Trent
remained there for over six years.

"*Vegas has been good to me, but it is a tough town. John Stuart is actually a great guy and I owe my career to him. When I was working with him
in 1996, I was making $3500 per week. Then I started* **The Dream King**,
*my current show, and made ten times what I made there with only five years
with my own production,*" Trent added.

Trent also won a contest in Montreal and met Martin Fontaine, an
Elvis performer who was also a judge for the competition. He has also
seen Fontaine's performance in **The Elvis Story**, a production based in
Quebec City, Canada. Trent found Fontaine to be very talented in a well-
done production. Trent describes his own **The Dream King** production as
similar, but a lot less theatrical with a whole lot less production support.

"*My show is a faster pace with a little more high energy. My show is one
hour and fifteen minutes to two hours and forty minutes depending upon the
audience. We have multimedia and lights. I do a more simplified version with
six costume changes of the different eras and we have some props. I run my
own agency, I hire and produce all of the shows myself,*" said Trent, "*so
unfortunately, that is a big difference for us compared to a full production
performance such as* **The Elvis Story**."

Trent has performed all over the world to sellout audiences. He
completed over 1,800 shows during his five years on the **Boardwalk** in
New Jersey. Trent's schedule amounts to over 300 shows a year plus the
other shows he books during his two months off, compared to his four
nights a week while at **Legends.** Trent Carlini, additionally, has produced a wonderful promotional video and CDs.

Trent now calls Las Vegas home and performs his show, **The Dream King,** nightly at **The Riviera Hotel and Casino**. What is in the future for Trent Carlini? Well, he claims that he is planning to retire at age 42. He will perform his last show and never do Elvis again!

"Elvis performed until he was 42 years old and died. Trent Carlini will perform until he's 42, but when we do our last production, it will be called 'The Last Live Performance,' and it will be done in a variety of different towns, and that will be it. It will be the last show," said Trent very seriously.

With his talent, videos, CDs, and the stage productions that Trent Carlini has, and continues to produce, it is hard to believe that he will really retire as a successful "Elvis Stylist" at age 42 in the prime of his life. But then again, the world, so full of Elvis Presley fans, has still not really accepted the fact that Elvis Presley, the person, is indeed gone.

PAUL CASEY

Paul Casey is best known as the official "Elvis of Las Vegas." He was awarded the endorsement from the **Las Vegas Business and Convention Authority** in 1989. It allows Paul the ongoing responsibility to represent Las Vegas wherever he travels, performing or not, as Vegas' goodwill ambassador. That is quite an honor when you consider how many Elvis entertainers perform in Las Vegas.

"I developed a rapport working for them, always making it successful for my employer, whomever I worked for. They continue to call me back and I've continued with that for five years now. I'm one out of six other people to have a contract with them. I travel all over the world for them. I'm always promoting Las Vegas," Paul said.

He hosted at the **Four Queens Casino** for seven years from the mid-1980s and on. Then in 1995, he worked for **Legends in Concert** until 1998 and from there, went on to Germany for its sister show, called **Stars In Concert,** where he has been for about four years now.

Last year, Paul put together a special show in Germany bringing together the **Sweet Inspirations,** Sonny West, Ed Bonja, and others. It is a venue that includes live documentation along with the music. The people that actually knew Elvis provide dialogue about Elvis' life right up to eight months before his death. Paul hopes to eventually bring this show to the United States.

"It's like 'Elvis in Concert' with all the original cast members. Sonny talks about growing up with Elvis, having known him since 1956. He is very straight-forward and sincere."

To Paul Casey, performing as an Elvis entertainer is like being an actor that includes a business investment. First of all, Paul has a few college degrees. He went from high school to a community college where he obtained a social arts degree. Then, he went to California State graduating with a Bachelor of Science degree. From Cal State, Paul went to law school and ultimately received his Juris Doctorate. He worked in a variety of law firms for several years in California. Although Paul continues his interest in law on a part-time basis, he would like to eventually practice full-time and focus on entertainment law.

Paul also worked in the music business for the **Academy of Country Music,** opening for such acts as Alabama, Ricky Nelson, Jerry Lee Lewis, Kenny Rogers, and others.

"I have been very fortunate. This business put me through all of my schooling. I've been able to enjoy my Harley Davidson, golfing, my two Rottweilers, my family, and my life in general. I've tried to lend my advice to many of the guys in this business. I tell them there are two different people in this world. There's Elvis and there's everybody else. If you're an Elvis act, you are not Elvis no matter what you do—have surgery, change your name, or whatever, but you are not Elvis. Some of these guys are like watching a bunch of male dogs around a tree trying to impress one another. Portray honesty and integrity. That will give you a genuine performance and that is what the audience will remember."

Paul has also produced a few motorcycle events in Palm Springs, which is where he lived for a while after law school. This event draws 25 – 30,000 people. By the way, Paul Casey sported a long ponytail for many years. He had to disguise himself by tucking his hair into the collar of his costume. Last year, he finally cut it off to enhance an "Elvis Special" that he put together.

"You know, I don't know what I'd rather do—a show or an event. An impersonator's life is like a shooting star. It's usually a short-lived thing. The only thing is you can learn from it, grow, and become yourself. Let's face it, Elvis' career only lasted a short time and then he passed away. The key is to

walk with integrity, and once you can't do that anymore, it's over. It's time to move on, and change is good."

Paul does not participate in the competitions, except for the one that he felt an obligation to enter because it was held in Las Vegas. He walked away from that contest $5,000 richer and the proud winner. He feels that the contests are too self-serving and someone is always walking away mad.

"I lived there and I felt it was time I stepped up to the plate. Yet, I still think the most successful Elvis entertainers are the ones working in the midst and, honestly, making the most money at it."

It is apparent that all of the education Paul received was an asset to the marketing and **Business of Being Elvis**. Paul recently released his CD, **Aloha From Hawaii**.

"I have agents who represent me, but I control my own destiny. Too many people allow someone else to drive their car for them and then they can't understand why they're not going in the direction they want to go or the car's not being taken care of."

In summary, Paul reminds the many new talents entering the **Business of Being Elvis** as an entertainer or tribute artist to *"stay focused, try doing someone else you admire, thereby learning that you don't have to be just like them, and always take control of the path you take."*

Paul also realizes that it is difficult to find good agents, adding, *"If they're willing to invest a lot of time in your act, they should also nurture you and not play games."*

IRV CASS

Irv Cass is the man you just can't help falling in love with. His charm and relaxed sense of humor would even impress Elvis. Irv is equally sensitive and respectful about the man, Elvis Presley; always reminding the audience how grateful he is to be able to pay tribute to the King. Though Irv has been in the **Business of Being Elvis** for ten years, his energy level is higher than ever.

"It seems like I'm always on a diet...and I just love good food...trying to stay in shape. I have to recognize that there is a lot of tough competition out there. There is some great talent amongst the ETAs and many of them are

*much younger than me. I perform full-time and as an ETA. This is my
livelihood and I take that aspect very seriously."*

Irv began his career in the entertainment business as a male dancer
with the Canadian Chippendales in Vancouver. He enjoyed traveling
with the dance troupe for 13 years before growing tired of it. Irv
accepts this part of his life as another learning experience adding:
*"there are parts of it I'm not proud off...it is easy to get too caught up in it
all sometimes."* In spite of it all, Irv still believes it is important to be
truthful about who you are.

*"If you can't be honest with yourself, then you can't be honest with any-
body or anything...and your life will just continue to be miserable."*

Irv started out in the Elvis business entering a contest in
Southbend, Indiana, at the **Ramada Inn.** With brown hair, no sideburns, and wearing a pair of slacks with a puffy shirt, he placed 5th out
of twenty-five contestants.

"I looked more like Tom Jones than I did Elvis," he laughed.

Irv entered the **Images of the King** contest in Memphis four times
before taking a first-place win in 1999. He was also a finalist in the
2003 **$50,000 Tribute to the King** contest held at the **Isle of Capri** in
Lula, Mississippi. Irv feels that contests present a great opportunity for
an ETA to promote himself. He also recognizes that, as in any contest,
there are winners and there are losers. You have to be able to accept
that when the contest is over. Irv's performed venues all over the world
including **Legends in Concert** in Las Vegas, Nevada; Myrtle Beach,
South Carolina; and Branson, Missouri, but perhaps his most memorable experience performing was the show in Beruit, Lebanon about six
years go.

*The promoter set our show up in a Muslim area...so even though we
had a couple of good shows with decent crowds, the ticket sales weren't that
good. We had the Lebanese army guys with us at all times, which gave us the
impression that we were pretty safe. All of a sudden the promoter started
arguing with the producers about not making enough money, saying he wanted some of his investment money back. The producers took this as a personal
threat and called the American Embassy. We were told to pack our bags and
meet in the lobby prepared to leave immediately. The Embassy sent five
armored vehicles, with our passports, to escort us to the airport and out of
the country."*

Irv would like to continue his career as an ETA for five more years. He recently qualified to instruct classes in permanent make-up procedures for licensing with a firm called **Boomers**. Irv describes it as a form of tattooing and says *"the money is great and I have real steady hands."* When, and if, he actually retires from the **Business of Being Elvis,** Irv wants to seek out an interesting sales position. He was employed in sales prior to becoming an ETA and was successful at it. I have no doubt about his ability to sell because he sells himself so well as an Elvis tribute artist. Many top corporations request Irv as an Elvis greeter for their conventions and private parties.

When Irv is not touring, helping out at charity events, or working with the **EEN** as a member of the board, he is always willing to offer advice to the guys just starting out in the Elvis business—as long as they are sincere about it.

Often, when Irv performs on stage, he is quick to give the audience a laugh, perhaps to prove that he is just a regular guy in real life, and not Elvis. Wearing a stunning jumpsuit, Irv begins singing *Suspicious Minds*. The audience is quiet while being drawn into the passion of the song. Irv approaches the front of the stage and bends down on one knee while stretching the other leg out to the side. The female fans gather to the edge of the stage hoping to feel a scarf draped around their neck.

"I'm caught in a trap...I think I split my pants...wooooooo... because I love you too much baby!"

That's Irv, folks....

STEVE CHUKE

One might describe Steve Chuke as a "diamond in the rough." A jeweler by trade, no pun is intended here, but rather, the phrase is used to indicate that Steve traveled a very different road than most Elvis entertainers travel. For one thing, you need to know some things about **Monmouth Street** in Newport, Kentucky, where Steve continues to operate his jewelry store. Monmouth Street, the main drag, was previously plastered with 13 strip clubs, plus every greasy spoon had a slot machine and gambling was so common it was generally assumed to be legal. Monmouth Street has since developed along the riverfront, while at the same time boasts of one-of-kind landmark shops.

It is easy to understand then why Steve went to work for Larry Flint, founder of **Hustler** magazine and owner of several of the strip nightclubs in the 70s. He ran Flint's nightclubs for nearly five years. These strip clubs actually had dancers performing, complete with the silk stockings, high heels and exotic clothing.

"*I did become a tremendous dancer, though,*" Steve recalls with a chuckle.

Even though Steve made good money working for Flint, he also eventually grew tired of the hard-core scene. Always a huge Elvis fan, exposure to the numerous live bands performing in the area led to the transition towards becoming an Elvis entertainer, a profession that Steve soon loved.

Now fifty-seven years old, Steve holds on to many memories of Elvis and performing Elvis tribute shows. He still likes to talk about his treasured purchase in 1994 of the RCA Victrola that Elvis used to play. There's one in **Graceland** exactly like it. As a bit of a skeptic, Steve attempted to have the Victrola authenticated by securing some original paperwork that traced it backwards through ownerships. He has some other rare pieces as well.

In 1996, Steve was injured in a motorcycle accident that nearly cost him his leg. This was one of the turning points in his decision to change direction as a promoter and a jeweler.

Steve is a very candid and outspoken individual. As a performer for over twenty-five years, he has earned that right.

"*I am truthful. You will always hear the truth from me. I tell it like it is in this business.*"

But just start talking about the contests and you will really get an earful.

"*I did one contest and I swore I'd never do another one. I tell people, it's not an Elvis contest. It's an ego contest, a male beauty contest. You won't win a contest if you don't know anyone. They just want the money they make off the whole thing.*"

Steve also believes that these are some of the reasons why the Elvis impersonators receive so much negative attention.

"I don't like being called an Elvis impersonator because that belongs to those guys that wear the wigs, put on the sideburns, the heavy make-up. The kind that make people look and just laugh. When I got into this contest, I thought these guys were going to be straight up you know. But those wigs! I said the only people that wear things like that are car salesmen when they want to sell cars on TV."

Steve, a fair-haired, natural sandy-colored blond, admits he has had to resort to coloring over the last ten years or so.

"I am still just Steve Chuke singing Elvis. I am not Elvis," he added.

As Steve's jewelry store, appropriately named **Jewel King Jewelers,** is sandwiched in the row of other historical shops, he still promotes Elvis every day. There is always a flier in the window announcing his next event and the line-up of who will be the featured Elvis entertainer coming to town.

By the way, if you're in the market for a TCB necklace, ring, or some other form of custom jewelry, just call **Jewel King Jewelers.** Steve Chuke will proudly answer the telephone. The many customers over the years will tell you that you can buy some jewelry, book an Elvis performer, or get in on one of Steve Chuke's many interesting stories which, of course, are free of charge.

DOUG CHURCH

Doug Church, known as **The Voice of Elvis,** is considered to be the best-known Elvis Tribute Artist in the world. Everyone that I interviewed for the **Business of Being Elvis** quickly connects the name Doug Church as synonymous with the voice of Elvis Presley. You merely need to play one of the many Doug Church CDs and you will immediately appreciate the fact that Church has legitimately earned his trademarked name of **The Voice of Elvis.**

"I started singing in high school. A friend of mine was an Elvis fan and I wasn't really interested in music. He turned me on to Elvis' music and, to me, it is the best music in the world…the greatest sound I had ever heard."

After graduating from high school, Doug enlisted in the U.S. Air Force at the age of 20. In 1982, he discovered that the Air Force held talent contests every year. With some persuasion from a buddy, Doug entered the contest.

"*I thought…oh, what the heck. I knew I had a good chance because I have a gift for mimicking.*" (Doug quipped out a version of Richard Nixon.) "*I won first place in two different categories, **pop potpourri** and **male vocalist**. Then I went on to the regional level and I didn't even place. But the judges felt there was something interesting enough, so they sent me on to the next level anyway. This was the talent contest* **U.S. Air Force Europe**, *which was the entire European command of all bases including Germany, Italy and France. I competed against a duo that sang folk music and played guitars. They were really good. I sang* **My Way** *and* **Love Me Tender** *with a guitar. I had also made my own costume just the night before. I went to the Base Exchange in Germany and bought a pair of women's white polyester stretch pants. I bought jeweled button covers, glued them onto the pants in a pattern of fairly good design…bought a white shirt and cut off the collar. Then I made a high Elvis-type collar with cardboard and covered it with white bed sheet material and sewed it on the shirt. I made a belt the same way. It looked like a jumpsuit…took me until 3 a.m. to finish it. I took my highest award in the Air Force with a first place trophy of a huge silver bowl. To this day, it is my pride and joy.*"

During the five years Doug was in the Air Force, he collected 13 first place trophies in a variety of categories. After leaving the Air Force in 1987, he returned home to the Midwest and continued to perform. It is difficult to believe that ANYONE could sound so much like Elvis without being Elvis but Doug is a true impersonator extraordinaire. In the Elvis impersonator documentary film, **Almost Elvis,** Doug duplicates 70 different and unique voice personalities.

In 1990, Doug's Elvis Tribute turned into his full-time career. He took second place in the ***Worldwide Elvis Impersonator Contest*** held at **Bad Bob's Vapors**. The following year, 1991, Doug won first place in **The Images of Elvis Contest**—now known as **The Images of the King Contest**. In 1993, he began performing with the **Legends in Concert**. Doug's performed a variety of venues all over the United States and Europe including Hong Kong, Bangkok, Moscow, Aruba, England, Germany, the Bahamas and Canada. He's performed with many of the great artists who worked with Elvis and is personally acquainted with many of Elvis' chosen few friends. In fact, Doug was presented with a bracelet by several of the **Memphis Mafia** (former employees of Elvis Presley, including those who co-wrote **Elvis, What Happened?**). The bracelet is inscribed with **"Krazy."** During Elvis' lifetime, the **Memphis Mafia** also presented a comparable bracelet to Elvis inscribed with **"Crazy."** Clearly, members of the **Memphis Mafia** hold Doug Church in very high regard.

A few years ago, Doug signed on with a major recording company to a 10-CD, five-year contract. His first double CD, **Kingtinued,** feature popular songs from the decade of the 90s including **The Wind Beneath My Feet** and **Candle In The Wind**. Doug presents the musical scores as he imagines Elvis would have. He also has a CD called **KingCountry**.

"I just recorded a **Live In Concert** *CD to be released in February 2003. I am doing many new shows on the east coast with a new agent that I met last year. Many new opportunities have presented themselves and my act is moving forward and up. I am very pleased with the professional crew I have working for me. They are a topnotch group!"*

Doug is the Vice-President of Musical Direction with **The Elvis Entertainers Network (EEN)**. There are three other VPs that include Irv Cass, Jerome Marion, and Ronny Craig.

"I enjoy working with Nance Fox (President of EEN). She has proven to be a force to reckon with in this genre. She treats the ETAs with professionalism and respect and works very hard to maintain only the highest standards in her performers. Our basic intent is to provide only quality performers and to raise the level of public awareness about Elvis and his many good qualities…and hopefully, erase the ugly stigma placed on Elvis' name and reputation by the media over the years. I look forward to Ronny and Nance's new opportunity as partners in **The Images of the King Contest***. I believe they will set a new standard of excellence and* **Images** *will prove to be the model for all other contests held around the world."*

This is my prediction for the future of the **Business of Being Elvis**, *from all angles: I believe that within the next decade or so, the genre will be recognized as a legitimate enterprise that is organized and run by professionals, not nutballs with no life…which seems to be the opinion of the general public. It will be considered a* **real job** *and not just a bunch of guys running around in jumpsuits and sideburns trying to* **Be Elvis***. It will be sanctioned by the powers that be and run like a union, with dues and privileges for being*

a member. Anyone wishing to hold a contest will have to pass stringent criteria before they are allowed to do so and all judges must fit certain guidelines
of Elvis knowledge. Contestants will also have to apply for the right to enter
the contest by providing promotional material in advance and they must be
screened. That's how I see things going in the near future…at least I am
praying for that."

MICHAEL CONTI

Originally from Texas, Michael Conti lived in Los Angeles for many
years pursuing an acting career and, as Michael puts it, *"working as a
waiter to survive out there."* He landed roles in the television dramas
General Hospital and **Santa Barbara**. He also made numerous appearances on several television shows, as well as commercials. In about
1994, a friend of Michael's convinced him to do Elvis for a Halloween
event after hearing him sing a variety of Elvis' songs at a karaoke event

*"It was a fluke. I never was into that in high school or college, but I took
the advice and here I am."*

That decision eventually brought Michael to Las Vegas starring in
the **"Legends in Concert"** at the **Imperial Palace.** He also went on to
perform **"Legends"** in Singapore, the Bahamas, Myrtle Beach, and several other locations. Though he continues to receive offers to travel
and perform on cruise ships, he doesn't want to do that anymore. The
idea of doing the same thing over and over doesn't provide the same
stimulus for Michael as it once used to. He is 40 years old and feels it is
time to look into the future toward a new direction, *"to expand my hori-
zons,"* he added.

He is currently involved with a group putting the **Michael Conti
Show** together. Michael will perform as Englebert Humperdinck with a
cast of other celebrity look-alikes, including the likes of a Tom Jones,
Dean Martin, Sammy Davis Jr. and a Jerry Lewis.

*"It will have some dancing, a little comedy, and offer a variety. I will
continue to do Elvis, of course, like the weddings here in Vegas and other
special shows."*

In the ten years that Michael has performed as an Elvis entertainer,
he has experienced a lot of things in the industry, both good and bad.

He especially doesn't appreciate the lack of respect for Elvis that he sees in many of the Elvis "impersonators." Though we all know the lack of respect can be very irritating, just imagine how irritating it must be living in the Elvis capitol of the world—Las Vegas?

"The way the Elvis thing is now is people don't care. You can stick a guy out there with sideburns who flips burgers. I studied and studied Elvis, his mannerisms, his talk, and his voice. I utilized all of the things I have learned from acting. Elvis will always be the number one entertainer in the world. I'm glad I've been able to do him."

Michael doesn't like the contests either. He did participate in contests in the beginning of his career, but his last contest was held in Las Vegas at the **Lady Luck Casino**. He was also invited to compete in **Collingwood**—only as a contestant. He declined.

"I'll never do another contest as long as I live. They're all rigged and I don't care what anyone says. I will go as a performer, not as a contestant. The biographies all read, '# 1 IN THE WORLD,' but come on. Were all the Elvis' in the world there to compete?"

Michael Conti, the performer, is enthused about putting his new show together. The addition of Englebert Humperdinck to his repertoire is like preparing for a new acting role. Michael and his wife recently became the proud parents of a baby boy. By the way, she does an impersonation of Reba Macintire. Michael Conti, the person, has settled in with his family in their home just outside of Las Vegas.

"I want to be a producer, an entertainer. I love entertainment. I am working out daily, taking better care of my diet and, most of all, looking forward to another new challenging role—being a good father."

RONNY CRAIG

Tall, dark, and handsome with a million dollar smile, Ronny Craig prefers the natural look these days. He still, on occasion, dons an Elvis jumpsuit minus the Elvis disguise. More than likely, you might see him in a **GQ** (**Gentleman's Quarterly**) persona wearing a spiffy jacket or pompadour. Ronny could also be described as the **Bob Barker** of the ETA contests because he acts as the host and master of ceremonies for numerous ETA events. He began his entertainment career as an Elvis impersonator in 1991 on a lark.

*"I decided to be Elvis for Halloween…thinking it would be fun and easy to put a costume together. I started researching for a suit, sideburns, glasses, scarf, and boots. At that time, there wasn't one simple source to purchase these items. I finally got it all together though…but I didn't want to put any of it on until I had everything. I colored by hair jet black, pasted some sideburns on, got a cheap jumpsuit…couldn't find white Elvis boots so I had to settle for white cowboy boots. I put it all on and looked in the mirror. I'll never forget the feeling I had…I felt like **Superman** and I thought to myself: 'My God, you are the King!' That's how crazy this **Business of Being Elvis** is."*

Ronny was also employed as a cattle buyer for a large meat packing plant in the small town of Norwalk, Wisconsin. His father, Ron, a statuesque, no-nonsense type of guy, was the president of the company. Between the encouragement of Ronny's brother and a successful Valentine's Day promotion in which he ran a classified ad "to sing to your sweetheart for fifty dollars," Ronny began to develop a different attitude about Elvis impersonating. While his mother drove him around town during a Valentine blizzard, *"having a blast"* and amazing himself that he was getting paid money to sing, he contemplated taking this business to another level. Ronny began to receive more calls to perform for a variety of events.

I started charging $300, then it was $500 to $1000 and, sometimes when I felt brave enough, $1500. People were willing to pay it without blinking an eye. This was my opportunity to get out of the cattle business…so here I am in the back of the plant buying cattle off the scale heading out toward the executive area of the building. I remember walking into my dad's office. He was sitting behind his desk signing checks. I walked up to the front of his desk and said 'I'm buying a real Elvis suit and I'm going to become an Elvis impersonator.' He looked at me (like any father would, especially your boss) *and said 'Craig, you just don't want to work anymore. Get your butt out back and grade some cattle.' I was so angry. I thought for sure he would think it was a great idea."*

From that moment, Ronny began to attend Elvis impersonator conventions and enter as many Elvis impersonator contests as he could find. To his own surprise, he was winning more contests than he was losing. In fact, in 1993, Ronny Craig earned 3rd place in the **Images of**

the King contest in Memphis. By then, Ronny and his family had relocated to La Crosse, Wisconsin. He began performing and producing a variety of venues with an area band called **The Headliners**. He also traveled extensively, which included a stint in Branson, Missouri. Ronny considers Branson as one of his first *"wake-up calls."*

"I met a gal in Branson who later became my fiancé. She was the first person to say to me 'you don't need this Elvis thing…just put on a pair of **Wranglers***, a country western shirt…and sing country…and be accepted for who you are.'* (Ronny Craig has recorded both country tunes and Elvis music, but claims he never felt that the Elvis voice was his strongest suit.) *"I guess that is what I really wanted to be…just myself. In Branson, especially, Elvis impersonators really end up at the bottom of the entertainment list. At the same time, I realized my living room had become an Elvis shrine. My friends were making comments to me like 'you are touched, why?' I can see, to this day, how people can get caught up in this Elvis business. I mean, you don't worship an entertainer, you worship God. Let's put it into perspective. Elvis is just a wonderful man that had a lot of talent and great music. It's your family that should matter. Have fun along the way…make some money even, but keep your feet on the ground."*

"I also started losing in the competitions. I was getting beat and that is huge on your ego. This is when I realized I'm NOT Elvis and I'm tired of being caught up in it. There were a lot of good impersonators coming along and we began to recognize them as Elvis Tribute Artists. It was getting tougher. I was feeling like an old hat…the new guys had the moves and were dedicated to perfecting their skills as an Elvis. I have a lot of respect for those guys that can really take it to a level that is a tribute to Elvis as an art form. I'm not saying you can't be a fan of Elvis, but how far do you take it? I'm not here to criticize the Elvis impersonator either…I mean I'm right in the middle of it. I do believe that in the 13 years I've been involved, there have been thousands in the business. You really can get burned out on this sometimes."

Ronny Craig is excited about his future. He will produce his fifth annual **Elvis Explosion** show in La Crosse, Wisconsin, which is also a regional contest and qualifier to the **Images of the King** contest. The show raises several thousand dollars each year as a benefit for the **Children's Miracle Network**, co-sponsored by the **Gundersen-Lutheran Medical Foundation**. This event has become Ronny's cherished project. He continues to work with Nance Fox at the **EEN** and has recently partnered with her in the *Images of the King* contest in Memphis with Doc and Jackie Franklin.

"I am looking forward to working with everyone on the contest. We all want to erase the negativity that so often shadows the contests...perhaps stricter rules, a higher sense of fairness and, in general, implement new ideas. I think the **Business of Being Elvis** *has never been stronger. I sincerely hope we can bring the image of the Elvis impersonator to that of a tribute artist. I'm sure there are many people in this business that want to be respected for their contributions."*

Kavan Creamer

Kavan, which means "Jupiter" in Persian, Creamer began singing Elvis' songs when he was only three years old. Although Kavan's parents do not sing, Kavan believes that his father was very influential in his life. He was told that his grandfather Creamer used to be a singer, but unfortunately, he passed away before Kavan was born. His maternal grandparents however, chaperone Kavan for all of the Elvis impersonator contests and shows. *"My grandpa is always with me,"* Kavan proudly states. Kavan's parents work in very demanding careers requiring them to put in long hours away from home.

"I think I just started watching a lot of Elvis movies and listening to his music for something to do. I knew other people impersonated Elvis and I decided that I wanted to do that...so I did. I have never had any singing lessons either."

Kavan, almost 16 years old now, has a natural Elvis look with his dark features and sincere smile, but he also has a humble attitude about the **Business of Being Elvis.** Kavan remembers hearing Elvis sing **Unchained Melodies** and thinking that was the greatest song he had ever heard. Kavan, obviously, wasn't even born when **Unchained Melodies** was originally released.

"My favorite thing about Elvis is that he was always loyal to his fans. He would always stand there and sign every autograph that everybody had. A lot of singers now-a-days don't think they need to do that...like they are too good to do that kind of stuff. I think that was a really good quality of Elvis Presley. So, I have to say that I give my fans a lot of credit for my suc-

cess as an ETA. I wouldn't be here today if it weren't for my fans. If the people don't like you, I don't believe you will go anywhere... especially in this business. There are times when I don't do so well at a show and my fans still cheer me on."

Another one of Kavan's favorite Elvis songs is **If I Can Dream.** When we discussed this particular song, Kavan very emotionally shared that, *"If I could dream...I would wish for world peace. I would also dream for Elvis to be alive...he had such a great talent. Out of all the superstars that have died, I don't believe there has ever been such a following...like Elvis. I wish he could still be here to sing and carry on his legend."*

LEO DAYS

Leo Days was born in Honolulu, Hawaii, in 1980. Leo and his family now reside in Michigan. The first time I saw Leo perform, he won first place at the Marquette, Iowa *Isle of Capri Casino* contest in September, 2001. The thing about Leo that first struck both me and my husband was how much he looked like my husband's son, Ryan. In fact, we introduced Ryan to Darren Lee in Las Vegas and Darren thought Ryan was an ETA. Secondly, Leo's other notable characteristic is how someone so reserved is able to become so alive when he walks on the stage? I just knew he would win this one. Then, when I interviewed Leo, I felt a strong connection to Ryan similar to a déjà vu experience. I also gained considerable insight into the tremendous impact Elvis Presley has had on Leo, and Leo's choice to follow a better road in life. I was deeply moved and felt a sense of hope...and hope for our son Ryan who is still searching.

According to Leo's mother, Karen, *"Leo had become a runaway when he was 15 years old. The kid was lost and confused. He was always shy and a loner, then when he hit his teen years, he began to get in trouble. When I, and Leo's stepfather, Jerry, finally got him back home, we had already purchased a Karaoke machine. Leo always liked to sing. As a young child, he always studied Elvis' moves in his concerts and movies. He admired Elvis very much and I was hoping that the Karaoke machine would give Leo an opportunity to spark that interest. As a mother, I had no choice but to try something. I love him very much...and that is how he got started."*

One day, Leo's mother heard him singing in the basement, but she was not certain whether she was hearing Leo or Elvis. She went downstairs to discover that it was Leo singing and performing moves just like Elvis'. She told him she thought he was really good and asked Leo if he might like to sing Elvis professionally. After some discussion, Leo agreed to sing and Karen agreed to make his costumes. Eventually, Jerry began running the sound equipment while assuming the role as Leo's manager. Whenever Leo is not in school, they are all on the road together. Leo returned to high school, graduated six months behind schedule, and received his diploma. He is currently enrolled in college.

Leo has a lot of big plans for his future and optimistically added, *"My first priority now is to finish college. Ultimately, I want to become a lawyer. I love performing Elvis and I would like to do this as long as I am able. I think it is important to have a Plan B, especially in the entertainment business. Plan B is my education. I am grateful to Elvis for his tremendous inspiration to me. He literally changed my life…giving me self-confidence and the opportunity to change my direction in life."*

Performing for benefits is one of Leo's favorite features of being an ETA. His first benefit was for the Muscular Dystrophy Association after he lost an aunt to the disease. Leo performs all of the Elvis eras and is careful to replicate Elvis in every detail. In Leo's six years performing, his fan base and bookings continue to soar. The entire family works and travels together calling themselves "the Michigan Mafia."

Leo has presented his production of **The Three Faces of Elvis** all over the world. He has headlined for numerous celebrity entertainers such as Peter Noon of Herman's Hermits, Gary Puckett of the Union Gap, The Rascals, Paul Revere and The Raiders, Clay Walker, Chuck Negron of Three Dog Night and many others.

With Leo's family and fans' continued encouragement and support, I have no doubt that Leo will become a successful lawyer, in addition to his career as an ETA. I am honored to have met Leo and to share his personal story with you. If Leo is able to help even one person turn his or her life around, then his purpose as an ETA is clearly more than simply performing as Elvis. Perhaps Leo will someday receive the "Spirit of Elvis" award, the most prestigious award given each year to an ETA at the **Images of the King Contest** in Memphis. From my perspective, Leo has already given the greatest gift of all…a piece of himself.

MICHAEL DEAN

Michael Dean and his wife, Gayle, own a successful and interesting business in Decatur, Alabama. They also perform together in their band called **Memphis**, where Michael performs as an Elvis Tribute Artist.

*"I tell everybody we build prisons during the day and play **Jailhouse Rock** at night. It can be difficult sometimes, though, especially when we get offers to do a six-week show in Branson, Missouri, for example, because of the business. Those shows are also very time-consuming and we can't be away that long. We book as much as we want to right now. Gayle is a great manager, she has a good business mind, and she provides a lot of talent to the band,"* said Michael.

As a young child, Michael learned to play keyboard, rhythm guitar, lead guitar, harmonica and trombone. He must have been a natural at building things with an **Erector Set** or **Lincoln Logs** as well. In 1992, while playing in his own band, a good friend of Michael's approached him about doing a Christmas show that would include some Elvis music.

"I grew up with the Beatles, not Elvis, you see, and therefore I had to learn some Elvis songs. It began as just a fun thing, you know. I found a lady that would make me an Elvis costume for about $250.00. We did this little show and from that we began to get all kinds of calls to do parties and such. I worked steady for six months or more learning and listening to Elvis music day and night. Once I got into the music, I fell in love with the talent and voice of Elvis. I'm a huge fan of Elvis now," he said.

Gayle and Michael have now been married for nearly ten years. What does she think about all of this?

"Oh, yes, I thought he had the talent. I just never dreamed I'd be married to an Elvis impersonator. The opportunity has allowed us to meet a lot of great people. Some of our best friends in the world are those we have met doing the shows."

They have also met many of the folks who performed or worked for Elvis. In fact, **Michael Dean and Memphis** presents an annual show with **The Stamps Quartet**. This also gives them a chance to share their many stories they have gathered over the years about Elvis Presley, the person. It is fascinating to hear some of them because they really highlight Elvis' fun side, his sense of humor and his generosity.

Michael doesn't really do contests, as far as contests go. He does a few of them mostly because he is asked to participate by personal friends. He just enjoys performing Elvis' music. Michael took first place at the preliminaries of **The $50,000 Tribute to the King** regional contest in Tunica, Mississippi in 2001. The **Michael Dean and Memphis – Tribute to Elvis** CD is now available.

"*I love the gospel music 'How Great Thou Art' and 'Help Me.' I also love 'Trilogy' as a three-part song, although I seldom sing it. But sometimes when I do, I know I'm doing it well when I give myself chills. I just literally get thrilled with the power and the presence of that song,*" Michael explained.

Dean also enjoys the diversity of his fans—from the little children who come up and sing with him to the ladies who can barely walk with their canes. He occasionally places a scarf around their necks and often sees tears in their eyes. He is also aware of some of the drawbacks but Michael Dean, in or out of costume, projects an aura of class. He and Gayle share a love and respect for each other that is clearly visible, even to the casual observer.

"*It is wonderful to have the life we have. I also understand how Gayle feels about certain things in this business. I know what my limits are and I stay within them. Once in a while, someone will sneak up on me and try to get past those limits. I get out of that situation in a hurry, and it works. I just try to be as close to Elvis as I can when I'm on stage. I want people to see that and to feel that, and to understand that. And if I'm not, I'm leaving,*" he summarized.

Gayle added, "*Someone once asked me about being married to the 'King,' and I said, I don't call him the 'King' at home.*"

And with his big, handsome, Southern smile, Michael mischievously adds "*…unless I've been bad and I've been dogged.*"

BUTCH DICUS

Butch Dicus truly is **The Heart of Elvis** in his appropriately named tribute to Elvis show. From several personal conversations with Butch, it is clear to me that he sincerely loves paying tribute to Elvis, as he's been impersonating the King since 1973. A native of Arkansas, Butch saw

Elvis perform in 1972 in Pine Bluff, Arkansas, and met Elvis at Graceland in 1974, and then again the same year, backstage in Pine Bluff.

"*When I watched the* **Aloha From Hawaii** *concert in January 1973…that's when I decided I wanted to impersonate Elvis. I dreamed of contributing to America what Elvis had contributed. Elvis was an American dream come true. I performed my Elvis act for free every moment I had until 1977 when I entered my high school talent contest taking a first place win.*"

Following high school graduation, Butch enlisted in the United States Air Force. He didn't think he would be performing Elvis tributes for a while, but much to his surprise, Butch ended up taking Elvis all over Europe during his military career. In Butch's sixteen plus years in the Air Force, he was stationed at a variety of different bases and was proud to serve his country and pay tribute to Elvis at the same time.

"*I returned to the Little Rock Air Force Base in Arkansas, I had the opportunity to perform for numerous city organizations and charities. I received two keys to the city of Jacksonville and a letter of appreciation from then-Governor Frank White of Arkansas for my volunteer work. Soon after, I was stationed in West Germany and had to give the performing days a little rest. In 1986, I arrived at Cannon Air Force Base in New Mexico. I immediately began performing for the various Officers Club functions. By 1989, I was stationed in the United Kingdom. It was there that I had the opportunity to work with a charity group in Bury St. Edmunds, United Kingdom, to help raise money for the orphans in Romania. It was a local talent show featuring 12 British contestants and one American…me. The grand prize for the winner was a guest shot in London for the Sky Television Network's version of Star Search. I won the local contest, went on to London to place second behind a 98-year-old man with a dog in his pocket…but the experience in front of live television was outstanding.*"

Butch's band toured and performed all over the United Kingdom with him as well. In 1993, he received orders to go to Yuba City, California, and soon after, was stationed at Nellis Air Force Base in Las Vegas, Nevada. A group of Butch's friends arranged a surprise welcoming for his Las Vegas arrival; they took Butch to the **Palace Hotel and Casino** to see a quartet and band performing in the hotel's lounge. Suddenly, the band's lead singer announced to the lounge crowd: "*We have an actual Elvis impersonator amongst us tonight.*" Of course everyone looked around. The lead singer announced Butch's name and called him up on stage. Butch performed one set for two nights with the lounge group. This is one of the many fond memories Butch shared with me about paying tribute to Elvis.

When Butch retired from the Air Force in 1994, he took a break from performing and scouted out the job market in the civilian world. Then, in 2000, Butch married Lisa Van Boven, a violinist with the Arkansas Symphony Orchestra. Butch and Lisa currently have six musically inclined children—three girls and three boys, plus one musical cat named Mozart who makes up this talented family group.

"With dad performing Elvis, mom playing her violin, the sisters doing their **N'Sinc/Britney Spears** *act, son Drew with his recorder and the other son John with his collar turned up and hair spiked…the* **Osbornes** *have nothing compared to us. And the rest, as you say, is history still writing itself."*

One of the greatest highlights of Butch's career includes his performance with the Pine Bluff Symphony Orchestra in November 2001. For the **Butch Dicus – The Heart of Elvis** performance, the Arkansas Symphony included 22 violins, 8 violas, 8 cellos, 5 bass violins, 4 trumpets, 4 trombones and an assortment of other brass and wind instruments in addition to a piano and drums. The Symphony's conductor, Charles Jones Evan, also holds the arrangements for the three songs that Butch sang with the symphony.

"The show was a pops concert and at the end, the orchestra played **2001 Space Odessey** *and then I came out and did* **That's Alright Mama** *followed by* **Suspicious Minds***. Now what was really funny was, I was having to depend on the violins as Elvis did. The guitars and the drummer scared me at first. I thought it was Ronny Tutt, he was that good."*

Butch has produced a number of CDs including several gospel, Christmas, and Elvis tributes, as well as a promotional video.

LANCE DOBINSON

Lance John James Dobinson is an exemplary young man at the age of sixteen. Lance is also a talented, up-and-coming Elvis Tribute Artist. Born in Collingwood, Ontario, Canada, he now resides in Nottawa, Ontario, Canada, where he lives with his parents, Sharon and John, and his 12-year-old brother, Kristopher. He will be a junior in 2004 at the Collingwood Collegiate Institute. Lance enjoys a variety of sports, but is particularly involved with soccer and hockey. He's played rep hockey since the age of seven and currently holds the position of defenseman, a position that permitted Lance to assist his team winning four OMHA All Ontario Championships plus one Triple Crown Championship.

"Aside from liking hockey at the age of seven, I also began to take an interest in singing and listening to music. I especially liked the band **Aeorosmith**. *I even performed some of their music at public school talent show. The following year, though, my grandmother had me tuned into Elvis Aaron Presley. I was amazed when I learned just how talented the King of Rock and Roll really was. His style was so unique from any other performing artist. From that moment on, I developed this strong desire to sing and per-form Elvis on stage."*

Lance first entered the **Collingwood Elvis Festival** in 1999 and par-ticipates in the contest and festival since then. It is apparent that his desire and ambition is paying off. Lance won first place in the **Under 16 Youth Division** in 2001 singing **One Night With You**. Then, in 2002, Lance placed in the top twenty of the semi-finals in the **Non-Professional Division** with a nice medley of **The Wonder Of You**. Lance has participated in a variety of events that include **The London Western Fair Talent Search** and **Brantford Elvis Festival** in Brantford, Ontario, Canada. I watched Lance do a terrific performance in a venue at **Don Cherry's** during the 2002 **Collingwood Elvis Festival**.

Lance is well respected among his peers, classmates and ETA fans. He volunteers his talent as an ETA by performing at numerous bene-fits, churches, schools and other local events. It is so wonderful, in my opinion, that Lance utilizes his abilities in such a positive manner. It is a great opportunity for Lance to be a role model that other teenagers can look up to. Elvis Presley would be as proud of you as we are, Lance. Keep up the good work.

"Being an Elvis Tribute Artist is not always easy because some people can be very judgmental. I believe that with the continued love, support and encouragement from my family, there really isn't anything else that matters. If you love what you do, then you should follow your dreams. There will

*never be another artist like Elvis Presley, but by paying tribute and believing
in his music, Elvis will always be alive in our hearts."*

ERIC ERICKSON

Although Eric Erickson has been paying tribute to Elvis for only
ten years, he is sometimes referred to as the oldest Elvis impersonator
at the age of 63. In the **Business of Being Elvis**, however, he is
respectfully known as one of the best Gospel singers. Eric entered the
Elvis entertainment world quite differently than most other ETAs.

*"It all started at my church one day while I was folding bulletins and
drinking some coffee. I was singing along with some Elvis Gospel music
when the pastor walked in and heard me. The pastor suggested that I begin
doing some solos with the choir. Well, up to that point in my life, the only
time I even sang in front of people was as a party guy while I was in the
service…just jamming and fooling around. I was scared to death at the
thought of performing on a stage. A couple of weeks went by and the pastor
came down with laryngitis and quickly informed me that I would have to lead
the singing…doing the chorus myself. Needless to say, I was a wreck."*

The following week, his pastor asked Eric to lead the chorus again,
only this time he insisted that Eric use the microphone so that the
entire congregation could hear him well. Eric eventually overcame his
fear of singing in church and graduated to performing in front of large
audiences. He has been invited to the **Elvis Collingwood Festival** in
Collingwood, Ontario, Canada, for the last few years to participate in
their Elvis Gospel service. The Gospel service includes a couple of
other ETAs and **The Sweet Inspirations** as backup. It is an absolutely
beautiful service. Eric also assisted the **Collingwood Festival** in organiz-
ing the Gospel program for the youth groups during the festival. Eric
has performed numerous Elvis Gospel concerts. Prior to his recent
move to Florida, he traveled throughout Michigan and surrounding
states to sing in other churches and their choirs. Each year, Eric volunteers to sing his Elvis Gospel music for **The Salvation Army** during the
Christmas season.

*"As with Elvis, Gospel is first and foremost with me, and always will be.
I am one that is very thankful to God for the gift of singing He has given me.*

I am thankful to Elvis Presley and his beautiful voice. Through the years, there have been many things to be thankful for…my wonderful wife, Cherie, the other ETAs I have met, the contests, the showcases, and for being one of the featured artists in the documentary **Almost Elvis.**"

One summer, Eric had the opportunity to sing some Elvis "tunes" at a drive-in theatre. He was reluctant at first because he had become so comfortable with Gospel that he wasn't sure he could sing anything else. Now he is glad that he did that little performance as it has brought him many other opportunities to sing Elvis' music, such as parties, nursing homes, and several benefits for special children, as well as, contests. Eric has been a finalist in the **Images of the King** contest in Memphis three out of the last five years.

"*My wife, Cherie, travels with me all the time to the different venues. She also sings backup with me for our* **Spirit of Elvis** *shows. We were married on August 16, 2000, in Memphis, Tennessee. As time has gone by, she has shown her love of Elvis, not only by her involvement with our show, but also by a few tattoos of Elvis on her shoulder and upper arm.*"

Eric often shares a photo of himself at age 12 because of the uncanny resemblance he bears to that of Elvis Presley. He loves the fans and their smiles. Eric and Cherie are excited about their move to a warmer climate in Florida and look forward to the many new opportunities to perform there. They plan to continue to stay in touch with the many fans they have already met as well.

"*My favorite Gospel song is* **How Great Thou Art**, *but like the Elvis song* **If I Can Dream**, *I would wish that everyone could love one another. As long as God allows me to, I'll share this gift with as many people as possible. I…we, enjoy every moment of paying tribute to Elvis.*"

PAUL FRACASSI

Paul Fracassi, known as ETA **Kid Elvis** is, at the ripe old age of 13, a mature and talented young man from Woodbridge, Ontario, Canada. Although Paul started his singing when he was five years old, he began performing Elvis music only about three years ago. Paul has already taken the **Business of Being Elvis** world by storm. Paul could be described as a little hunk of rockabilly charm. He was recently the cover feature in **The Toronto Sun**, featured in Joe Warmington's column **The Night Scrawler** in **The Sun,** and additionally received a rave performance review in **The Montreal Gazette**. Paul, as a young actor, recently wrapped up the movie **Crime Spree** with tough guy and **Oscar** nominee Harvey Keitel and actors Gerard Depadieu, Johnny Hallyday, and Kiefer Sutherland. He was cast as a son of a mob boss with a 10 to 15 minute part. The movie is expected to be released in the summer of 2003. And, according to Paul, he owes it all to Elvis.

"I was performing in an Elvis tribute show in Oashawa where someone from the movie saw me. I guess they liked my stage act because they called me in for an audition. I also found out that Johnny Hallyday began his career as the Elvis of France way back in the days when Elvis was still alive (Paul is like a walking encyclopedia when it comes to Elvisology). *But I haven't talked to him about that. I have never acted before so I had to learn to read lines. I've never done commercials either. But I've always been up to challenges."*

Paul is the 2002 **Collingwood Grand Champion Youth** as well as the 2002 **Brantford Grand Champion Youth**. He has appeared on several television programs including **Good Morning America**.

"I was just really happy I won a Canadian championship. My day was going crazy and my mom was crying. I just think Elvis was a great performer. He was a nice guy and he bought people cars all over the place. Elvis was such a giving person. I'd like to be an Elvis impersonator for a long time and eventually make my own songs."

Heading for the 8th grade, Paul studies hard to maintain his good grades. He is currently taking extensive voice training lessons. He plays several musical instruments and continues his achievements in Kempo Karate. His hobbies include hockey, basketball, and golf. As you can see, Paul has an extremely active and busy life. Then add Elvis. He sings over 100 Elvis songs performing all of the Elvis eras at weddings, charity events, conventions, private parties and **Legends**-like concerts. Paul is in the process of producing a promotional video and hopes to have his own CD out soon.

"At first my friends at school teased me, but then they thought it was kind of cool that I get to go on TV and be on the front page of a newspaper. Now they are all learning Elvis is the King and they listen to his music too.

In Canada now, I usually have security on the stage. The fans want to have scarves and I had this suit with tassels…and they tried to pull my tassels. I was scared. I love to carry on the tradition of being an Elvis impersonator. I like Elvis' songs…to me it's like trying to make a better world for all of us without racism and all the other bad stuff going on in the world right now. I would just like to say Elvis lives—he's the best. Elvis will never die."

His parents, Gianna and Peter, were observers to the world of Elvis but *"we never expected our son to be a part of it."* They escort Paul to events throughout Canada and the United States. In August, 2002, the entire family, including his older brother, Peter, traveled to Memphis. It was Paul's first glimpse of **Graceland** and a chance to compete in the **Images of the King** contest. He owns several re-creations of Elvis' costumes, each costing $500 dollars or more. Paul has an agent for bookings, generating numerous offers that include auditions for **The Sopranos** sitcom and possibly another movie with Harvey Keitel. With Paul's dedication and his family's continued support, I believe this tremendous investment in the **Business of Being Elvis** will ultimately reap great rewards for Paul.

STEPHEN FREEMAN

Stephen Freeman, a native of Thomasville, North Carolina, was only six years old when Elvis passed away. His parents had tickets to see Elvis perform in Greensboro, North Carolina and he begged his parents to let him go along.

"They told me I could go next time and, in a pouting retaliation, I said Elvis will be dead by that time. And strangely enough, Elvis passed away the very next day. For a long time, I thought I actually killed him. I believe that kind of triggered my obsession with Elvis, in a sense. I experienced a form of guilt I guess without really understanding it. My parents didn't really understand the obsession and probably thought it was just something I was going through. I never would have believed I would go to the extent I have with it."

Although preoccupied with thoughts of Elvis, Stephen always dreamed about three careers that he wanted to pursue when he grew up. He wanted to be **Superman** (because of his black hair), Elvis (because he liked his music), and a police officer (because they always helped people). Stephen, now 41 years old, actually fulfilled all three of his dreams.

In 1993, he became a police officer. Stephen often sang at the police department Christmas parties, opening with one of his favorite Elvis songs, **Blue Christmas,** and performing at other private events as well. He didn't dress up as Elvis then but he did sing Elvis' music. It started as something fun to do. Eventually, Stephen started to receive a lot of booking opportunities and his career as an Elvis entertainer rose to the forefront of his old dreams. After six years with the police department, Stephen quit his job in 1999.

*"I decided one day to go for it...to take the risk...leaving behind my pension. I just gave it all up. I bought some new sound equipment, bought myself my first authentic Elvis costume...***The Aloha Eagle***, and became really serious about it. Initially, my parents worried about me making a career out of this, but now they are my biggest fans, doing everything they can to help me with it. My buddies from the force still come to all my shows too. As a police officer, you see a lot of things you really don't want to take home with you. The key is to leave it at work, and it is tough to do that sometimes. I learned so much about people and their reactions...that is why I believe that performing as Elvis provides a great opportunity to do something good as well. My shows offer an escape for people to forget about their problems for a while, maybe go back to a happy point in their life. To hear a certain song that relates to a fond memory. People tell me that after seeing my shows. That is one of the reasons I do this, is to make people happy."*

Stephen works out at the gym on a regular basis, following a strict schedule to keep in shape. It is critical because he performs the very early 70s era of Elvis, requiring a tremendous amount of energy. He doesn't believe that people want, or need, to be reminded of Elvis toward the end of his career when his illness began to affect his performance, adding: *"I think that is the biggest thing a lot of the impersonators do and it just creates a really negative image, especially on the young people. That's not who Elvis really was and that's not why he became who he was. My goal is to try to show people why he was so successful."* Stephen takes the **Business of Being Elvis** very seriously.

"I intentionally take breaks away from this business...where there is no Elvis around. I just try to clear my head so it doesn't get old and Elvis is

always fresh to me. Because when you do this as much as I do, you can take for granted what Elvis did accomplish. I don't want to ever do that."

Stephen produces most of his own shows, **Echos of a Legend**, performing with his band, **The Centennial Station**, complete with back-up singers and percussion. His most recent show, **All Shook Up**, is a special production and a joint effort between himself and the owner of the **Centennial Station Dinner Theatre** in Hotpoint, North Carolina. A sold out show of 275 people, this production is more like a play. Each act represents a different era of Elvis complimented with dialogue, while producing a concert atmosphere at the same time. Stephen will be returning to Hotpoint for a 20-day engagement in March, 2003. He feels that his band enhances his show: *"thus bringing more people and more interest."* His new promotional video, excerpts from the **All Shook Up** stage show, provides a powerful exhibition of his ability to pay tribute to Elvis. He is currently working on a new CD at the request of his fans and is a new member of the **Elvis Entertainers Network (EEN).** Stephen's ultimate goal is to perform Elvis in another country.

"The fans are great. I even have a lot of young ones from age seven or twelve or so. The secret with fans is to be honest with them. I tell these young people to stay in school and don't fall victim to other people's opinions because everybody's got one. It's easy to change your style and focus based on what other people tell you or think you should do. If you have a vision of something you want to do and you are successful to a point, then I think you should stick to it. I am happy and feel blessed to do what I thoroughly enjoy doing."

Well, Stephen, it appears that you fulfilled all three of your dreams...police officer, Elvis...and **Superman** *"because that's just Elvis with a cape on,"* according to Stephen.

ROB GARRETT

Rob Garrett was born in New York City, Manhattan, and raised in the borough of Queens. His first opportunity to see Elvis perform live came in 1972 at **Madison Square Garden**. In 1974, Rob's father received a job offer in Las Vegas, Nevada, and the family moved.

Between Elvis' **Madison Square Garden** performance and Rob's move
to Vegas, Rob attended an additional eight live Elvis performances. All
told, Rob's opportunity to attend 23 Elvis live performances earned
him the nickname of "Elvis aficionado."

*"It was great time to move to Las Vegas. So much was happening then.
There was a lot of opportunity to make money as an Elvis impersonator.
Elvis will always be big business in Las Vegas because of his popularity and
the fact that he's become more than a legend. He's become mythical—like a
folk hero. He is the only entertainer that has made that change over from
icon legend to folklore. With my entertainment background and the fact I
was already impersonating some celebrities in my act such as Elvis and Neil
Diamond, it was a natural for me."*

Rob has been an entertainer for nearly 24 years beginning with his
own band, **Rock 'N Roll Heaven.** They specialized in 50s, 60s and 70s
music performing in Las Vegas as well as other parts of the country for
15 years and provided Rob the good fortune to perform as Elvis with a
live band. He also became good friends with ETA Jonathan Von Brana,
at the time an Elvis entertainer for **Legends in Concert** in Las Vegas.
Jonathan performed in Vegas for several years until the late 80s when
he decided to move to Hawaii.

*"There were no **Legends** in Hawaii at the time and it turned out to be a
very wise move for Jonathan. He started his own show and became very successful there. Jonathan performed as Elvis and his wife (at that time) performed together. Then, Las Vegas started getting flooded with Elvi and I was
looking for a change, so I called Jonathan to see if the show would be interested in hiring me for a Neil Diamond act. Jonathan thought they might, so I
sent my promotional videotape out to Hawaii. Jonathan's boss was Paul
Revere of **Paul Revere and The Raiders**. He was running the show. He
was a great boss, the best boss. Well, they got my tape and they liked it, but
they weren't hiring at the time. They said they were making some changes
and would call me back. I thought it was the brush off, but about nine
months later, Paul called to inform me that he and **The Raiders** were coming to Las Vegas. He wanted me to do a live audition. We did the audition
and Paul asked how I would feel about coming to Hawaii. I thought about it
for two seconds. It was supposed to be a two-month job and I ended up
being there for three years performing as Neil Diamond while Jonathan performed as Elvis."*

When Rob returned to Las Vegas, he went to work for John Stuart performing with **Legends in Concert**. Later, he also worked with Stewart and his staff in the office and assisted Stuart with some of the scheduling duties. Rob respects John Stuart and the opportunity Stuart provided him. Yet, after a while, Rob still wasn't getting as much work as he wanted with **Legends**.

"I started to have too much time on my hands and I thought to myself…rather than wait around for John Stuart's phone calls including the ones he's not returning and the promises he wasn't keeping… I said I can do this myself and decided to form my own booking agency. So, in 1998, I formed the company **ImerpsonatorScentral**. *John Stuart wasn't too happy about that, but it turned out to be pretty lucrative. Back then, there was a lot more opportunity, now it has become much more political because so many corporations have taken over what was once mostly private and family owned businesses in Las Vegas."*

In the likeness of his former band's name, Rob's company is now known as **RNRH Entertainment**. The company provides a troupe of over 100 professional impersonators and celebrity look-a-likes for hire. They range from Elvis, of course, to political figures including the likes of Bill Clinton. Prices range from approximately $150 for a meet-and-greet Elvis to roam the room shaking hands and picture taking opportunities at a convention or private party, to $1000 for an hour-long stage show. Corporate groups are generally the most lucrative because they generally have larger entertainment budgets. Elvis is, and probably always will be, the most popular impersonator.

"Most of the Elvi are not complimentary to the image of Elvis Presley and, unfortunately, that is the majority. There are very few that can make a good living at performing Elvis. The rest of them know to keep their day job. Even I know that I am **NOT** *Elvis."*

Rob continues to perform as Elvis, but only in Las Vegas. When he is on the road, which is quite often, Rob performs as Neil Diamond. In between his own appearances, Rob is very busy booking engagements for his own roster of impersonators. Rob recently joined the Board of Directors as a member of the **International Guild of Celebrity Impersonators and Tribute Arts (IGCITA).** He is very proud of his opportunity to be one of the presenters at the **Cloney Awards.** Rob is also proud of his association with Fil Jessee and Bea Fogelman noting that *"Bea is like a second mom to me."*

"I'm actually too busy to even attend other shows or go out to scout for new talent. I receive an unbelievable amount of promotional packages from performers and, unfortunately, most of it never makes the grade. I will tell the impersonators and I will say this to people who are just searching on the Internet for an impersonator, specifically Elvis. There are a lot of Elvi out there, but most of them are awful or unkempt. Be sure to provide, or request as the case may, professional promotional kits. Send only quality photos and videos with references. If you work for free or if you can hire Elvis for free, you will probably get just what you paid for."

Rob Garrett, whether as Elvis or Neil Diamond, or as an entrepreneur in the entertainment world, continues to be a major influence in the **Business of Being Elvis**.

TONY GROVA

Anthony Grova, Jr. began his journey into the Elvis arena at the age of eight in Brooklyn, New York. He attended Catholic schools, sang in the church choir, and loved *"doing my little Elvis act"* at school dances. His mother was a big Elvis fan and Tony literally wore out her Elvis 45s record collection. It was Elvis' infamous **1968 Comeback Special** on television that became the final turning point in his desire to perform Elvis' music.

In 1975, Tony was blessed with the opportunity to see Elvis live in concert at the **National Coliseum** in New York:

"I guess besides being a role model for me, Elvis had this thing about him with people—the charisma, the charm that just captured the audience. It is hard to describe."

Then, in 1977 when Elvis Presley died, it hit Tony like a ton of bricks. He was performing as an Elvis entertainer at restaurants and clubs in Hoboken, New Jersey (Frank Sinatra's hometown).

"I was very upset like everyone else, but I actually went into seclusion for a while. I guess I was just mad at the world because the one thing I loved in life was gone, outside of my mother and father. Elvis is the next biggest thing in my life. It's just something I grew up with. But I'm still my own person."

Tony has done a few contests in the past but mainly because he was asked to do them. He doesn't want any part of them now. He also feels that the contests are *"rigged"* in some way and that the *"conclusion is obvious."*

"There is no contest because there's only one Elvis. You can take every Elvis impersonator, no matter how good they are—including myself—but that will still not make them an Elvis Presley. The contests will always continue because it's a matter of money. Elvis is a big money business now days. Unfortunately, it's not done for the right reasons. I wasn't doing Elvis just for the money. I'm a union carpenter by trade."

Tony receives a lot of calls from other Elvis entertainers seeking his advice. He reminds the young guys starting out that *"there is no competition because Elvis is Elvis. Go out there and be yourself. Be an entertainer, and make the people see the love. Never let the fans see or feel that you are only up there because you're getting paid for it."*

Tony doesn't want new Elvis entertainers to think that they're all going to make a living off of this business, even though there are many that do. He believes that too many of the impersonators think that getting into **Legends in Concert** is the ultimate goal. He also feels that a person is, in his or her own right, a professional when he or she gets paid for it. Tony has a terrific promotional video and a variety of CDs. He is well aware of what it takes to survive in the **Business of Being Elvis**.

"Elvis is a part of my life. I'm Tony Grova without Elvis Presley. Elvis provided inspiration. My parents provided guidance and Elvis was just another person that helped to guide me. Rather than hanging out on some street corner, Elvis gave me some values and provided an outlet that kept me focused and busy."

Tony is his own agent and performs a tribute called **Tony Grova's Memories of Elvis**.

He was recently hired as a consultant by a Hollywood director to teach Harvey Keitel how to perform Elvis for the movie **Finding Graceland**. Tony loves being an entertainer and he enjoys the *"unbelievable high I get when I'm on stage in front of people performing, especially Elvis."*

In closing, Tony Grova recites his trademark phrase and philosophy:

"There have been many kings and queens and presidents too, but never again in this lifetime or any lifetime to come, will there be

another man or entertainer as the one and only Elvis Aaron Presley."

RAY GUILLEMETTE, JR.

Ray Guillemette, Jr. has been an Elvis fan since he was eight years old. By the time he reached high school, his friends had nicknamed him Elvis. Ray had a natural look of Elvis with the slicked back, black hair and sideburns. He would sing Elvis music and hang Elvis posters in his locker. During his college years, he even did the Elvis thing for Halloween. Then he went on to graduate from The Culinary Institute of America in Hyde Park, New York. A chef by trade, out searching for a job, he happened upon a classified ad in a Boston newspaper looking to hire a Michael Jackson or Madonna impersonator. Ray followed up with the idea that they might also be interested in an Elvis impersonator. It turns out the agent already had one, but hinted that he might call Ray back. Ray thought this was basically a dead lead. But a few months later, the agent did call him. His Elvis impersonator was unable to attend a booked engagement and so he asked Ray to fill in. Ray had a feeling this might be his first big break and, ultimately, it was. Ray, now 12 years later, is still working with **Imposter Bostonian** and is one of the most requested tribute acts.

"*Actually, I got into this business because I didn't want to. I didn't have the chance to see Elvis in person, but I had seen a few impersonators when I was younger. I wasn't impressed with the way they presented themselves, not necessarily on stage, but as I felt compelled to connect with them. I wanted to talk to them, get their autograph and I really just wanted attention from them. That is where they fell short. Then as I got older, I would see these guys and people began making fun of them...they gained a bad reputation as Elvis impersonators. I didn't want any part of that. I admired Elvis way too much to get put into that category. So when I did step into the* **Business of Being Elvis**, *with a lot of encouragement and opportunity of course, I was going to make sure it was done with respect and pride. To change, as best I could, the stigma of negativity that in part, was created by Elvis impersonators.*"

In 1991, Ray began to concentrate on putting a first class Elvis show together.

*"So I thought…what am I going to do? What am I going to call it? Am I going to change my name? I don't want to change my name. I am proud to be Ray Guillemette, Jr., my father's son. I also respect Elvis enough not to throw in a name that's not mine. With the help of some of my friends, we got together and started tossing a few ideas around. Someone said…'Elvis a Ray'…meaning a variety of songs so as in array of something. Then I kind of blurted out 'A Ray of Elvis.' I said bingo, that's it! That's about as positive as I could title my show. It could be anything…a ray of tunes, a ray of light, a ray of something positive. So from that point on, I wanted to make sure that when I was on stage, I paid attention to not only the music or the style, but also the people. This is something I discovered in the hospitality business as well. To me, Elvis conveyed that and that is exactly what I wanted to connect with when I was a child. I wanted to make sure that is what I gave on stage **and** off stage. **A Ray of Elvis** is a full picture. You can't be on stage and be a superstar, then get off the stage, jump into the dressing room and fly away. You've got to give people the connection that they couldn't have with Elvis any more."*

For the next couple of years, when Ray could get time off from the restaurant he was employed with, he performed primarily at private parties. Then one day following a routine show at a birthday party in New Hampshire in 1993, a disc jockey who happened to be there preparing to register the **New Hampshire Elvis Fan Club** with **Graceland**, approached Ray with an idea—an idea that would turn out to be Ray's biggest break in the **Business of Being Elvis**.

*"He said, 'Listen, I have got to take you to this contest. I have never seen the likes of anybody like you.' And I was so green. I had no idea what he was talking about. I only knew this guy two weeks and there we were… getting in his car and driving to Memphis. We were on a wing and a prayer. We got there and I competed for five days at **Bad Bob Vapor's** in the **Images of Elvis** contest. I didn't know anyone in the business and I'm sure they didn't know me."*

Ray Guillemette, Jr. evidently took the contest by storm becoming the 1993 **Champion** of the **Images of Elvis** competition. This undoubtedly would create a major change in Ray's personal life and as an ETA.

"I was overwhelmed. All of a sudden I was thrown into this crazy world as you've known it and seen it. A lot of impersonators there were sort of

shrugging me off, giving me the cold shoulder because I came out of nowhere. I personally felt like...wow, this is wonderful to win. I was so proud of the whole situation. Although some accepted me, many others were scratching their heads and making comments about the contest being fixed or that someone was paid off. I was feeling pretty hurt at the time, but excited as well."

Needless to say, Ray stepped away from the restaurant business in 1993 and became a full-time ETA. For the next couple of years, Ray reaped the tremendous rewards that often follow a win in this internationally recognized contest that **Images** is so noted for.

"All of a sudden my telephone is ringing and ringing...I am booking show after show...until about 1995. My telephone wasn't ringing as much anymore and I started to think...well, maybe I've gone as far as I'm going to go as an ETA. I asked myself, what should I do? I began to realize that this is like any other business. You've got to pick up the telephone yourself. You've got to start promoting yourself...send out literature...put together a quality promotional package with photos and create my own opportunities. The business isn't just going to come to you. I started contacting various festivals, charity events, and other organizations that hire entertainment, which eventually paid off."

In 1995, some more wonderful things happened to Ray. He was named **International Grand Champion** at the **Collingwood Elvis Festival** in Collingwood, Ontario, Canada. He also met a pretty young lady named Delora, a native of the area. She was only 16 years old at the time. Elvis-loving mothers brought them both up. The pair stayed in touch over the years and eventually started dating seriously. While Delora attended the University of Guelph, she would travel to the United States to see Ray during her school breaks. By 1998, Ray had acquired seven "number one" awards throughout the United States and Canada. Ray, to date, is the only ETA ever awarded with such documentation and accreditations!

Now a singing sensation, Ray fulfilled a personal dream by purchasing a **Harley-Davidson Softail Classic** motorcycle in 1998. It seemed like life just couldn't get any better.

Then one evening in July, 2001, Ray decided to take his **Harley** out for a nice, leisurely ride. Before he even realized what was happening, a drunk driver in a pickup truck struck his motorcycle in the rear.

When he came to, he was in the **Hartford Hospital** in Hartford, Connecticut.

"*I had a very good team of 10 to 12 doctors. I learned that my left leg was basically ripped apart. The doctors tried everything to save my leg. At one point, they took an artery from my right leg to connect the veins and things in my left leg. Then I developed an infection in my leg. After five or six weeks of pain without results, the doctors started talking about fusing the upper and lower bones together, which would mean I would have a permanently stiff leg. This ultimately led to the discussion of amputation. I was beginning to get tired of not having any control, becoming frustrated with having to depend on others to do anything. I finally decided I wanted to learn more about amputation. I started speaking with people about it…learning to say and accept the word amputation. A lot of positive people came to speak with me…telling me that life goes on and, yes it does suck sometimes…so does the pain. 'We're not going to paint a pretty picture here, but it is your personal strength that will get you through this.' The doctors explained that they could amputate in a few days, get me measured for a prosthesis in five days…I could begin therapy right away, and within two weeks I could be home. That was it for me. I made the decision to go forward with it. I felt good about taking control of my life again. I believe that this was the turning point in my healing process as well.*"

The prosthesis was good news, but it was the support system that came from many aspects, which evolved into the most positive effect. During the 56 days in the hospital, Gail, Ray's friend and business manager at the time, visited Ray at least every other day. Ray would keep her informed about everything and then she would promptly post all of the news on Ray's website.

"*She would literally take people through my day-to-day progress, including my drops, in a very compassionate way. People were writing back about using their lunch hours or coffee breaks to read my updated site. It became sort of a soap opera for people that couldn't be there physically, could still feel like they were there with me. Every day I would get letters from people and I must have gotten 500 to 600 e-mails every day. I received cards, gifts and flowers. What was once a fear for me…when I decided to lose the leg…was now an agenda. If I can get back on that stage again, even one show, I will have met my goal and call it a day.*"

In December, 2001, when I first interviewed Ray at a Christmas benefit being held for him, I expected to see Ray in a wheelchair. I was pleasantly surprised when he answered the door walking tall, as they say. Handsome and confident as ever, Ray walked back into the room and sat down next to Delora. After only a few months out of the hospital, it was difficult for me to imagine how Ray could successfully overcome his handicap so quickly. At that time, he had just learned that he might be a candidate for a new, more advanced, computerized prosthesis. Ray excitedly described the device as *"an opportunity to become a 'Bionic Elvis.'*

Ray was feeling very humbled about attending another benefit on his behalf.

"The fellow ETAs, fans, Nance Fox and others involved in putting this Christmas production together…is so astonishing to me. It is such an honor. There have been so many people coming together to raise money…even Canadian artists and friends. When I thought people would pull away, they stepped up to the plate instead. I'm usually the fundraiser and so to be on the receiving end is very strange, but it is also flattering."

Shortly after that interview, in January of 2002, Ray was accepted as a candidate for the new bionic leg. **Hangar Prosthetics and Orthodics**, a distributor for the German manufacturer and inventor of the **C-Leg** device, worked extensively with Ray's therapists to determine his physical and mental qualifications before making a determination. They viewed Ray's promotional videos to observe the range of motion he used as an entertainer and understand that it is somewhat complex when it comes to performing Elvis—from hip swiveling to karate stances. Although Ray was already on his feet, **Hangar** was confident they could help Ray return to the stage as Elvis.

The design of this prosthesis was embraced in other European countries and was just recently approved for the last few years by the **FDA** here in the United States. The **C-Leg** is all programmed by a PC and has microprocessors in the knee section. This tells the leg to execute stance control (stability) on uneven ground; you can set your own pace when walking along with numerous other functions. **Hangar** has sponsored Olympic athletes, rock climbers and skydivers to promote its product…now the sponsor, Ray!

*"Unfortunately, insurance covers very little of the expense for prosthetic devices. They don't really consider an amputee disabled. It is basically discriminatory, but that is the system. So when **Hangar** was willing to sponsor*

me, I was elated. They help to defray the cost of the leg, but in exchange for that, I agree to promote their product. I do a lot of shows for them, as well as my own, and I demonstrate my leg. I am a motivational speaker for them, which has turned out to be the best therapy in the world for me. In my own shows now, I make mention of my situation…sharing with other families who might be dealing with this issue. I do a lot of things with the **Shriners**, as I always have. Children totally amaze me with their spirit and drive to overcome obstacles.

"I think I have smiled more on the outside and inside on stage than the audience realizes. My life is not over…it is a rebirth, so to speak. I am perhaps a little less spontaneous and flippant when I perform. I have to plan it out a bit more now in my mind…like maybe 30 seconds, but I can still do all of the moves that I used to do. I have evolved myself as Elvis evolved. From originally doing mostly 50s, I now do 68 – 70s era. I'm comfortable with it. The manners and nuances about Elvis are different. I really enjoy it. As for any pain presently, well… what they call phantom pain/sensation is always there and always will be, but I will continue to deal with it. Phantom pain/sensations is the by-product that follows amputation. It is a mysterious pain, but your mind is so powerful. You learn and teach yourself to block it out."

Ray has also become associated with the **Amputee Coalition of America (ACA)** as a **Regional Representative** (somewhat of a mentor and advocate for amputees). He was recently the feature story in their trade magazine **InMotion** (Jan/Feb 2003 issue) including a color ETA photo of Ray on the front and back cover. Ray is available and willing to talk to anyone who has questions, needs information, or seeking advice about amputation. Ray's motto is simply **D-I-S-ability…DIS-COVERY-INSIGHT-SUCCESS!** Anyone seeking more information about the ups and downs of life as an amputee or related orthodic concerns can go to www.amputee-coalition.org.

On April 1st, 2000, in Collingwood, Ontario, Canada, and then again on July 13, 2002, in Hamilton, Ontario, Canada, Delora Skelton and Ray Guillemette Jr. tied the knot. Collingwood is where their early romance started. This was a small and intimate ceremony in celebration of that. They were married again in Hamilton near Niagra Falls for all of their family and friends to attend. Delora graduated from McMaster University in Hamilton and currently is seeking to finish her masters degree in English. She also assists Ray with his very busy schedule. In addition to his many supporters out there, he credits Delora for a great portion of his positive demeanor.

*She may be ten years my junior, but her actions and wisdom are ten years my senior. Delora is a very patient and understanding person. She is very beautiful as well. I am lucky to have her by my side. In addition, I will always be thankful to this **Business of Being Elvis** and for the inspiration that Elvis has given me."*

You might say **A Ray of Elvis** has also become **A Ray of Hope** for the entire world. Ray's future brings **A Ray of Light** as well. January, 2003 was Ray's biggest booking month in eight years and the rest of the year is likewise. He continues to enjoy his ride in the Elvis arena as well as on his recent purchase of his second **Harley Davidson**, a **2003 Anniversary Edition Heritage Softail Classic**. He rides with the assistance of a **klicktronic** shifter fitted to his left handlebar. Designed originally for **Grand Prix** racing, it has evolved to help disabled motorcyclists to continue to enjoy their love of riding. I love his CD **20th Anniversary Tribute— I'll Remember you.** Ironically, my favorite song on that CD is **Got a Lot of Living To Do.** As for the future of the **Business of Being Elvis**, here is what Ray had to say: *"I haven't been involved with contests for a long time now, but I have judged a few. I judge hard, friend/acquaintance or not. The judging aspect of contests has always been controversial, even when I won. I think that it is wonderful that organizations continue to identify the need for improvement. I know it is a big machine to fix and start changing. It won't be easy, no doubt, but I think they will give it a shot in the arm and let it evolve to the next level. There's such a mass influx of Elvis impersonators that something has to be done. Its just chaos with some people getting so caught up in Elvis they lose themselves and their perspective. It's a circus sometimes when I look at some of these people. There's got to be regulation to bring the standard up. I know many entertainers that impersonate celebrities other than Elvis. They introduce themselves to people and the people think it is great. I tell them that I'm an Elvis impersonator, they snicker. Why is that? I am proud to personify Elvis and bring a positive **Ray** of him to the people. I know I am not Elvis... I love being... Ray Guillemette, Jr."*

PAUL HALVERSTADT

Paul Halverstadt was only five years old when his interest in music started. By the time he was 15, he already had his own band and was dreaming of becoming the next **Boots Randolph**. The band played primarily instrumentals with Paul leading on the saxophone. He still loves to play the saxophone but never mixes it with Elvis, however.

"The saxophone is an instrument you can do so much with...really make it talk. Well, I played with that band for about 13 years. We all worked full-time jobs and were booked every weekend. One day, I realized I had gotten burned out on the whole thing so I just quit the band. Sold all my equipment to the band members. I kept in touch with them and about three years later they asked me when I would be ready to come back. I thought for a minute and said **right now**.*"*

Paul reunited with the band for another ten years until he met up with friends Tom and Carmen. They were very familiar with Paul's performances with the band and especially enjoyed his renditions of Elvis. Tom and Carmen persuaded Paul to listen to some CD tracks of Elvis' music and to also sing along. This convinced Paul to focus on his ability to be the best Elvis tribute artist that he could be. They decided to produce an Elvis show of their own calling it **Memories of Elvis** and produced under the name **TCP Productions**. Tom is the host/emcee of the show. Ensuring that each performance would offer variety and freshness, Tom also prepares the song arrangements specifically for each show. Paul doesn't even know exactly what song he will be singing or in what order until he arrives at the venue. Carmen is the sound engineer, monitoring the quality of each song. Then there is the addition of another Paul, who is the technical engineer. Paul tells me he can fix anything. **TCP Productions** became the umbrella for all of the additional family members who also work behind the scenes.

"Carmen's wife is very good with the spotlights, especially because I move around a lot on stage. My wife and teenage daughter work the 2400 watts of stage lighting...everybody gets involved. Tom and my daughter also merchandise my CDs after each show while I greet the audience and sign autographs. It's pretty amazing how great they all are and how well we all work together. In fact, Carmen also works as a professional tailor, making tuxedos for weddings and proms. April and May are her busiest months so we cut back on

our shows during those months. It would be like driving a car with one wheel off. We really need everybody to pull off a first class show."

Memories of Elvis is indeed a first class production. For the last five years, the **Memories of Elvis** show has been a regular at **Jim and Jacks Club** which is a 350-seat dinner theatre located in the heart of Cincinnati, Ohio. Cincinnati, by the way, is just a stone's throw from Paul's home in Covington, Kentucky. About a year ago, the newly renovated **Cabaret Club** opened up. The new owner heard about Paul's ETA show at **Jim and Jacks** and promptly booked Paul to do one show each month.

It's hectic sometimes. Since 1977, I have worked as an auto mechanic specializing in suspension, alignments, and a/c problems. If you break down and need tie rods, I've got 'em. My wife is a nursing administrator. We have three children...15, 2, and 3 years old. We are currently renovating our 103-year-old house...completely gutting it. We've got all this on our plate. Plus the **Business of Being Elvis***."*

Paul does not enter many contests simply because he is so busy. He enjoys attending them whenever he can, however, for the friendship and camaraderie of the other ETAs. In July, 2002, Paul won first place at the **Bluff's Run Casino** in Council Bluffs, Iowa and looks forward to returning this year. Paul has a live CD **Aloha From Hawaii** that is an exact recreation. He is working on another live CD from his venue at the **Cabaret Club** that will be a recreation of Elvis, only this time Las Vegas style. Paul is looking forward to the future and the opportunity to perform as an ETA, and trying to keep the **Memories of Elvis** alive. He is also excited about Nance Fox and Ronny Craig's partnership in the **Images of the King** contest in Memphis.

"They have already brought a lot of professionalism to the industry. In the **Business of Being Elvis***, Nance could be compared to Marge Schott, the owner of the* **Cincinnati Reds***. She isn't afraid to do what it takes to get a ball club up and running."*

KEITH HENDERSON

Keith Henderson, as most ETA fans know, found himself $50,000 richer last year when he won first place in the final competition of the

2001 **The $50,000 Tribute to the King** national competition held at the **Isle of Capri Casino** in Biloxi, Mississippi. Interestingly, Keith has only entered six contests during his twenty- five-year career, meaning that Henderson was one of the very few ETAs performing when he first started in **The Business of Being Elvis.**

Maybe this explains why Henderson takes this business of performing his Elvis Tribute **Illusions of the King** show so seriously.

"My family tells me that I started my interest when I was three years old. As I grew older, I had this dream of singing with Elvis. So my dad, who can play practically any instrument as well as sing, told me 'well, if you want to do that, if you ever get the chance to sing with him—you need to know everything about him, to where you are like kin,'" said Henderson.

Keith grew up with his entire family singing and learning harmony together so it was natural that Keith passed that tradition on to his own family. Henderson's wife, his high school sweetheart, convinced Keith into performing his first tribute to Elvis for their high school talent show in 1978. Now, Keith's entire family is very involved in his Elvis business. Both Keith's mother and his 93-year-old grandmother continue to make his outfits. Additionally, his wife manages the soundboard while his son is responsible for the lighting when he's home from college, and both his daughter and his father sing with Henderson's band. It is a family enterprise!

"I had always been able to sing like Elvis, it's my style. I don't try to sing like him or sound like him. I'm doing my own thing and for me, it's similar enough to Elvis; my looks, the way I react to the songs and to the audience," Henderson said.

In addition to his Elvis career, Henderson is employed full-time in an engineering firm. He acts as his own business manager and, with his band, presents his show, **"Illusions of the King."** In his spare time, Keith's recorded a variety of CDs, including my favorite, **Love and Inspiration**. Recently, Henderson was absolutely thrilled to present his "tribute show" at the North Carolina State Fair as the opening night's headliner.

"It takes money to do this business. I don't have to do it. I do it for the love of Elvis and his music. There is so much negativity in this world that I want to represent him, and myself, in a positive way," stated Henderson.

Is Elvis still alive?

"There is no way that Elvis is alive," Henderson answered quickly. *"I try to do my show as if Elvis were in the audience. I would want him to be proud. Whether I am on or off the stage, I am Keith. My wife is my world, and my family will always be a priority."*

ROBIN KELLY

Robin Kelly is a Canadian based ETA. He is also the younger brother of ETA Darren Lee by five years. They were both involved in music at a young age. Robin thinks he is more like mom and Darren is more like dad. The brothers are supportive and encouraging of each other. Robin and Darren share their love for each other and Elvis' music. Both are extremely talented, yet respectfully unique.

When I interviewed Robin in Memphis, he was preparing to compete in the August 2002 **Images of the King** contest. He had just won as the **Grand Champion** at the July 2002 **Collingwood Elvis Festival** in Collingwood, Ontario, Canada, yet he was still nervous about competing in the **Images of the King** contest.

"It's hard to believe that I used to have such stage fright. I would literally faint...pass out in front of crowds of people. So I started out not knowing if I would really be able to do it. I didn't think my voice was that good. One of my first big jobs was actually performing with Darren. My voice was horrible; you would have walked out of the show. Now, I am here and I have Darren Lee the 1997 **Images of the King** *winner, which could make me look that much worse. Having Darren for a brother can be good and bad in this* **Business of Being Elvis**. *Don't get me wrong; Darren is very supportive of my endeavors. He understands what it's like and what I am going through because he has been there. I honestly don't like contests, but I feel they are a good way to get your name out there. It is tough to decide what songs to sing...I think the judges like to hear you sing some of the more difficult Elvis songs. I wonder, is the contest going to go against me because I am Darren's brother?* (Robin did make it as a finalist in the competition.) *It's ironic that Darren won Memphis on the 20th anniversary of Elvis' death and I won Collingwood on the 25th anniversary of Elvis' death."*

Robin feels he has a great manager who travels with him on the road. In 2001, they were on the road for eleven months traveling all over together. In 2002, the schedule was about the same, but they traveled mostly in Canada. Robin reads everything he is able to find about Elvis; the legend, the man and his music, His knowledge of Elvis helped him to develop the show, **One Night With You – starring Robin Kelly – The Ultimate Tribute To Elvis**. Robin would love to find work in the United States and dreams of one day having a show with his brother.

"I am still on the road all of the time, performing all across Canada. I've been reorganizing my company **Robin Kelly Productions,** *located in Vancouver, British Columbia. I want to add more agents and promoters to the ranks. Unfortunately, I'm not at liberty to divulge who they are at this time. I want to bring my company to the level of a top notch entertainment company."*

Robin is in the process of producing a video and CD, adding: *"I am very, very fussy...thus until I have a finished product I am satisfied with...I will keep working on it."*

Another exciting highlight for this year is that Robin is scheduled to perform at **B.B.King's** in Memphis, Tennessee, in August, 2003.

"In the **Business of Being Elvis**, *it helps to have a good agent. Meeting the right people who believe in you is the key. Mom is our biggest supporter—you can't buy that. I think if you stay busy enough, the money is good. The ETAs with the highest profile make a better living."*

In a final note, Robin said: *"There are two Canadians that have won* **Images**: *My brother Darren in 1997, Stephen Kabakos in 2001 and I want to be number three."*

MATT KING

Matt King started singing when he was 13 years old. When he was in high school, he also worked in a costume shop breaking up boxes and such in the warehouse. It was then that he got the idea to dress up as Elvis for a Halloween dance. Matt started saving his money to buy an Elvis jumpsuit and a wig. The party included Karaoke so Matt naturally took his turn at the microphone and sang some of his Elvis tunes.

"Well, at first, it was just to be funny. I was always kind of like the class clown. I could do a bunch of other impressions then, too. My friends at the party started telling me that I was pretty good. They would ask me to come to their party dressed like Elvis and sing. It evolved from there. In fact, one of my first greatest moments was getting paid to perform as an Elvis imper-sonator. In 1993, I bought Elvis' album **Madison Square Garden**, *which I used to lip sync at first. I think that is when I seriously realized how great Elvis' voice was. I really fell in love with his music and became a die-hard Elvis fan. When I was 18 years old, and in my second semester of college, my goal was to enroll in the police academy. I wanted to become a police officer. It so happened that my aunt was the director of promotions for a major pharmaceutical company at the time. The company she worked for ended up hiring me to do a six- week tour performing four nights a week. I had the opportunity to entertain at the* **Stratosphere Hotel and Casino** *in Las Vegas, the* **Civic Center** *in Dallas, and bunch of other big shows all over the place. It was a huge success, as well as a big break for me."*

In 1997, Matt started to enter Elvis impersonator contests. He won the 1998 title of **International Grand Champion** in the professional division at the **Collingwood Elvis Festival**. In 2002, he received the **People's Choice Award** at the **Elvis Fantasy Festival** in Portage, Indiana. Matt has also been honored with numerous other prestigious awards throughout his young career. He appeared on several interna-tional television programs and was a contestant on **The Ricki Lake Show** for the **King of Kings** competition. Matt is also the co-founder of the **Michigan Elvis Fest**, in his home state. In 2002, the fest brought over 30,000 Elvis fans together for the two-day event.

"One of the biggest highlights as an ETA was when Joe Esposito, Elvis' road manager, hired me to perform in Collingwood, Ontario, Canada doing a replica of Elvis' last concert. I was heavier then. I did the show and when I got off the stage, Marian Koch, Elvis' nurse, was crying. She was emotional about my rendition of **Unchained Melody** *that I sang while playing the piano. That experience just meant more than anything to me."*

Matt continues to work hard as an ETA in the **Business of Being Elvis.** He credits not only Elvis for his success, but his fans and the opportunity to meet and perform with other great ETAs. Matt includes the likes of ETAs Travis Morris, Quentin Flagg, and Irv Cass as his friends. He feels that his fans are his friends as well. Matt is proud to mention that he shared the stage with several stars during his career; including Merle Haggard, Eddie Holman, Jack Green, and Michael Twitty, Conway's son.

In closing, Matt King shared the following poignant comment: *"If I could dream, there would be world peace. I especially hope we can solve our problems with the Middle East. I am sure that the impending war with Iraq is on everyone's mind."*

KJELL ELVIS

Kjell (pronounced Key-el) Henning Bjornestad, known as Kjell Elvis, is **the** Elvis of Norway. He has been a big fan of Elvis since he was a child. Kjell, along with his family of two brothers and two sisters, would sing in church on a regular basis. He started imitating Elvis when he was 19 years old and finally in 1997, Kjell was able to become an Elvis tribute artist professionally on a full-time basis.

"I remember watching the movie **Love Me Tender** *on a black and white television. I was overcome by his voice and his moves. My life is to sing Elvis, but I do not live like Elvis. I don't collect Elvis' items and I don't have any Elvis pictures on the walls in my house. I work very hard to portray Elvis' personality and his voice when I perform."*

Kjell performs a variety of different Elvis shows ranging from a one-man show with professional sound and lighting engineers to a full-blown Elvis concert type of show. The Elvis concert show includes a live band with 22 members. The large venue is expensive to produce, but it also draws sell-out audiences. There have been several filmed documentaries about Kjell as a person and an entertainer. One of the documentaries was specifically a biography and tailored to Kjell's life as an Elvis tribute artist and was aired on television throughout Norway, Sweden, Denmark, Germany, and Australia.

"I am fortunate to have the best band in Europe…I also have a great manager. We all work hard together to be professional on stage with Elvis. We have constantly so much work that often our performances are our rehearsals. I am also all the time promoting myself. I take the **Business of**

Being Elvis very seriously. I know that I am the man behind the show…to sell myself always…on the stage and off. I don't like so many impersonators out there trying to be Elvis all the time. They make it a joke sometimes, giving Elvis a bad name. I have too much respect for Elvis. I want always to portray Elvis as someone good and kind…very generous with his time and money."

Kjell is, obviously, very talented as an ETA and acts as his own public relations manager. Kjell Elvis is evident everywhere in Scandinavia, from television to the covers of European magazines. Kjell averages about 50,000 hits a month on his website, proof of his popularity and his ever-widening circle of fans. There may be 35,000 Elvis impersonators in the world, but in Norway it seems that Kjell Elvis is the only one. In 2001, Kjell earned the title of **Best Elvis Imitator** by winning first place in a European Elvis contest. He also established an **Elvis Festival** in Norway that will soon be approaching its third year.

"This was a dream come true. The first year, we took a television crew on a plane to Memphis. We went to Sam Phillip's house (the founder of **Sun Records***). Then we visited Dee Presley (Vernon Presley's 2nd wife). We went to see James Burton and brought him and his band back with us to Norway."*

Although not very well known by the general public, James Burton is acknowledged by many in the music industry as one of the best and most influential guitarists of the rock era. Born and raised in the south, he was a regular on the famous **Louisiana Hayride** radio program in the 50s as a back-up musician for many country and western stars. Burton developed a guitar picking style similar to the guitarists who recorded on the **Sun Records** label such as Scotty Moore and Carl Perkins. He had a long collaboration with Ricky Nelson until he was recruited to work with Elvis Presley in 1969 up until Elvis' death in 1977. He also worked with Gram Parsons until his death in 1973, then the **Hot Band** formed by Parson's girlfriend, Emmylou Harris. Burton continued to work with John Denver and host of other celebrities in the music industry.

"We had **The Stamps Quartet** *at the festival also. In 2002, the festival got even bigger and better. We had the* **TCB Band** *and other stars from Scandinavia. There was a big wedding chapel set up for couples to get mar-*

ried in. We invited Elvis impersonators from many countries to enter in the Elvis contest. The festival has gained a lot of attention here and in Europe now. I am looking forward to the next festival."

Kjell has sold thousands of his hot CD **ELVIS: In My Way**. His voice is complimentary to Elvis leaving no trace of his heavy Norwegian accent. Kjell recently formed a new company, **Golden Voice**, producing high quality sound tracks specializing in Elvis music.

"*I am very serious about my work as an ETA and the* **Business of Being Elvis**. *Nothing has come easy for me. I have to work very hard for everything. I always am singing Elvis in my car, listening to his wonderful voice. I don't listen too much at home though because I also enjoy the peace and quiet. I am a loner that way. It is important to me to leave Elvis on the stage. I dream someday of performing and producing a musical show about Elvis' life…to show respect and to honor him.*"

I sure hope he will consider bringing his show to the United States.

SHAWN KLUSH

For nearly seven years now, Shawn Klush is content in reaching his comfort zone with his family at his side and performing at the Myrtle Beach **Legends in Concert**. He also occasionally rotates into their Atlantic City, Branson, and Las Vegas showrooms. It is a rigorous schedule working for Legends and John Stuart.

"*John Stuart is a foot soldier,*" said Shawn, "*but he never steers us wrong. I don't think he puts us in any situation that he couldn't handle himself, so you have to respect him for that.*"

Shawn has been an entertainer since he was 16 or 17 years old, playing with his own band in a variety of bars. Shawn was under age when he played in the bars, but it brought money to the club owner. His father was a disc jockey so music was always part of Shawn's life, especially Elvis' music because "*he was the biggest thing going,*" Shawn said.

Born and raised in Pittston, Pennsylvania, a small coal-mining town, Shawn's road to success is similar to the Loretta Lynn story. He encountered many difficulties that young people who are trying to make it as an entertainer experience.

"*But being impressionable, you go with the first chance that somebody offers you. They say they can do this and do that. Unfortunately, I drew a lot of zeros. It wasn't bad, really, it was a learning experience, and it was a stepping stone,*" explains Shawn.

He even tried his hand at the contests. One experience was very good, and one was very bad. The showcase in Montreal landed Shawn a second place win for $5000 and the attention of a soon-to-be new agent/manager. The other was the first contest he entered. He was discouraged by the reaction of the people regarding his performance.

"*I saw how the other guys were doing their show. I got up and did what I did. They didn't respect what I was doing and I didn't respect them. I thought, o.k,. I guess they didn't understand what I was doing. But what I was doing was coming from the screen, if you will—the book of Elvis. I studied the music and videos of Elvis.*"

But the good thing was the Montreal event connecting Shawn with Dan Lentino, an accomplished musician and businessman.

"*Dan has done a lot for my career. There are a lot of things that go on behind the scenes in this business. Dan handles them very well. I would trust him with my own kid. About four years into this business with Dan and they were knocking down my door to get me to come back,*" Shawn noted. "*That's why I don't do contests anymore, nor do I like them.*"

It may be true that Dan helped pave the way to **Legends** for Shawn, but Shawn has also demonstrated that he has the drive and dedication to be there. He has evolved into a polished entertainer and committed as an Elvis tribute artist. Shawn has recorded CDs, (**Live at the Foxwoods**)is my favorite), and he has performed with several of Elvis' former band members. He has also portrayed Elvis in the television mini-series **Shake, Rattle, Roll.** Klush plans to continue pursuing his acting career. Shawn Klush also performs annually in the **Elvis Birthday Tribute Tour** held each January.

During a Shawn Klush performance, I happened to hear an excited fan describing him simply as **"*Shawn is sooooooooooo Clutch*"**!

CURTIS LECHNER

Beginning in about May of 2002, everything that 32-year-old Curtis Lechner did in the **Business of Being Elvis** was a first time experience for him. He was an insurance claims adjuster for quite some time but he had always been a big Elvis fan. As a young child, he used to run around the house with a towel draped around his neck pretending to be Elvis wearing a cape. Curt has always played the guitar and sang Elvis songs around the house just for fun, but performing as an ETA never seriously occurred to him.

"*My nephew Robbie has a friend named Vince, whose mother happens to be a good friend of Nance Fox. We always get together during the holidays and every year, Vince would try to convince me to call his mother because her friend Nance is really into the Elvis stuff. Finally last year, I called Darlene, Vince's mother. She told me to grab my guitar and come over to her house, which was only 25 minutes away. I just really believed I wasn't good enough. Darlene videotaped me singing and then she said 'I think you can do it.' Then she arranged for me to sing a couple of songs on stage with the* **Wolverine Brothers**, *a band playing at the* **Radisson Hotel**. *She videotaped that also and presented it to Nance Fox and the* **Elvis Entertainers Network** *for their opinion. It was my first time on stage and I didn't think I would be nervous, but I really was. But once I got out there…your personality changes and your whole attitude changes. The band only knew a couple of Elvis songs and I had never been on stage singing with a live band before, but it ended up o.k. I started to feel comfortable up there. Now, the more I do it, the more I like it. Being on stage gives just a small taste of what it must have been like for Elvis.*"

Nance Fox liked what she saw on Darlene's videotape and invited Curt to attend the **EEN Annual Elvis Convention** in June of 2002. This would be Curt's first convention, the first time he performed at the famous **Sabre Room**, the first time he performed with the **ExSpence Account Band** and the first time he would perform with other ETAs. He participated in the seminars conducted by a variety of professionals in the industry. He had the opportunity to learn more about marketing himself as an ETA, techniques in how to improve his vocals (provided by ETA Doug Church), and the importance of professionalism as an entertainer.

"*I thought I would be intimidated by the other ETAs, but that wasn't the case at all. I really enjoyed the convention. I met a lot of great people, got the chance to meet some really good ETAs in the business. I realized that they all do this because they love Elvis. They offered me advice and helped me to improve my performance. They made me realize that you just do the best job you can do. I had such a good time.*"

In July, Curt made his first trip to Memphis and the **Images of the King** contest. He watched all of the ETA's performances.

"*I was just getting into this so everything was pretty overwhelming. It was just something else...hard to describe. I'm a natural blonde and my sister, who is a beautician, persuaded me to let her dye my hair black. I told myself I would change it back after I returned from Memphis. Well, I started getting more work so it is still black. Part of the business I guess. Funny story... I was wearing a new pair of sunglasses, similar to Elvis' but with a little different style. When Irv Cass saw me with them on, he said 'Wow, man, those are really great, I've got to get a pair of those,' and I told him to go ahead and take 'em and wear 'em out. We both laughed. ETAs like him keep it fun. It also makes you much more aware of what's out there and how big this **Business of Being Elvis** really is. I can't wait to get back there next year. Hopefully, I will have time to see the tourist attractions this time.*"

In October, Curt entered his first Elvis contest at the **Isle of Capri Casino** in Marquette, Iowa. His future plans include getting more involved with the contests. He feels that contests are a positive thing and, at this point in life, he hasn't found any negative things about the business in general. He is working on a new website and has future plans for a CD of his own.

"*When I first dyed my hair black, my ten year old son would look at me and say 'where's my dad?' I take him to see some of my shows if they don't last more than an hour or so, otherwise he gets bored. It turns out he enjoys the fact that I am an ETA. Recently, he told his music teacher about me. Then, the school called and asked me to perform Elvis for the 4th and 5th grade music class, which I was happy to do. After that, the teacher wanted the class to learn to write letters so they practiced with me. I received about 50 letters in the mail. You might say that I now have my first fan club, too.*"

DARREN LEE

In 1997, on his fifth trip to Memphis, Darren Lee became the first Canadian to win the **Images of the King** contest. He started performing at the age of ten, and now claims 16 years as an entertainer. Darren is the older brother of ETA Robin Kelly. They were both raised in an environment full of love and Elvis music. His mother used to sing on the radio in her youth and Darren describes her as the third **Everly Brother**. Darren even remembers jumping around to the song **Hound Dog** when he was just four years old.

"I think I got really serious about music in the 6th grade. I sang in the choir and started taking guitar lessons from a nun at the Catholic school I attended. The choir sang Gospel music, but we sang really non-traditional Gospel songs. It was a 73-person choir singing the newer contemporary Gospel tunes, so it was a really fun choir. With that, I took an interest in the guitar. This nun would teach me basic chords on the guitar, and then I would go home and practice the chords along with Elvis' records. When I told her what I was doing, she started teaching me the chords that were on Elvis' records. Eventually, I just naturally began playing all of Elvis' songs. By the time I was 15 years old, I was performing Elvis, Eddie Rabbit and Buddy Holly in various lounges."

In 1998, Darren finally entered an Elvis impersonator contest in Edmonton, Alberta, Canada, taking 2nd place. A chance meeting with another Elvis impersonator led to an audition with the **Elvis – Elvis – Elvis Show**. One day, the Elvis impersonator called Darren and asked him to join the show.

"I told him that I had been singing Elvis, playing the guitar, for quite a while now, but I never really performed just Elvis. He asked me to send him a tape anyway and we'll see what happens. I sent him a tape…it was a bad tape I thought, but I sent it anyway. Well, he called me back and said, 'You are hired and you have one week to prepare.' My brother Robin and I sat in front of a video screen watching all of Elvis' moves. Robin would automatically get up and do Elvis perfectly. Then I would get up to do them and trip over my own feet. It was like I had two left feet…it didn't even feel natural. The singing part was easy for me, so I concentrated the most on learning those moves. By the time I finished the show a year later, the Elvis moves became second nature to me."

Darren then formed **Rock N' Roll Heaven**, a tribute show that featured Darren in the roles of Elvis, Ricky Nelson, Buddy Holly, John Lennon and Ritchie Valens. The show toured for seven years. In 1994, Darren won an Elvis impersonator contest sponsored by the **Elvis Presley Museum** and his win evolved into an eight-month tour in Australia with the museum.

It may have taken Darren 14 years to get to Las Vegas, Nevada, but he finally made it! He has been performing as Elvis in the **American Superstars Show** at the **Stratosphere Hotel and Casino** for the past three years, sharing the stage with impersonators of **Madonna, Charlie Daniels, Cher, Michael Jackson** and a host of others.

"There are many people who have helped me along the way in my career. Aside from my family, I owe credit to my former manager, Neal Peterson. We were together for about eight years, traveling together all around Canada. He would book the jobs, drive his van to the shows and be my soundman, too. We weren't even making that much money then, but he stayed with me. The memory of that time keeps me humbled. Now, here I am in Las Vegas."

I sent out numerous videos and promotional packages…making several attempts to get an audition for a major show here in Las Vegas. As it turns out, those kinds of shows send out scouts to watch different entertainers perform. Ultimately, I guess that is what happened to me. Donny Moore, producer of **American Superstars***, found me and approached me about a job with them. I'm glad now that I didn't do* **Legends in Concert** *because you get shipped out to their other venues a lot. At* **American Superstars,** *I have the ideal situation to be able to stay right here in Las Vegas.* **Superstars** *is also very loyal. They encourage the performers to stay with the show."*

Darren will always be proud of his 1997 win with the **Images of the King** contest, but he is quick to tell you that he is happy not be doing contests any more.

"When I won **Images***, there were a lot of people that were not too pleased about it. Being a Canadian I guess…but mind you, I traveled to this contest in Memphis all the way from Canada for five years straight. I felt like my only fan was my brother, who was with me to share the joy. I was extremely impressed and elated that Ronny Craig came forward to shake my hand and congratulate me. I will never forget that."*

Darren and his adorable wife, Allison, are still on their honeymoon. They both love Elvis music, but they are more in love with each other. They are such romantics that they had two wedding ceremonies. Although they miss their Canadian homeland, they are enjoying Darren's success with one of the biggest shows in Las Vegas...where the **Business of Being Elvis** is the most competitive in the world.

The **American Superstars Show** presents two performances on Wednesday, Friday and Saturday at 7:00 pm and 10:00 pm; one show on Sunday, Monday and Tuesday at 1:00 pm; Thursday is black. All of the **Superstars** are there to greet you immediately after each show for autographs and photos, adding a very special touch to the show, I think. They also promote their own merchandise. Darren has a great CD, **Walk A Mile In My Shoes** with 24 songs, including my favorites **My Baby Left Me Behind**, **Treat Me Nice**, and **Smoke Gets In Your Eyes**. Just between you and me, sometimes when Darren is not performing, he retreats to his own personal Elvis museum. He likes to relax in his museum by listening to Elvis music, enveloped in a headset and admiring his wall-to-wall **MatchBox Collectables**.

DAVID LEE

Although David Lee began his career as an ETA in 1995, he really began to take the **Business of Being Elvis** world by storm in 2001. The kickoff was his win as the **Canadian Grand Champion** at the **Elvis Fest 2001** in Canada. Following his Canadian win, David went to Memphis, Tennessee, and placed third in the international **Images of the King** contest. He followed his **Images of the King** win by winning first place in Ronny Craig's **Elvis Explosion** in La Crosse, Wisconsin, in September. David Lee's list of ETA achievements just seems to keep growing.

"I guess I really just started to get serious about performing Elvis a few years ago. I was a manager at a **Wal-Mart** *store... up until the traveling as an ETA took hold and I began entering contests. Contests are a good way to get your name out there and they are good marketing avenues to acquire paid bookings. My goal was to be able to dedicate myself as a professional Elvis entertainer. I decided it was time...shape up or ship out. I am happy I made that decision and I believe the hard work is paying off."*

David, his wife, and his four-year old daughter call Birmingham, Alabama home. With his Elvis tribute show, **Burning in Birmingham**, a lot of folks around Alabama have dubbed David as "Birmingham's Elvis." David is an electric Elvis entertainer. His energizing spirit is apparent the minute he hits the stage. Wearing the glitz of an Elvis jumpsuit, Davis is polished and confident about his presence. But it is David's reverberating voice that really draws his audience into the illusion that he is reviving the memory of Elvis.

When I watched David Lee perform at the **Elvis Explosion**, I was able to get a glimpse of his tremendous following of fans. Like an entourage of groupies chasing a celebrity, it is not unusual to also see a caravan of cars followed by an emblazoned **David Lee Fan Club Greyhound** bus. The bus passengers are all proudly decorated with David Lee memorabilia. Sally Morgan from Erlanger, Kentucky was just one of David's dedicated devotees. She was more than eager to explain the phenomena of being an Elvis fan and a follower of the ETAs, especially David Lee: "*My girlfriend and I left Kentucky at midnight to drive here. I am confident that David Lee is going to win tonight. He has the voice and that is most important to me. I don't pay that much attention to how an ETA looks. Too many of these guys concentrate and worry about their looks…but that is not enough. It is definitely the voice and David has it. I also have to say that Steve Chuke from my home state is a favorite, too. He owns* **Jewel King Jewelers** *and makes a lot of TCB necklaces and rings for the ETAs. His whole store is in an Elvis motif.*"

Sally and her family had just returned from their first trip to Memphis, Tennessee to tour **Graceland** and attend the **Images of the King** contest. According to Sally, "*It was the most moving experience in my life, especially the* **Candlelight Vigil** *filled with Elvis' ambiance. People often ask me why a 25-year-old girl would travel all over to see these guys perform and I tell them…well, you haven't been touched by Elvis yet…By the way, do you want to see my Elvis tattoo on my back?*"

David Lee has continued on his ETA journey, winning numerous contests and adding a first runner-up in the **Professional Division** at the renowned **Collingwood Elvis Festival** in Ontario, Canada. He produces most of his own venues, often sharing the stage with fellow ETAs. Most recently, he performed with **Michael Dean and Memphis, William Stiles** and **Todd C. Martin** with a special Cruise ship performance celebrating their 30th birthdays together. David also hosted his third annual **Elvis In Dixie Land** contest in June, which is a preliminary for the ***Images of the King*** contest. This contest offers $2000 in cash and prizes and is a charitable event for ***The American Cancer Society***. David is a proud member of the **Elvis Entertainers Network**. David's association with Nance Fox and Ronny Craig and the **Elvis Entertainers Network** provided David the ability to draw from a wealth of professional expertise in organizing his contest.

"*If I could pick one reason why I became an ETA, it would be for the love of the music. Elvis was just so strong worldwide with everybody. Something about it just touched me…I identified with it. Elvis, the person, is hard to describe…there are so many wonderful things about him I enjoy listening to all of the stories about him from the people that knew him and from the books I've read about him. I give a lot of credit to his fans after 25 years and still so loyal. I appreciate my fans as well. They are so supportive of me and my family.*"

David Lee has a terrific CD, **The Magic of Elvis** with his band **The Promise Land.** He additionally offers a diverse line of David Lee merchandise through his **CafePress** known on the Internet as www.cafeshops.com. He clearly understands the necessity of the total package in the ***Business of Being Elvis***.

In closing, on September 20th, 2001, when David first talked about his future, he said, "*If I could dream…to be happy and move forward with the opportunities in performing as Elvis. It's been a good time so far. I'd like to see my role as an ETA continuing on and maybe one day, down the road, to have a successful career as a well-known and respected ETA. The whole picture…just doing a good job in Elvis' name.*"

MARK LEEN

A native of Ireland, ETA Mark Leen proudly refers to himself as the **Emerald Elvis**. His personal connection to Elvis Presley goes back to 1979 when he was nine years old. It is that sense of spirit that stays with him today.

"*There was a lot of unrest in my country then… a lot of reciprocation of feelings going on. My father was like a freedom fighter with strong beliefs. It was like a civil war here filled with battles and troubles, and it landed my father in prison. My father was my best friend. My mother got very* *depressed about it all, trying to raise me and my sister as best as she could. Elvis passed away in 1977 and suddenly his music was everywhere. My mother taught me to sing and I clung to Elvis. I had pictures of Elvis all over the place...only one picture was of **Easy Rider** on the bike with Fonda, Hopper, and Jack Nicholson. Then, one day I heard **Hound Dog**, and the drum roll in the song sent me into ecstasy. I would listen to it over and over. Elvis was wonderful and I became massively influenced."*

Mark went on to become a traditionally trained actor, attending one of the top drama schools in the world. He soon discovered, however, that acting jobs were few and far between. In 1997, Mark was asked to do a tribute show marking the 20th anniversary of Elvis' death. The audience response to his show was overwhelming. So many people wanted to see his Elvis venue that they stood out in the street because couldn't get in. Mark's 1997 performance was his initiation into a full-time career as an Elvis Tribute Artist and he has since traveled to France, Holland, England and, of course, Ireland.

In his heavy Kerry Irish accent, Mark traces a few of Elvis' songs to Ireland: *Danny Boy made it into the top three on the charts here, along with **I'll Take You Home Again** and **My Boy**, written by Irishman Phil Colter. I continue to sing those songs in my shows, especially when I perform in pubs. I put my heart and soul into Elvis. As an ETA, I am always reminded, however, that I am not Elvis. I'm so used to being me looking out through my own eyes, I forget that I have sideburns and jet- black hair until I get on the stage. People want to see Elvis perform, but when I am not on stage, I speak in my native accent and I am Mark Leen."*

Mark has performed in many wonderful venues in Europe. One of his favorites includes his tribute performance on the 25th anniversary of Elvis' passing when he performed with a 21-piece orchestra and two other ETAs in Black Pool, England. He met David Stanley, Elvis' half brother, while he was England. David Stanley was so enamored with Mark's voice and his similarity to Elvis that he asked Mark if he could get up on the stage and sing **JohnnyBGood** with him—which he did. The 25th anniversary venue was viewed by an estimated half a billion people. Literally, hundreds of women waited in line to get a scarf from Mark. Mark's performance also gained him the attention of a talent scout representing **BMG Records**, the European arm of **RCA Records.** The scout reported back to **BMG** executives, describing Mark's aptness and portrayal of Elvis, as well as his ability to captivate and draw his audience into the illusion of Elvis. The executives felt that Mark would be ideal for a new promotion they were planning.

"They hired me to do a two- week promotional tour for the newly released **Elvis Gold: 30 #1 Hits** *album. I traveled throughout the United Kingdom promoting the album, appearing on European television and radio programs. I had to wear my gold lamé jacket and I had my Cadillac painted gold to empha-size the gold record. The promotion began with a really exciting 'launch party' to kick off the tour.* **BBC Wales** *was there along with many other celebrities. It was one of the highest and most respected achievements in my life."*

The promotion was, indeed, a huge success. The sales of the album skyrocketed and continued to be number one on the European charts indefinitely. This kind of recognition from **BMG**, actually **RCA**, gives an Elvis tribute artist an entirely new level of recognition in the Elvis world. In personifying an impersonator of Elvis through direct associa-tion with Elvis Presley and his music, it is ultimately an acclamation of an ETA's benefit to the **Business of Being Elvis**. Mark was awarded a framed, triple platinum disc from **BMG** for his contributions and com-mitment to the success of the promotion. To my knowledge, this is the first such endeavor to literally explore and link the entities together.

"I would never say anything on stage that Elvis wouldn't say. I may say things that make people laugh, but I would never make a joke about him. I draw from Elvis' spirit. A good ETA needs to be encased in a set of rules…to never say or do anything demeaning to Elvis Presley. Also, if you are going to be in the spirit of Elvis, there is a price to be paid. It is o.k. to be paying tribute to Elvis…whatever level you go to, you must remember Elvis' charitable heart. Always, in the spirit of Elvis, to give honestly of yourself."

On January 14, 2003, Mark produced his venue called **Aloha From Killarney – Killarney, Ireland.** The show was promoted as a special, once-in-a-lifetime recreation of the historic 1973 worldwide broadcast of *Aloha From Hawaii.* The **ExSpence Account Showband** performed the replicated musical arrangements with Mark. The two-day, two show event produced sell-out crowds of 20,000 people, while the finan-cial success of the show benefited several Irish charities in the name of Elvis. Mark performs for numerous charitable events.

Mark will be returning to the **Collingwood Elvis Festival** in Canada this year with a performance on the main stage. He currently has a CD **Just Pretendin'** and two videos/DVDs, **Aloha From Killarney** and **The Irish Tigerman**. Mark will also be playing a lead role in a film about an Elvis type character called **Whiskey In A Jar**.

"I am honored to be an Elvis tribute artist, but I am also grateful for my opportunities in Elvis. My family, especially my daughter, is always supportive of me. I never put Elvis in front of God and family. In fact, when I sometimes face a difficult challenge, I just pray or sing one of Elvis' inspirational Gospel songs."

During our interview, Mark recited some of the lyrics to the song **Black Velvet** written by Allana Myles about her loss of Elvis Presley. **Black Velvet** is her symbolic reference to Elvis. Perhaps it is the deep-rooted passion of being Irish that gives Mark the eloquence that clings to his every poetic word. In describing Elvis, Mark shared one of his favorite passages from the **Book of Proverbs**:

Store up riches for yourself, not here on earth where thieves can break in and moths can whither away, but store up riches for yourself in heaven. Let the season of good will not pass you by. Do it here and now.

"That was Elvis. That was his generous spirit."

RICK LENZI

ETA Rick Lenzi was 19 years old when he made his Elvis debut in a contest in Southbend, Indiana. He is a dynamic performer and is extremely committed to his re-creation of Elvis. Rick captures both the young, rebellious Elvis, and the seasoned, charismatic Elvis. He exemplifies his energetic performance with the moves and vocal abilities of Elvis.

"I listened to Elvis Presley all my life. My grandfather was an Italian officer in the Service. He liked the music of Frank Sinatra and Dean Martin. My grandfather was born in Tuscany, Italy in 1917 and he is still my biggest supporter. In fact, he's one of the reasons I got into singing...doing the Elvis thing. Elvis was such a humble man...a shy and humble country boy. Even when he became famous, he never lost that. I bring this to the impersonation of Elvis. I am really a very shy person too. Some people mistake me for

being arrogant because I am shy. It is just difficult for me to talk to people. I am working at getting better at that though."

Rick has attained numerous achievements as an Elvis tribute artist including earning a semi-finalist slot on Dick Clark's national television show, **Your Big Break**, first place wins in a variety of contests across the country, an appearance on **Entertainment Tonight** and, with other ETAs, the opportunity to work with Kevin Costner and Kurt Russell in the motion picture **3000 Miles to Graceland.**

*"I like being able to travel, becoming well-known. I enjoy the contests and the conventions. It is a great opportunity to meet and hang out with the other ETAs. They are all like family. We all look forward to getting together. You don't have to worry about who wins in these contests. At least, that's my opinion. One of the most fun contests was at the 2000 Elvis **Explosion** in La Crosse, Wisconsin. I tied for 3rd place."*

In 1999, Rick formed his band, **The Memphis Kings,** and began the production of his own venues. He presents his shows both in clubs and for community events. Rick works with **Celebrity Impersonators,** a booking agency that promotes a variety of celebrity look-a-likes. They produce and promote **What A Show**. Rick also had an opportunity to meet and audition with John Stuart of **Legends In Concert**. He has produced some of his own CDs along with a complete line of Rick Lenzi merchandise, available through **CafePress**.

*"There is one thing you have to understand about being an Elvis impersonator and that is the fact that you are not Elvis Presley. You are just here to create a part of Elvis. If you take everybody that is an Elvis performer and put them all in one bowl, you might get part of what Elvis Presley really was. In this **Business of Being Elvis**, I like the fact that the fans are not judgmental toward any Elvis impersonator. They treat them all equal. They may tell you that you are the best, but they know deep down that no one is as great as Elvis himself. We are not here to re-create really, but to create. You can't take his place by putting on a jumpsuit."*

Rick is proud of his family, which includes his wife, a daughter and a son. He is very happy and feels that life just couldn't be better.

"My goal in life is to take care of my family and to be able to perform Elvis to the best of my ability."

JOHNNY LOOS

Johnny Loos is not only **The Sound of Elvis,** as his show's title suggests, but he is also a statuesque and in-the-flesh silhouette of Elvis.
Though John bears a resemblance to the King, it is his personality that
most communicates Elvis to his audiences. Born in Cheyenne,
Wyoming, it is easy to envision John riding a horse in a great western
movie almost easier than it is to picture him on a Las Vegas stage as
Elvis. By combining both images, you have a great look of Elvis anyway. To know that just a few short years ago, John was driving a truck
delivering bread and snack cakes just adds to his homespun, almost
southern, way about him.

*"It all started because I loved Elvis all of my life. It was the first music
that I can ever really remember. I used to sing along with all of my dad's 8-
tracks and somehow, through the gift of God, I developed the ability to sound
a little bit like Elvis. I've always been really shy…terrified even, for anybody
to hear me sing. But one day, I was singing in my bedroom and some friends
of the family heard me. Well, then they asked me to sing at their wedding. I
couldn't even imagine doing that. After some convincing and a chance to
make $75, I somehow managed to do it. I guess that was just the beginning.
Well, through this, I was prompted to enter an Elvis contest…never even
placed. You know, I look back on that video now and it's like…ah pitiful!
One thing led to another. I started doing a lot of Karaoke and my father
backing me. 'You know,' he said, 'you're pretty darn good.' And with his
encouragement, which he also helped get my first Elvis costume. It was the*
68 Comeback Special *with the black leather."*

John continued to practice and perfect his voice and enter contests. Only now, he was winning them. When I first interviewed John
during the 2000 **Elvis Explosion,** he told me he was going to try this
Business of Being Elvis for three more years and give it his best shot.
It didn't take long for the taste of success to come his way. In January,
2001, he became the **Las Vegas World Champion.** Elvis work has been
steady for John since his win. John also has produced four of his own
CDs. He refers to them as promotional because he is never really totally happy with them.

*"I listen to them and I'm my own worst critic. You know, every time I
see myself or hear myself, I always see room for improvement. Not what I*

have accomplished, but what I could do better. But, people like my CDs. I like to sing some of Elvis' lesser-known songs. I get tired of the same songs over and over. Songs like **Fool** and **I'll Remember You.** My favorite Elvis songs change from day to day or week to week. It's really weird. I'm a fanatic. If I like something, I run it into the ground. It's the same way with music. I'll hear an Elvis song that I've heard hundreds of times and all of a sudden it will just click either in my mind or in my heart. It will become my favorite song and that's all I'll play. Today it happens to be **Don't Cry Daddy.** It was something that just hit me. Tomorrow, who knows?"

John loves to talk about Elvis and enjoys hearing stories about him. He says that Elvis intrigues him. Although he believes some people look to Elvis for strength and treat him as if he were a god, or something above human, John knows that Elvis was not.

"They sort of classified Elvis as white trash in the beginning. Elvis was Elvis. He always had something humble about him. He was just a man. Even when he became a star, he never forgot that. I guess that's what I love about him. It's not childish to act like a kid. Elvis just knew how to have fun. I heard someone say how bad they felt that Elvis died so young. One of Elvis' bodyguards was standing nearby at the time and he turned and said 'Don't feel bad for Elvis. I guarantee …anything you ever wanted to do in your whole life or any place you ever wanted to see…Elvis did it a hundred times over. He lived more in his short life than you will if you had three lives.' I thought, that's a good way to look at it. I mean, I can't think of anybody who ever lived a more fulfilling life than Elvis Presley. Even though it was a short life. The guy touched more lives than anyone, other than Jesus Christ…you know…in a good way. It was phenomenal!"

John continues to enter contests when he is not performing his own venue. He continues to perform for his fans and for the happiness it brings them to watch an Elvis sing.

"Contests are fun, but it is the winning that makes you feel good. It's a boost for the ego I guess. So many of these guys walk around like they are the best. No one is the best because you are only as good as the person watching you thinks you are. So a lot of the time winning a contest is just the luck of the draw and who's judging. My greatest moment is actually performing for the fans. There is nothing greater than being up on that stage doing something that you love to do. When I sing, my heart is in it so much. Then, when you get a reaction from the crowd, watching the people smile *and having fun…there's nothing like it. I especially enjoy the little children. They aren't critical of what I'm doing. They just see me as a star, something really special. They just wear their hearts on their shoulders. It takes so little to make them happy. When they appreciate what I am doing, it just makes my life feel complete."*

John has dreams of being successful in the **Business of Being Elvis**. It seems to me that he is well on his way. He credits the support of his family, especially his wife, Cindy, for giving him the opportunity to be an ETA.

"I want to always be able to provide for my family in a way that I can hold my head up with pride and I would love to be comfortable enough to be able to do something special for other people. Especially people in need. One time, Cindy and I were in Nashville. I was walking down the street by myself and bumped into this homeless guy. He asked me if I had any change and truthfully I did not. I had eighty dollars on me, but I didn't have any change. So I told him no so he lowered his head and walked away. I thought about it for a minute and felt so bad that I turned around. I said, 'You're probably going to go get drunk or whatever, but whatever you're going to do, enjoy yourself. Here's eighty dollars.' He started crying. I started crying. He gave me a big hug and said 'God bless you.' Turns out he was just down on his luck, lost his job and going through a divorce. He said, 'I'm going to go have dinner and get a room for the night.' That made me feel so good. Well, I told Cindy that I met this guy on the street and I gave him some money. She knows that I do this all the time and she keeps reminding me that there is a limit to what you can give. Finally, Cindy asked 'How much did you give him?' I told her I gave him everything I had which was eighty dollars. She said, 'You know, if you keep this up, you're going to be the guy on the street that is homeless and asking for money'".

I think that is just a perfect example of what John Loos is all about. Sounds a lot like Elvis Presley, too!

CHRIS MACDONALD

With respect to Elvis, ETA Chris MacDonald is wearing his **blue suede shoes** singing **go cat go** all over the country. Chris credits his love of music at a young age to his mother. He has been performing for almost 11 years now, but confesses that he *"considers the first four years as start-up."* For Chris, the **Business of Being Elvis** began when he was 23 years old. He dressed up like Elvis for Halloween and performed a tribute to Elvis. Initially working with tracks and eventually with his own band, he utilizes both arrangements. He refers to himself as a song and dance type of performer.

"I've been fortunate. Music has always been a natural for me. I know to sing from my diaphragm and from my heart. If you study something, it's like homework…and it makes it sound like homework. This is something I did as a child. I looked at Elvis like a hero. The perception…looking up to Elvis as someone special, strong, a leader and a father figure. Elvis had a great sense of humor. I love watching his movies and I still laugh. That expression on his face sometimes. You could tell what he was thinking…like 'I can't believe I'm gonna say this, but I'm gonna say it anyway and then I'm going to laugh about it.' He was great!"

Chris has worked with John Stuart and the **Legends in Concert** shows in Las Vegas, Nevada, and Branson, Missouri. Working with the **Jordanaires**, **D.J. Fontana** and **Scotty Moore**, Chris also tours with his own production show called **Chris MacDonald's Memories of Elvis**. Chris performs all of the different Elvis eras and uses both a live band and tracks to recreate the illusion of Elvis. He has taken his show to many parts of the United States and is optimistic about a return tour to Japan and England.

*"I have gained a great deal of experience in the music industry. I love country music as well as Elvis' music. In fact, I am currently working on a CD of original country music with songs written by two of my band members. I also learned a lot working with John Stuart. He knows what he wants and what he's looking for. He knows what is dynamic in a show and has a good vision of how to make it work. With **Legends,** you do two shows a day, six nights a week, but it gives you that structure of doing a production show. There are certain places you have to be on stage, there is set timing for everything, working with the dancers and understanding what it takes to put a full stage production show together. It is valuable experience."*

On occasion, **Legends In Concert** will contact Chris for an engagement, but he is generally already scheduled to perform. For the fifth year in a row, **Chris MacDonald's Memories of Elvis** tribute show will be performing at the **Heartbreak Hotel**. This is an extraordinary endorsement for Chris to attach to his memorable Elvis résumé because he is under contract with **Elvis Presley Enterprises**, the owner of **Graceland, The Plaza** and the **Heartbreak Hotel.**

"*I sent my promotional package to* **Elvis Presley Enterprises** *and they hired me to do a tribute show. They liked what they saw and I've been coming back every since. When I perform at* **Graceland,** *I wear casual 50s style attire. When I sing Elvis' music, it is not overdone. Some entertainers do that and I really work hard not to do that…it's not a caricature. It is a tribute to Elvis and it is me. It is really a fusion of the two. Anytime that I can be working with* **EPE,** *it is an honor. No matter what I've got going on, I will make the time to involve myself for the memory of Elvis.*

"*Elvis is like a* **Cinderella** *story. He is the all-American dream. That is really the basis of why Elvis is so strong. He is* **every** *man. That is why Elvis touched everyone, even at a time when some people didn't like him. Later on, they loved it. It was something different, something new. He was just doing his own thing with the influence of the black musicians and friends…including rhythm and blues. This is the era he lived and the area he grew up in. The roots of his music derived from the culture in which he was raised…poverty, the blues, and gospel music forged his style. It wasn't contrived. He just sang the music from his heart. That is why I enjoy his music so much, it's so close to the heart.*"

Chris doesn't get involved with contests, adding: "*Most of the contests are made of amateurs who are fooling around with it. Some of the contests do not project a good image for an ETA. And when it comes to the organizers and politics, they are as bad as a beauty contest. Some pretty shady characters.*"

Chris MacDonald is his own manager. He feels that most managers are really working for themselves making the money the entertainer should be making. He also believes that he is in control of his own destiny. It is obvious that he knows the right combination for mixing his musical ability and business savvy to create a winning formula for success.

"*Well, I thought about it his way. I have something to offer and this is just like a regular business. This is* **my** *livelihood. You have an investment of time in putting out a quality product. You have an investment of money for sound equipment, costumes, merchandising, marketing and other things. In this* **Business of Being Elvis***, the product and service you are delivering is* *songs. I perform for small crowds and for big crowds. I have a great time performing. When I finish the show, I get applause and at the end of my day of work, I get a check. Where else can you find a job like that?*

"*This is all very important to what you do…and you must always remember the fans. They are your loyal following. It's about making people happy. You want them to have a good time and the opportunity to see a great show. That is what they come out for and that is the reason they will come back to see you. The fans are really wonderful.*"

Some upcoming and exciting events for Chris and his **Memories of Elvis** tribute show include a performance for the **100th Anniversary Celebration of Harley Davidson** in Milwaukee, Wisconsin in August, 2003. Chris just happens to possess his own **Harley**. The event organizers expect over 250,000 people in attendance. Chris will also be the headliner for Michigan's **Alpena College** celebrating its 50th anniversary. And this August, following his shows at **Graceland's Heartbreak Hotel**, Chris will be performing his annual full production tribute at the **Broward Center of the Performing Arts** in South Florida. Chris also performs for all of the snowbirds on some of the cruise ships during the winter months, which gives him the opportunity to spend more time with his wife and children. Chris has several videotapes and CDs. My favorite videos include **Live in Concert – August 16, 2002,** the **Silver Anniversary Memorial Tribute: Broward Center of Performing Arts** and **Live From Branson: Chris MacDonald— "Memories of Elvis."** A couple of great CDs include **Chris MacDonald's Memories of Elvis in Concert** and **Baby What You Want Me To Do By Request.**

RICK MARINO

Rick Marino, Elvis entertainer and author of **Be Elvis – A Guide to Impersonating the King**, believes that, "*It's a career that found me.*"

According to Rick, most people don't start out intending to be an Elvis impersonator. He feels it is something people do as a "hoot" and perhaps that is one reason Rick wrote his book, but he is very serious when it comes to talking about the **Business of Being Elvis.** Rick has been performing all of his life and that includes performing in his own

show, **The Elvis Extravaganza** for nearly thirty years. He is the original, and current, president of **The Elvis Presley International
Impersonators Association** (EPIIA) established by promoters, Ron
and Sandy Bessette. The EPIIA organization includes over 300 members worldwide and hosts an annual convention in Chicago and Las
Vegas that awards outstanding individuals with its own version of the
Emmy or Oscar. The EPIIA also raises money through a variety of benefits for charity in Elvis' name.

*"My father was a big band singer and nightclub entertainer, so I grew up
behind the scenes learning the business. He sang in front of audiences of six
to seven thousand people, big concerts. I had the opportunity to meet numerous celebrities. I was in a band of my own in junior high school and in the
choir in high school. I also took vocal lessons and wanted to be an opera
singer. Eventually, I was a member of one of the top nightclub acts in
America. We did three shows a night, six nights a week for fifty weeks. The
show grossed a half a million dollars a year for seven years*, Rick said very
proudly.

Rick went to Nashville for a while and acted as a record producer
and co-owner of a production company. His company produced George
Strait's first song **Amarillo By Morning,** and Rick also worked with
T.G. Shepherd, helping him in the production of his show. Rick has
traveled all over the world, learned to fly airplanes, and is the proud
father of one son, Trevor.

*"I've enjoyed a lot of nice perks as an Elvis impersonator—otherwise I'd
have to be a millionaire to have done all the things I've done. I am always
saying, 'Thank-you Elvis!'"* quips Rick.

Rick is very aware of the inherent power of being Elvis—that
incredible occurrence that happens when he transforms himself from
Rick Marino into Elvis and dons his Elvis attire to the moment he
walks off the stage. One of the best examples of that power, and one of
the more memorable for Rick, was his three-month show in 1988 in
Inchon, Korea, located about fifty miles from Seoul on the Korean
coast.

*"I was one of three performers contracted to do a show 'Elvis, Elvis,
Elvis' which toured Asia with two other performers based on three different
eras of Elvis' career. There were three thirty-foot Elvis-like figures in the
front of what was the fourth largest nightclub in S. Korea that were suppose*

to be us. No one could speak English, and yet we were very well received. We even recorded a hit record in Korea. It was great. But the best, which we didn't know at the time, was being part of the featured entertainers to participate in the Olympics Song Festival. There was Julio Iglesias representing Spain, Englebert Humperdink and Duran Duran from England and Ireland. The audience was filled with athletes with a live broadcast viewed by more than 500 million people—except America because of the 14 hour time difference, unfortunately. We were featured in America on The Today Show, Good Morning America,—all three news network new programs making us somewhat celebrities when we got home. Incredible."

Rick played roles in several movies including **Honeymoon in Vegas** and **Finding Graceland,** starring Harvey Keitel with Priscilla Presley acting as one of the executive producers. Rick performed as a technical advisor for the film. I had the opportunity to see Rick Marino on the television show, **To Tell the Truth,** and although he was quite convincing, he wasn't able to stump the female member of the panel.

With Rick, the list goes on and on of where he has been and what he has achieved as an Elvis impersonator. He believes his best asset, as an Elvis entertainer, is his relationship with his fans.

"Elvis genuinely appreciated the fact that those fans were out there. That they took a night of their life and spent their hard earned money and went to see him. It matters so much that he spent every ounce of ability and energy he had to make sure they (fans) forgot whatever was wrong in their life for a few hours, which is what being the consummate entertainer is all about," Rick stated.

Unless you are prepared for an emotional response from Rick, it is wise to not bring up the subject of the media with him. He maintains, and probably always will, very negative feelings about how the media treated Elvis Presley. He really dislikes the way the media uses its influence to make fun of Elvis impersonators, even though he is quick to suggest that out of the thousands that exist, many are, to be truthful, not really very good. This is perhaps another reason why he wrote his book, **Be Elvis,** of which sold over 35,000 copies.

Rick may play a role as a judge for some future contests but he does not enter contests as a contestant. He does not believe that the majority of judges are truly qualified to act as judges nor does he think that an Elvis entertainer has anything to gain by participating as a contestant.

"I don't have any desire to beat my friends, and I certainly don't want to lose to them," he added.

"To sum it all up," Rick concluded "I do Elvis because I enjoy it and I make a good living at it."

Another perk that Rick likes to share is his luncheon experience with Nicholas Cage during the filming of **Honeymoon in Vegas**. Rick asked Cage, "What is it with Elvis? You did four movies in a row that had to do with Elvis."

Cage responded with, "Well, I'll tell ya' Rick. I am a major fan of the big 'E'."

We all know that just has to be true!

JEROME MARION

Jerome Marion, in the **Business of Being Elvis** for over 15 years, hails from the Chicago-land area. Presenting his version of Elvis in nearly every state of the United States, Jerome's ETA performances additionally include his 1984 three-week tour in Leningrad, Moscow, Russia, as a Goodwill Ambassador for the United States. The Russia tour benefited the Chernobyl Nuclear accident victims. Jerome traveled to Japan as well. An additional highlight of Jerome's ETA career includes his talent contest entry and his selection by John Stuart to perform with the **Legends in Concert** in Las Vegas.

"I've talked to most of the guys who have done **Legends**. They tell you that **Legends** is overrated because it is so Vegas. You are impersonating Elvis wherever you go. Realistically, you can make good money at this. I've made a good living, so I really can't complain. I would have made great money, but I didn't want to give my whole life to Las Vegas. There is a lot of control there…what to wear…what song to sing. It's not your own thing in **Legends**. I did the cruise ship thing too. For only one weekend. Some of these guys actually do that for six months. Claustrophobic! All you do is eat, relax and perform. It's not as enjoyable of a lifestyle as people think."

Jerome, always an Elvis fan, learned practically every Elvis song singing along with his mother's Elvis records. His first so-called performance was a 40-minute show at a sock hop with a rented Elvis costume from a Halloween shop. People thought he was lip-syncing.…

"That's the best compliment anyone could give you in this business," Jerome added. Jerome's rented costume was soon followed by a **Sears** 8-track sound system and his first custom costume made by *"a woman who did-n't know what a costume was…used it in one show and then it turned into pillow cases."* Jerome's ETA journey was fueled by his dream of being a singer, maybe even a star someday, because he loved to perform for people. At first he didn't think he could make a decent living as an Elvis impersonator and, in 1984, when he quit his job just two years into the Elvis business, he thought he might be crazy. Jerome was just beginning to realize that the **Business of Being Elvis** was big business. By 1986, Jerome hooked up with his first live band, **The ExSpence Account Showband**. It was the right mix and they developed an exclu-sive arrangement for Elvis tribute shows.

"**The ExSpence Account Showband**, *as you know, is the most recog-nized and authentic Elvis band in the industry. They are excellent musicians. We were one of the first groups to bring the impersonator to the level of Elvis tribute artists. We developed a recorded sound. With the development of Karaoke, there may be the opportunity for more music, but there is nothing like singing with a live band. In 1988 or 1989, when we did the first Elvis Convention in Las Vegas, we just clicked like a clock…grew together from then on…for 12 years. That's when I cut them loose. I couldn't keep them busy enough anymore because I was already starting to wind down my performance schedule."*

Jerome's résumé includes his membership as one of the original members of the **Elvis Impersonators Association (PEIA)** with founder and ETA Johnny Thompson. Following Nance Fox's purchase of the **Elvis Entertainers Network (EEN)** from Johnny Thompson, Jerome immediately took an active role in the **EEN** organization and is now a Vice-President and Director of sound engineering. Jerome brings to the table his invaluable experience in the entertainment business With the addition of fellow board members Doug Church and Ronny Craig, **EEN** has earned the professional recognition it rightfully deserves and is now diligently involved with establishing guidelines to achieve high-er standards in the **Business of Being Elvis**.

Jerome is also the owner of **Celebrity Impersonators**, a celebrity look-a-like booking agency and, additionally, works full-time as a dis-trict sales manager for a light bulb wholesaler. Jerome's busy schedule now limits his ETA performances to mostly weekends but he is highly

respected as a person and for his many accomplishments as an ETA. In
his quest to succeed, he ultimately paid a price for the lessons learned.

"*My family is the most important thing in the world to me now. I want
to spend more time with my wife and my two stepchildren. We do things
together, take vacations and building that retirement plan. It's real life. This
is a tough business. You are an average guy and all of a sudden you walk up
on stage and you've got 1000 people screaming at you, women throwing
clothing at you, passing phone numbers…temptation is very strong and I
don't care how hard you try. A majority of the Elvis impersonators who were
married when they started out in this business have ended up in divorce.
Including me, twice. Some of these guys in the business will give up their
wives, their jobs, their careers and they struggle from week to week. I
learned in life that it is not worth losing what you have over a small journey.
I think you should go after your dreams, but you better think everything
through before you do it because this is a short life. Don't make this
Business of Being Elvis such a phenomena in your life that it overpowers
you. You are not Elvis. There are a lot of impersonators out there that
haven't woke up yet, they haven't fallen. Today, in this business, you can
walk into a job and make $2000 and the next day you're working for $150
again because you have to do it. Fans are looking at the image you portray.
They are not looking at you. They want that Elvis. And when the jumpsuit
comes off, you're not Elvis anymore. You have got to focus on what life is
really all about.*"

Jerome has a great voice and a great sense of humor, which he now
tries to incorporate into his shows. He's produced many of his own
CDs and plans on continue performing as an ETA into the foreseeable
future. He enjoys assisting new ETAs, who often seek out his professional advice. A recent addition to Jerome's ETA résumé includes his
January 12, 2003, performance for the Inaugural Ball for the newly
elected Governor of Illinois in Springfield, Illinois.

"*The security was extremely tight so I wasn't allowed to do the meet and
greet, plus I had to be on site almost seven hours in advance. I was hired to
sing four songs, one of which was to the Governor's wife, and I shook the
Governor's hand. They had a large overhead screen for the backdrop and I
worked in the studio with the production company to create some video
footage prior to the event. Then with this large overhead screen, they put up
the red Elvis flashing sign. Then, with a silhouette of me turning toward the*

screen, it created the visual effect of me walking through the screen and into the event. At the end of my 15-minute performance, they projected a close-up of me typing a letter to the Governor, which said:

Good luck and keep taking care of business.
"E"

TODD C. MARTIN

Todd **C**. Martin is an Elvis tribute artist and a lawyer, but he is not Todd Martin, the famous tennis player. While Todd attended law school, he also owned a small coffee shop/bar/restaurant. One Halloween, his grandmother made him an Elvis jumpsuit. Todd added, *"It was so good of her to do that for me, but it was far from professional at the time."* He attended several costume parties and won, so the jump-suit must not have been too bad. A short time later, a customer came into his coffee shop and asked Todd if he might be interested in buying a Karaoke machine.

*"Well, I tried it out, sang a couple of songs and I thought—hey, this sounds pretty good. That was in about 1997 and I figured since I owned the place, I could just sort of force myself on people. It just went on from there. As with anything, practice gets you there. Customers would come in and say 'I'll give you fifty dollars to come and sing at a party…for a grandmother's birthday or an anniversary.' You're willing to pay me for this? I started going to nursing homes and picking up some private parties. Eventually, I worked up to better costumes. Now, I get them from **B & K Costumes**. You just work yourself into this…start working more…and then buying more, I guess."*

Graduating from law school in 2000 with an emphasis in civil law, Todd is currently not dealing with domestic issues. From his perspective, domestic issues tend to be too stressful and emotionally draining at times. Based in Monroe, Louisiana, Todd is 30 years old, single and looks forward to having a family of his own some day, although he real-izes that a family commitment requires a different set of commitments. At this point in his life, Todd believes it is the perfect time for him to have fun paying tribute to Elvis full time but he continues to keep a couple of cases going to hone his legal skills. Currently, he is primarily involved with real estate transactions because they *"are mostly just paperwork…contracts."*

"I enjoy practicing law on my own and being able to take some time away from it to perform. I'm going to New Orleans soon to take a continuing education course in entertainment law. I want to remain in law, but I think it is a good time to take a sabbatical somewhat. I am having so much fun with the Elvis thing right now. I want to take a couple of years and really push that…see what I can do with it. Then, at some point, fall back on the law career. I've talked to a lot of the ETAs out there. It is amazing how much diversity there is. I mean there's every kind of background you can imagine. Then, I talk to some of the young guys getting into this and they think 'no, I'm not going to college. I'm just gonna do Elvis.' BAD IDEA! For one thing, you don't want to be sixty and doing this. This is your job. You've got to have some other identity, I think."

Todd has been entering contest for a few years now and thoroughly enjoys them.

*"In this **Business of Being Elvis**, I wouldn't be where I am now if it weren't for contests. The secret to contests is how much you are willing to put into them. You have to pick **contest** songs…totally gearing yourself for a contest. You only get 15 minutes to perform. No one can show everything they can do in 15 minutes. Contests are a whole 'nother animal. You can be a great show performer and awful at contests or visa versa. I figure if I make it in the finals, I've already won. This year, I placed in nearly every contest I entered. Last year I made most of the finals. The year before, I was lucky if I made it to the finals. The contests give me an opportunity to learn a lot from the other ETAs. It is fun to meet everyone and share some camaraderie. They are an opportunity to get known, pick up bookings…especially in other geographical areas. They help to build confidence as well."*

At 6'1" and 190 lbs, Todd is able to perform all of the eras of Elvis. He feels he is fortunate to have that much flexibility in his Elvis act. Todd is gifted with blue eyes and natural dark brown hair but he used to color his hair black for special shows and contests, that is, until recently. Todd picked up a hot hair tip from Williams Stiles while attending one of the contests; black hair spray. If your hair color is dark, black hair spray just sort of helps to fill it in. Todd also learned to finalize the black hair spray with a dose of **AquaNet Hairspray** to prevent the dye from running down his face when he perspires under the hot lights. In my case, I wonder if the spray will work to cover up the gray!

"The fans are the best part of it all. I have never had a bad experience. My fans are also my friends...they are loyal and respectful. I think what keeps the balance is that when I walk off that stage, I am completely Todd. I keep it normal. Some of the guys in this business get lost in it. It's like their one claim to fame and they are trying to find Elvis. They become more than Elvis sometimes...almost forgetting the whole reason they are doing this...becoming an object rather than a person. I keep my private life separate from the ETA life. I have even dated girls that didn't even know I performed as Elvis. I think the best ETAs are the ones that have their own identity. They put their personality into their performance. The fans like to see some of your own interpretation of Elvis as well. I love watching the reaction of the audience when they listen to me. For a moment, I get to feel a glimpse of what Elvis might have felt.

*This **Business of Being Elvis** is not a job to me. It is interesting to me because Elvis is so interesting. Elvis is an original and that is why so many celebrities have copied him. Elvis was a social and musical revolution."*

RICHARD MESSIER

Richard Messier is a French Canadian who hails from Quebec City, Canada. He is not fluent in English, except when he performs as an Elvis tribute artist. I met Richard at the 2002 **Collingwood Elvis Festival** where he performed in several venues, but not as a contestant. He has a great voice and sincerely loves Elvis music. Although a performer for over 11 years, Richard did not launch his Elvis tribute shows until about four years ago. With the translation assistance of his wife and promoter, Nathalie, I was able to briefly interview Richard.

Why did you become an Elvis impersonator?

"Because when I sang with my Elvis discs, my wife told me I have the same voice as Elvis, so I bought Karaoke and started practicing. Eventually, I started going out performing with a live band."

What is your favorite Elvis song and why?

"It is **Now Or Never** *because I think everybody likes this one and always will."*

What is your favorite story or thoughts about Elvis Presley, the person?

"His angel voice and generosity. That is what makes him a demigod"

How are you most like Elvis—his looks, talent, personality, lifestyle, soul...?

"First, it is the voice and then the look. After that, the taste for things in life."

What was your greatest Elvis moment?

"The last show I made at the end of June 2002. When I started singing **Now Or Never***, the way the people looked at me from the front rows. Their mouths were dropped open. They made me cry on the stage."*

What do you like most about your fans? Who are they?

"The way they appreciate me making their idol live. They come and talk to me after the shows sometimes coming to see me again and again."

Like the Elvis song, If I Can Dream... How would you finish that sentence?

"First my family, some friends and the people who come to the shows and call me to find out where and when I will be performing next. Making a show that most of the people (Elvis fans) will come to see. First in Montreal and then a tour, I hope."

Richard performs in Montreal as an ETA with his band, **The King's Band**. Nathalie clarified that *"His specialty is to recreate the original songs in the sound of Elvis, then also in the proper key. Always in the proper voice."*

EDDIE MILES

When you talk about the **Business of Being Elvis**, very few in the business, if any, have managed Eddie Miles' accomplishments.

Although an entertainer most of his life, Eddie's pursuit of Elvis music is based in his fervent belief that Elvis' music is still the best music ever recorded. Following a four-year stint in the military, Eddie focused on a full-time career in music.

Raised in Kentucky, for the last ten years Eddie has lived in Tennessee. During the mid- to late-eighties, Eddie was primarily involved in road tours, performing at countless fairs. Eddie and his investors decided it made financial sense to settle in a permanent location and have the people come to them.

*"I was in Pigeon Forge (Tennessee) and we tried a theatre there. Not far from Dolly Parton's **Dollywood**. It was quite successful."*

Throughout the nineties, Eddie maintained theatres in major towns throughout the United States including his first, **Memories Theatre,** which he opened in 1990. Eddie opened additional theatres, including Myrtle Beach, in the late nineties and his **Eddie Miles Theatre.** Unfortunately for both Eddie and his fans, persistent back problems forced him to lay low for over a year while he endured two back surgeries to correct his disintegrating disc. Fully recovered, Eddie now performs one show a month at the **Southern Nights Theatre** in Pigeon Forge while maintaining a rigorous tour schedule traveling from one end of the country to the other.

"Since then, I've just been touring. I do some things with a big band, but it is very costly—especially if you want to do a reproduction of Elvis' band correctly," said Eddie.

Although he has had numerous opportunities to work with **The Jordanaires, Scotty Moore, DJ Fontana** and other former Elvis band members, Eddie continues to work primarily with digital music backing tracks, calling it his *one-man show.*

I really enjoyed **Eddie's One Man Show** at the famous **Orpheum Theatre** in Memphis. Eddie is both candid and warm on stage and creates an intimate rapport with his audience. As he performs a variety of Elvis music, one is always aware of his respect for Elvis Presley and that it is Eddie Miles singing Elvis music. Immediately following **Eddie's One Man Show,** and every single show, I am told, Eddie heads for the lobby to greet every fan and politely signs autographs.

Eddie acts as his own creative engineer, manager and of course is his own person. He markets a comprehensive line of "Eddie Miles'" merchandise as well including several videos, CDs, shirts, hats, buttons and more. After all, this is the **Business of Being Elvis**.

Most of the ETAs consider the **Legends in Concert, American Superstars** and other major productions to be the ultimate path in their career and, for some, it is a very positive step.

"I looked at those avenues because I thought it would be steady work, but I could see that the producers were telling the guys how to be Elvis, their interpretation of Elvis, most of the time it was just showbiz run-around," according to Eddie's perspective.

Eddie admits he is very critical of this business. It seems reasonable that when a performer, such as Eddie Miles, earns $7500 – $20,000 per show, that they have earned the right to be critical of the business.

"I don't mean to sound so harsh, but I so dislike anyone who thinks all Elvis was, was black hair, sideburns, and a jumpsuit. They think 'if I can do that, I can do Elvis,' and the sad thing is that so many of them get away with that."

Once, Eddie entered a contest under an assumed name just to see what it was like.

"When I did it, I was so embarrassed to be involved with something like that. It was probably the worst performance I ever did because I wasn't in my own element.... Then to see other guys get up there and join the contest that are so horrible, it makes the contests a joke," according to Eddie.

Eddie also tried his hand at an Elvis Festival and observed the ETAs spending the entire day competing. According to Eddie, this particular Elvis Festival was neither well organized nor well scheduled. In fact, Eddie's performance was scheduled for 8 p.m. and he didn't make it on stage until after 11 p.m. and that was after he was unable to get a sound check earlier in the afternoon. For the professional ETA, failures in organization and scheduling do not make either the entertainer or the fans very happy.

"It was such a beautiful town, a great area—but for the people who bought tickets to see me to have to wait so long...they were all tired by then. While I was waiting through all of this, there were so many of those Elvis Impersonators with the Halloween type of thing. I just couldn't tolerate it," he said, barely suppressing his resentment.

In February, 2003, Eddie Miles was a finalist in **The $50,000 Tribute to the King Contest** in Lula, Mississippi. The **Tribute to the**

King contest continues to attract big acts such as Eddie Miles but who in their right mind can turn down the chance to win $50,000?

Eddie Miles is definitely his own person. He refuses to make any public appearances that requires him to show up in an Elvis costume... He is well aware of his self worth and commands a price tag to match. Some of the ETAs he respects include Martin Fontaine, Trent Carlini, and Doug Church. If the opportunity presents itself, make certain you see an Eddie Miles show...you won't be disappointed!

DAVID "JESSE" MOORE

David "Jesse" Moore considers himself an illusionist rather than an Elvis impersonator. Personally, I see David as an *inspirationalist*. David shares his love for Elvis and his heritage as a proud Native American (his father is Cherokee), when he performs his Elvis tribute and has been perfecting his ETA craft for over 13 years now. David's show, **The Heart Of Elvis Tribute**, along with his band **Double Eagle**, is considered to be one of the most unique and informative in the business. David carefully re-creates the image of Elvis, while weaving his own personality and skill into each performance. He also tells some great Elvis stories as told to him by many of Elvis' friends. First released in 1997, David's CD, **Road To America – USA,** is filled with his compositions and reads like a book of Elvis poetry. The CD is the product of his 20th Anniversary Tour in England which, by the way, was booked by the same agent that handled **The Beatles**. **Road To America – USA** includes **Rockin' Heaven** and **Going From Graceland to Heaven's Door** and both songs became big hits in England. David re-released **Road To America – USA** in 2001 and included additional compositions. The title track, **Road To America**, is dedicated to those who lost their lives on September 11, 2001.

Flying down south on a 727
Gotta get to Graceland or make it up to heaven
Jumped in a Cadillac, pressed it to the floor
Ran up to Graceland knockin' at the door
The King is gone, he's not at home

He's up in heaven, playin' at the throne
And he's rockin' heaven...
Rockin' Heaven

David "Jesse" Moore

David's original compositions demonstrate both his sensitivity and creativity as he shares his sense of loss with his listeners, but his music and lyrics also reflect his love of God and of his country. Each of the eight songs included on **Road To America – USA** are both inspirational and timeless. David's music reminds me of the first time I heard Ronnie McDowell's **The King Is Gone**. I could actually feel McDowell's, and the entire Elvis world's, sense of loss and sadness at Elvis' death.

David's **The Heart of Elvis Tribute Show** is definitely a family affair and David likes it that way. The show features David "Jesse" Moore as Elvis, but additionally includes Justin Lee, David's son, as the Young Elvis. You might also catch Justin Lee appearing as Buddy Holly and Ricky Nelson. **The Heart of Elvis Tribute Show** also features David's daughter, Krista Lyn, singing songs made popular by Britney Spears, Patsy Cline, Shania Twain, Leanne Rimes and others. The show's special guest is always **Cricket** from the movie **Elvis—That's The Way It Is.** David's wife of 27 years is a schoolteacher, so I am sure she helps keep everyone organized.

David was the first ETA to perform at **Graceland's Wilson World Hotel**, now owned by **Elvis Presley Enterprises** and renamed **The Heartbreak Hotel**. Located in Memphis directly across from **Graceland**, David performed there each January and August for five years. When the original owners built the new **Wilson Hotel and Suites** on Cherry Road, David was once again requested to perform. David is a regular performer in his home state of Oregon as well including the annual **Portland Rose Festival**, which hosts the 2nd largest Rose Parade in the nation. Other highlights of David's ETA résumé include opening for several celebrity acts including **The Beach Boys, Chubby Checker, The Kingsmen** and **The Tokens**. He is also involved with a variety of charities including **The National Organization for Missing and Exploited Children.**

*"I recently purchased my own tour bus calling it **Out Of This World**. I will be bringing it to Memphis again this year in August. I also have two*

pink Cadillacs. One of them is fully restored and the only difference between mine and Elvis' is that his had a white leather interior. His was also one of the 200 that had factory air, mine does not. My son will have to restore the other one someday. It is a '55 Fleetwood Cadillac. I don't have another year and $20,000 to put into it. I had never planned to get that involved in the car, but I always believed in whatever I do for Elvis…whether it's my show or what not…it has to be the best the best that it can be. I always give. I feel it is my responsibility. There can be ten people or 10,000 people, I still put out the best performance I can."

David owns several re-creation jumpsuits, but my favorite includes the **American Indian Suit** that David designed. David is wearing his **American Indian Suit** in the color section of this book. When Sonny West first saw the suit on David in Memphis, Sonny shared with David, "If Elvis would have seen that, he would want it." David was quick to reply, "If Elvis was alive, I'd give it to him."

"I have a family that I love and I have a gift from God to be able to perform in Elvis' name. It's a passion that I love doing. That is why I have to do this. The one thing I love about Elvis, that Elvis taught me and I teach my children is…Don't sing with your head, or sing from your throat, sing from your heart. You don't get rich… because I put everything back into my shows.

"Oregon is sort of different state. It's like the west…we're like the cowboys out here and like to do our own thing. One of my dreams is to have an even bigger Elvis collection. I've got two of Elvis autographs and I've got two scarves. My TCB is one that came from Mike MacGregor before he died, which came out of the original mold that Elvis gave him. I now have 65 guitars in my collection—one of them has an American Flag painted on it. I guess that is another reason I love Elvis so much…he loved America too!"

Motherhood, brotherhood
And things you don't see
Thanks to the brave who kept us free
United we stand, divided we fall
They gave their lives for one and all…

Road to America
David "Jesse"Moore

TRAVIS MORRIS

Travis Morris has been an ETA for about 11 years now. Concentrating on music in high school, Travis sang in church with his parents and was a constant target of his peer's teasing since he looked so much like Elvis. Travis never considered himself an Elvis *fanatic* even though he thoroughly enjoyed his music. He was also very shy, so the idea of impersonating Elvis wasn't even a consideration.

*"That's what got me into this **Business of Being Elvis** ultimately. People just would not leave me alone about my looks and then, one day, somebody must have convinced me I could make a living at it…otherwise I would have gotten into this when I was 15 years old instead of waiting until I was 30. I always thought it was a joke. For example, my wife's best friend married a guy in Florida that worked for **Universal Studios**. They moved back here to the Chicago area and he had some footage of a guy who was making a living at impersonating Elvis. It was horrendous. He probably weighed 350 lbs., didn't look anything like Elvis, and couldn't even sing a note. I started to think,'boy, I'm in the wrong business.' One day, a bunch of my co-workers at the factory talked me into dressing up like Elvis so they could take a picture of me out on the docks. They sent it to Chicago's **Hollywood Look-A-Likes**. In 1993, I was chosen for the lead role as Elvis in **Picasso at the Lapín Agile** by Steve Martin. It is a comedy about Picasso and Einstein meeting in a bar in France in 1904 and talking about how they are going to change the world and what the future holds. At the end of the play, Elvis travels through time and comes into the bar. Elvis gives his perspective on what the future holds. It was a blast. This was my start in the business, acting and singing Elvis full-time."*

Travis performed in the **Picasso at the Lapín Agile** production for six months at **The Steppenwolf Theater** before the play closed according to the theater's schedule. To this day, Travis continues to exchange Christmas cards with Steve Martin. One year after **Picasso at the Lapín Agile,** Travis was singing to an audience of 3000 in an **Elvis Birthday Tribute** at the **Holiday Star Theater** in Merrillville, Indiana. In 1998, he won first place in the **Images Of The King** contest.

"You do what it takes to survive in this business if you're going to be a professional full time Elvis tribute artist. I usually sing with tracks, but on occasion I perform with a live band. I primarily work the areas of the

Midwest, but I have traveled as far as Portland, Oregon. too. The further I travel, the more it costs the client. I'll go to the moon; it doesn't matter to me where I go. I've done shows before an audience at **PGA** golf events in Columbus, Ohio for say $5000.... I go there and perform, everything is all set up for me. Then, there are gigs that are really close to my house...a club called **The Pit** and I get $250. I like that, too, because it's fun and most of the customers are my age This is more like a party and entertainment, not to Elvis-ize so much. My point is that you do what it takes. If you have a date open, rather than leaving it go because you don't have a $1000 job to go to, you take the $250, which is a big deal, too. I used to make $350 a week in my job. To some of these guys, this is chump change, but to me, I'm almost making more in one night than it took me all week to earn."

Travis' ETA performances are primarily of the Elvis' 50s era although he added one of the 18 songs from the **Elvis – 30 #1 Hits** CD to his repertoire. He does not participate in contests unless it is a charitable event in the Chicago or Milwaukee area. You may see him at one of the contests, but Travis is not there to compete.

"I went to Ronny Craig's **Elvis Explosion** a couple of years ago just so I could meet up with the other performers and hang out together for a while. To me that is just sort of a party, and I treat it as though I'm giving myself a night off. I don't expect to win anything because that's the way you should go to a contest anyway. Contests are a very fickle beast. They are based on someone else's opinion and, more often than not, there is some sort of politics involved...whether it be the local Elvis performer or the judges... So, if you are in this **Business of Being Elvis** to make a living, contests are for fun, not to be taken seriously. Another thing is that there are always contests held during the anniversary week of Elvis' death or of his birthday, but as a professional, those are also the best times for me to have my own bookings. Not every performer can go to Memphis.

"I think it is great that most people get into this business for different reasons than I have. There are a lot of guys that are part-timers and they do this because they love Elvis. Some just like to perform in front of an audience and they are good at what they do. There are a handful of guys who got into this business just for the money and you'll be able to find those guys...they're all the ones who go to the extremes—plastic surgery and all that."

Travis and his wife have a 15 year old daughter and an 8 year old son. During the week, Travis acts as Mr. Mom since his wife works full-time for a pharmaceutical company. He is proud of his role as *Mr. Mom* and is dedicated to his family. He handles the majority of his own bookings, but also works with a several agents since Travis does not see the need to be exclusive with anyone. Travis' current CD is sold out, but he is working on a new one.

MIKE MORRISSETTE

Mike Morrissette, from Ottawa, Ontario, Canada, has been singing for as long as he can remember. He grew up in a household where his mother played Elvis' music all day long while she did her daily chores around the house. You might say Mike grew up in an Elvis household because the entire family was Elvis fans.

"My father would blast out **How Great Thou Art** *every Sunday morning. I just kind of sang Elvis to myself all these years; learning every word, studying every note, expression and slur. About a year ago, my brother Maurice, we call him Moe, heard me singing Elvis to some tacks. Moe asked me if I was imitating Elvis and I told him no…that is me singing. He didn't believe me, so he made me turn the volume of the music up and down while I kept singing. Moe said, 'Get ready, we're going to the* **Collingwood Elvis Festival.'** *I knew he was serious because Moe is a cop, he meant it. I was so nervous. I had never done Karaoke or even sang with a live band before."*

Mike and Moe headed off to Collingwood, an experience that would change Mike's life forever because it turned out to be the opportunity of a lifetime. He sang on the main stage with **The ExSpence Account Showband**. The reaction to his performance from the Elvis fans was overwhelming for Mike. *"It's totally amazing, the fans are incredible,"* he added. Needless to say, Mike came "out of the Elvis closet" at age 36 and has been singing ever since.

Mike is a full-time bus driver for **Executive Coach Charters**, which primarily transports groups of people to the area casinos. The regular riders have gotten to know Mike pretty well these days.

"Many of my customers call me Elvis now because I am always singing. I just sing Elvis the whole way there and back. Some of my senior ladies want to sit behind me so that I can sing an Elvis song to them. Occasionally, they bring me Elvis memorabilia as gifts. They are so sweet.

"I would say that the reason I will continue to do this is for the fans and my love of performing for them. When I headed to Collingwood, I thought it would be a weekend thing and that's it. But the response of the fans and the fact that they continue to follow me to other shows...men and women crying as they listened to me sing...hugging me and kissing me. It just blew me away. They say that I sound so much like Elvis. If this is true, then I owe it to these fans, Elvis fans, to continue on my journey of singing Elvis to keep his memory alive. Elvis has given so much to me that maybe this is an opportunity to give something back. There was only one Elvis and there will never be another. But, if I can bring them back to that time, you just can't imagine how that makes me feel. It is from my heart that I sing Elvis, it is not just for money."

Mike and his family recently established the first annual non-profit **Ottawa Elvis Festival** to be held June 27th – 29th, 2003, in Lansdowne Park. The proceeds from the festival will be donated to the Children's Hospitals of Eastern Ontario, Canada. The three day festival will include **The ExSpence Account Showband, The Jordanaires, The Sweet Inspirations, Al Dvorin** and an Elvis contest with guest ETAs Ryan Pelton and Shawn Klush performing. It is an indoor festival with a seating capacity of 11,000 and an expansion area offering an additional 10,000 seats. The **Ottawa Elvis Festival** will include nearly 200 vendors offering food, Elvis merchandise and accessories. In a city with nearly 2 million in population, the festival expects to draw 120,000 fans. Although Mike will not compete in his own contest, he will perform in the **Ottawa Elvis Festival** in the first official Elvis jumpsuit, **The Sundial,** designed by **Kathy Lee Creations.**

*"It will be most exciting for me and my family to be part of a new festival. I am looking forward to my future in the **Business of Being Elvis.**"*

CRAIG NEWELL

Craig Newell, in **The Business of Being Elvis** since May 3rd, 1993, received his first paycheck as an ETA while he was employed as a New Jersey bartender. He advanced his entertainment career by performing in small clubs and for private parties on the New Jersey beaches playing the piano and the guitar and singing a variety of songs, including, of course, Elvis Presley songs. Eventually, Craig's piano and guitar playing evolved into performing with live bands all along the east coast.

"*At that time, the most you could make was fifty to a hundred dollars after playing all night. I picked up the phone book one day and thumbing through the* **yellow pages** *I hooked up with a couple of entertainment booking agents. They sent me to some private parties to perform as Elvis. My first hit record was* **Happy Birthday To You**," Craig chuckled. "*Then, I got my first big break, landing a contract to perform every weekend at an amusement park on the beach in New Jersey. My career as an Elvis tribute artist seemed to snowball after that.*"

It did not take long before Craig became the featured Elvis for dinner show entertainment in several small restaurants in Atlantic City, New Jersey. Craig was extremely popular among the dinner show crowds and generally sang to sell-out audiences. The restaurateurs increased their advertising expenditures as well as the price of a ticket. The enhanced publicity advanced Craig Newell's career and enriched his wallet as well. Craig's popularity led him to consider a marketing campaign of his own. He placed an ad in the **yellow pages** of both the New York City and Philadelphia telephone books and promoted himself as an Elvis entertainer willing to sing and perform at private parties and such. The ads proved to be very effective.

"*All of a sudden I was bombarded with phone calls. I had no idea that the demand for Elvis entertainers would be so great. I had so many bookings that I had to hire additional Elvis performers. The money was good, but I began to think about another challenge. It occurred to me that the next logical step was to jump into the Las Vegas arena. All of the sid burns lead to Las Vegas where some make it ...and most don't.*"

The Fitzgerald Casino and Hotel in Las Vegas, looking for an exclusive **Fitzgerald** Elvis for their Lounge shows, decided to host an Elvis contest, a 'star search' so to speak. The grand prize included a two year contract with the **Fitzgerald Casino and Hotel**. I can't even imagine how many Elvi flocked to Las Vegas with the hopes of fulfilling their lifetime dream of being a full-time paid Elvis performer in the Elvis capital of the world. Craig Newell soon realized his dream when he won the contest.

"*It seemed like every Elvis guy in the world came out for this contest...including those in Las Vegas. Each guy was allowed 20 minutes to perform and it took nearly two months to determine the winner. In my final performance, I received a standing ovation. I thank God I was such a hit that night. I feel fortunate and lucky that I was there that night...the right place at the right time.*"

Three years after winning the "star search," Craig continues to perform **Craig Newell's Tribute To Elvis** at **The Fitzgerald Casino and Hotel**. His shows run from Thursday through Monday at 7 p.m. and 9 p.m. and includes a wonderful mix of Elvis' music and Elvis' humor. Combined with Craig's talent, looks, and personality, his show is a memorable and entertaining tribute to Elvis.

Although Craig has enjoyed winning a variety of Elvis contests around the country, he no longer participates in contests. In reciting the names of several well-known contests, Craig believes most of them are corrupt in one way or another, adding, "*I'm sure all of the ETAs you have interviewed tell you that, even though most of them still participate in the contests anyway.*

"*My kind of street is business, not contests. I love living in Las Vegas. I'm 36 years old. I'm a single parent and I'm very comfortable with this* **Business of Being Elvis.** *My son Sam has been performing Elvis since he was two years old because he loves it and he's good. We have a lot of fun together. He has been in a few international and national television commercials already.*" I believe that Sam is now ten years old.

Craig's ETA list of accomplishments includes his appearance on **Ricki Lake's Show—The King of Kings** contest in 2002 and his appearance in **3000 Miles To Graceland** sharing the silver screen with Kevin Costner and others. Craig hopes to venture into producing his own shows in the future and currently has both a CD and a video featuring himself that he markets. Both were obviously well received by his fans since he was sold out of both at the time of our interview.

KRAIG PARKER

Although ETA Kraig Parker was born in Belmont, Texas, he spent most of his life based in Dallas. Well versed in computer technology, Kraig is also a graphic designer. Kraig believes his graphic design expertise is a tremendous asset in the entertainment industry because he is able to create his own promotional literature and maintain his websites with regular updates. In the **Business of Being Elvis**, his ETA slogan is **Elvis Lives!**

"It's incredible. I never had any idea…well, the perception when you start this business is if you are really good and you want to make money, then you've got to live in Las Vegas. But that's not really the reality. The reality is if you are in a big metropolitan area and you're good at Elvis that's what it takes. Elvis was the entertainer of the century, people still love him and that's who people want to have at their party."

Kraig recalls his roots to Elvis as a child, but his journey into the entertainment world didn't include Elvis or, at least, not in the beginning.

*"I used to listen to my collection of Elvis 45s. Then, with my hair slicked back, I would ride my bike around singing **All Shook Up.** Of course, I grew out of that and got into the harder rock…got into having my own band in high school playing at parties and dances. I went through that phase of long hair and leather and stuff. Actually, many of my peers nicknamed me Elvis because I kind of have that look and charisma…goofing around about Elvis with them. I never once imagined I'd be doing Elvis. I guess about eight years ago, I just decided to take some time off from doing the live band scene. I had been recording an album and it takes a lot out of you. Then, of course, we didn't get the record deal. It is frustrating and hard to make it in the music business."*

Kraig decided to throw a Halloween party one year, rent an Elvis costume and have fun with the idea. A few weeks later, showing some pictures of the party to one of his co-workers, his colleague suggested that Kraig do Elvis for another co-worker's birthday party.

*"That is really how it all started…as a gag. It felt really good though when everyone at the party freaked out about how good my Elvis perform-ance was. Since I had some spare time on my hand, I decided to take a clos-er look at this **Business of Being Elvis.** I started working with about a dozen booking agents in Dallas and throughout Texas. They probably have two or three Elvis entertainers in their data bank. They call me or whoever is available. I get referrals. I also have my own **yellow page** ad and my web-site. Everybody involved in the whole Elvis world has this kind of warmth about it. My fans are great. I've got some that follow me around from show to show, keeping track of my schedule on the website. They pop up every-*

where, many of them I know by name. I also do a tremendous amount of private parties. I wear the look of Elvis all the time. My sideburns are natural and my hair is black, styled like Elvis. I do dye it to keep it black because it is one of the best means of advertising. I have a wife and children. In fact, my wife does Priscilla. I taught her how to sing with my live group act. She is more talented than she thought she was. My 15-year-old son is my 'roady' or technician, which works out real well for my solo party gigs."

Kraig believes he is fortunate for his opportunities to perform all over the country. Recently, an attorney client flew Kraig to Hawaii to perform for his wedding. The attorney found Kraig from his website.

"He told me he had looked at about 50 or 60 different Elvis on the Internet. He zeroed in on me and we got talking through e-mail. Finally, he said, 'I don't want to go anywhere else.' That particular gig was a two-hour performance. I charged him $2500 plus the airfare and the three-day hotel. He was very happy with the whole thing and that makes for another great referral. That is how it all works."

Kraig offers advice to anyone who wants to get started as an Elvis performer. He reinforces the fact that an ETA must take it seriously. ETAs must respect the fact that they are performing as Elvis Presley and must focus on the aspect that this is, in fact, a business. Kraig's dedication to the **Business of Being Elvis** resulted in his first place win at the Dallas, Texas **Hard Rock Café** contest in January 2000 and at an **Isle of Capri Casino** in November 2002.

"I would say that anyone wanting to get into this should do contests. They are a good place to start. You get to see what other guys are doing and the ones that are winning the contest. Watch how they act, sing and move when they perform as Elvis. Find the top people in this business, why they are doing it and try to mimic that as best as you can. You also need to understand contests. They all have their own set of rules and most of them are relatively legitimate. There are many that are not judged fairly. No one is better than anybody else. I have probably $50,000 dollars invested in this. I am a Christian guy. I was really a serious recording musician before I started out. There's a whole lot of people who think these Elvis acts are a joke…that's what they think of impersonators. When I really stepped into it, I saw the love and appreciation from the fans when you perform a good act. That is what turned my view around. I really respect the guys that have done this for a long time and keep the memory of Elvis alive. You also have

*to have a cross point where you stop trying to act like Elvis and start enter-
taining the people."*

Kraig's CD, **The Ultimate Tribute to Elvis: Live at the Plaza,** was
recorded live with his band **The Royal Tribute Band** at *The Plaza
Theatre* in Carrollton, Texas, on August 18, 2001. Kraig is currently
working on a new CD and maintains some nice video clips on his website. Kraig's wonderful **25th Anniversary Salute: Elvis Lives! Show**
commemorating Elvis' death, was produced by Kraig. With a sell-out
audience of 3000 plus, Kraig clearly understands what the **Business of
Being Elvis** requires.

ED PARZYGNAT

Rather than try to pronounce Ed Parzygnat's last name, most people identify him by one of his better-known stage names. He is
Fabulous Eddie P, Ed Elvis, or **Ed – The Monkey Man.** For over six
years now, Ed's performed his Elvis tribute show for birthday parties,
festivals, weddings and various corporate and charity events. Ed, and
his wife, Annette, also make up the **Ed and Annette's Monkeys and
More Show.** This show, hosted by **Ed Elvis** and Annette, is a very
interactive, educational and entertaining show. It isn't just monkey
business either! They work very hard at óperating their own sort of
humane society shelter in Chicago, Illinois.

*"I've been working with animals for nearly 24 years and my wife has
been working with animals for nearly 11 years. Our "no kill" animal shelter
means that most of the animals we have were given to us by people who no
longer wanted them or were going to be putting them to sleep. We bring live,
exotic animals to schools, libraries, nursing homes, day care centers, cub
scout meetings and any other special occasion someone might be having. It is
not a circus act."*

The show is interactive because their animals are all available for
petting or holding by members of the audience. The show is educational because Ed and Annette share information about each of the animals with the audience. They talk about where they come from, what
they eat, who their enemies are, their habitats, life span, why they
don't make good pets, and which animals are or are not endangered. It

is extremely informative. Add a great Elvis performer and you've got a fun and entertaining show.

"*I am an Elvis tribute artist for the love of Elvis. Definitely for the love of Elvis! I also love animals, especially caring for rescued animals. Of course, I perform without them. too. But our total show is so gratifying and rewarding…watching people interact with the animals and learning about them. Most of them have never petted animals like these. My wife and I enjoy doing this together. The animals, after all, are our children. We take care of them, feed them, house them, provide veterinary care and love them.*

"*We have close to 30 animals. We would have more if we could, but unfortunately our present site is too small for many more or larger animals. We would love to take in more because there is going to be a need for more animals in need of shelter. That's our future goal. To name a few of our animals: we have Ajax and Priscilla – named after Priscilla Presley of course, our Weeper Capuchins; one of our monkeys named Jordan who owns his own Elvis jumpsuit; an American Raccoon, Rocky, our North American Raccoon; Charlie, our Chinchilla; Flower, our chocolate and white skunk; Fancy, our Fennec Fox; Ricky, our Ferret; Rascal, our North American cougar; Sneezer, our Albino Burmese Python; Julia-Squeezer, our Boa Constrictor; Suzie and Tommy, our large tortoise; and Terry our Tarantula…just to give you some idea.*

"*I perform as an Elvis impersonator because we are both big Elvis fans. We love being part of something that is entertaining with Elvis. The second it stops being fun, or people would ever even think that I am making fun of Elvis, that is the day I would stop impersonating.*"

I think that Ed and Annette are excellent representatives of the **Business of Being Elvis**. Elvis Presley would have truly enjoyed their act and would also have been proud that his presence was being utilized in such a positive and charitable manner.

RYAN PELTON

The **2001 Worldwide Images of the King Contest** in Memphis, Tennessee, was my first visit to Memphis plus my first attendance at an Elvis impersonator contest. I remember it like it was yesterday. I've never sought out an autograph prior to my Memphis visit, or a scarf, for that matter. I still don't! But when Ryan Pelton walked into that crowded room filled with over 100 Elvis contestants plus their fans, I had to get an autographed photo. It only cost me five dollars. This was my first exposure to the world of the Elvis entertainer merchandising. At that time, I did not even know his name.

My later interview with Ryan Pelton was like a breath of fresh air, which is difficult sometimes in this business because it is so flooded with egos. Ryan and I met in the quietest place we could find in the **Imperial Palace Casino** in Las Vegas where Ryan performs. He had just flown into Las Vegas, returning from a trip to Ohio and it was after midnight when we met. As tired as he must have been, he couldn't have been more gracious.

"I think when I look at myself and what I'd like to do, I realize that I'm so new at this and I'm still learning the ropes. I really am," Pelton said.

The most fascinating aspect of Pelton's career path is that it never did include a music career. He is college educated, started his own computer graphics business, and served in the **Marine Corps**. While in the **Marines**, Ryan, with his head shaven, still earned the nickname 'Elvis' from his drill instructors.

Following his military career, Ryan's mother challenged him to enter an Elvis impersonator contest. He'd been told numerous times since he was 13 that he looked like Elvis, but looking like Elvis was one thing and singing and performing like Elvis was another. Ryan decided to take up his mother's challenge and he walked away as the winner. So, as the saying goes, 'the rest is history.'

"I changed my direction because this is kind of my own thing. I'm really a computer geek. I had a chance to get on stage, and I went wild. This is the first thing I've done in my life that didn't come natural, to be honest. It's a challenge. You've also got to have some dignity in portraying a character."

Learning the **Business of Being Elvis** was not as easy as it sounds for Pelton. In the beginning, Ryan encountered a variety of people who thought they saw a perfect opportunity to take advantage of this young, perhaps naïve, entertainer.

"I knew nothing about this business. I literally had to spend tens of thousands of dollars in court just so they're not selling my picture with someone else's name on it. It seems crazy, but I will say that for every hundred agents or managers, 99 of them are lacking something," Ryan explained.

He is aware of the many other potential negatives of performing Elvis.

"The women trying to live the Elvis dream, the guys just in it for the money, the romper room attitude of the contests and some of the performers, or the people who just like the power of being a control freak."

In his effort to become a better and better performer, Ryan confessed, *"I'm embarrassed to say how much I rehearse. You might say 'he should be a lot better.' I also watch a tremendous amount of videos and listen to music. I have all the DVDs, I can take them with me on my laptop computer and every night go to bed playing my DVDs."*

Obviously, Ryan's hard work is paying off. He is currently touring the **Legends in Concert** production and has toured all over the world with various venues. Ryan was the winner among seven other Elvis contestants in an episode of **The Weakest Link** game show. A few ETAs that know Ryan say that he raked in the $150,000 prize to outwit Anne Robinson. In June, 2002, Ryan was one of the first ETAs to be granted permission from **EPE** and allowed to film inside the gates of **Graceland** with his commercial for **Volvo**. More recently, Ryan was approached about doing some modeling for a major fashion designer.

When Ryan won the **Images of the King Contest** in 2000, John Branston, a writer with **The Memphis Flyer** newspaper concluded that *"Ryan Pelton is such a dead-on young Elvis that he may well become the Tiger Woods of this singular art form."*

Yet in all of his success, Ryan Pelton, the person, remains unchanged. He is genuine and projects the charisma so much like Elvis Presley did in his own real shyness.

*"I've been lucky. I like being an entertainer. I have a great manager, Dan Lentino. Though I enjoy performing **Legends,** I would someday like to be involved in a production that tells a story. Like in a theatre similar to Martin Fontaine in **The Elvis Story.** Elvis is a cool story. It is a tragedy how it all ended, but it is cool how it all started,"* Pelton summarized.

Ryan has truly taken the **Business of Being Elvis**, and himself, to a level far beyond that of impersonating Elvis. Mixed with his humble personality and astute business savvy, Ryan utilizes his talent to mold his career path to be filled with an optimistic future. On a personal note, Ryan does not forget those who encouraged him and, perhaps assisted him, during his successful journey. He genuinely expresses his appreciation to those individuals in a variety of thoughtful ways. Ryan's humility and ability to share his success and advice with others continues as a breath of fresh air in the **Business of Being Elvis**.

STEVE PRESTON

From Lancashire County located on the Irish Sea, Steve Preston is from Haslingen, Rosendale, England. When Steve was ten, his father gave him an old six-string acoustic guitar and, according to Steve's recollections, he listened to the songs on the music charts and watched on television the frenzy created by Elvis Presley's appearance. Steve enjoyed music but it was clearly not the passion of his life and performing as an entertainer of anything was never a serious consideration for him. Steve's life substantially changed following high school graduation.

He enrolled in the **Bolton Art College** to study graphic design. While in college, Steve performed with his guitar on weekends with a local band and accompanied the band on vocals. Steve's generation is usually associated with the music of **The Beatles** and **The Rolling Stones** and this was the music that Steve knew well. However, he was also following the music of Elvis Presley and the music intrigued Steve. Steve's weekend gigs and his increasing fascination with Elvis' music started to surpass his original career choice and, with time, he switched from graphic designer to entertainer.

Against the wishes of his father, Steve dropped out of college to pursue what, by now, was his dream to become an entertainer. Eventually Steve's entertainer dream would materialize into a passion, a passion that Steve needed to pursue. In 1986, Steve organized his first Elvis Tribute show. Steve's tribute show, immensely well received and popular, became so well known among club-goers on the **Northern Club Circuit,** that he presented his show throughout the area, an area that covered the entire United Kingdom. Steve's **Northern Club Circuit** success appeared for a while to be the end of his dream because it took Steve an additional five years before he landed another big break.

"Elvis has always been popular all over the world, especially in the Western World. The Elvis tribute thing, though, didn't really take off until about 10 to 12 years ago with the **Stars In Their Eyes** *television series* (in

England). *It was a show for people to sing the person they sounded like or looked like. From that time on, the popularity of ETAs has grown and grown. In 1992, I signed a contract with the United Kingdom version of* **Legends in Concert**. *Although I never appeared on the* **Stars In Their Eyes Show,** *I toured with the winners of the show throughout Europe, including New Zealand."*

In 1994, Steve received a cigar lighter previously owned by Elvis Presley and presented by Philip Schofield on the television show, **London Weekend**. Steve received his gift, along with a certificate of authenticity, live in front of millions of viewers. Currently, the only other Elvis memorabilia Steve owns is a pair of tickets to an Elvis concert on September 26, 1977, which, obviously, never took place.

"I planned a holiday to America in 1995 to see all of the major sights...Memphis, Dallas, the Alamo...everything I could see. One week before I was scheduled to leave, I received a phone call informing me I was required to perform for the Queen on the **Royal Variety Performance** *at the* **Domminium Theatre** *in London on November 20th, 1995. I probably drove 4000 miles around America in four days to see as much as I could. It was such an honour to perform for* **Her Majesty, The Queen.** *This is certainly the highlight of my career. Back stage, I also met American composer Marvin Hamlish and we chatted about Elvis for a while."*

Another major highlight in Steve's ETA career includes his December, 1999, performance in the arena of the **Scottish National Conference Centre**.

"In all the years I've been singing Elvis, there was nothing quite like the feeling of performing in that arena. There were about 10,000 people there and as I walked toward the stage, I could hear the musicians playing **2001 Space Odyssey** *and the deafening noise of the crowd. It's the same kind of venue that Elvis would have played. There I am, dressed in my white suit and flanked by officials. It is about as close as you can ever get to relate to Elvis' performing.*

In 2001, I was hired to perform at the **Gran Palace** *in Spain. I don't just sing to the Spanish. There is a mixture of nationalities out there. Most Europeans speak English these days, but it wouldn't matter because Elvis is universal anyway. I'm quite sure there is an Eskimo in an igloo playing an Elvis hit right now. As far as my British accent goes, you won't know it when I sing Elvis. In fact, recently, there was a sales company here who* decided to put on a competition for their employees...like an incentive. The prize would be a trip to Las Vegas. The company wanted an Elvis impersonator to phone up as a surprise to congratulate the employees who had won. An agency notified me about the audition, but by the time I called the company they had already made their choice. So, I continued my conversation on the telephone in my Elvis voice. I ended up getting the job.

"My wife, Linda, and I have two children. I have worked in Europe a lot in the last few years and it's not the best industry to be in when you have a family. It's not the ideal situation but we have survived a long time. I met Linda in 1977 and we married in 1982. We are apart a lot, but we make it work. I've recently been performing in Ireland and, at the moment, I am preparing to do some work in Malta, a little island off of Italy."

From his original aspirations to become a graphic artist with no particular desire to become an entertainer, Steve is currently considered one of the world's leading Elvis performers. In fact, the **Official King Elvis International Fan Club** critically acclaims Steve's current show, ***The Best Elvis Show in the World...Ever!*** for his talent in recreating the excitement and essence of a live Elvis Presley performance which is a substantial endorsement indeed. Presently performing in Europe, Steve remains the unrivaled number one Elvis act in the United Kingdom. Steve's future goal includes bringing his talent to the United States. He is currently working with a spokesperson to represent him and assist him in promoting a future venue in the States. You may contact the Steve Preston's website in the United Kingdom at http://www.elvistribute.org/ or Solo Angel in the United States at http://mywebpage.netscape.com/soloangel10/page1.html for his upcoming schedule. I know Steve would love to have you visit!

"For an Elvis impersonator from the U.K. to play in America...it really is **the** place to play. I've played some pretty big places over here, but I'm quite sure that compared to Memphis or Las Vegas, the U.K. can't compete...simply because that is where **the man** himself walked."

AARON SKILTON

Aaron Skilton, **The Blonde Elvis**, will be seven years old this year. His parents, Sandra and Brian Skilton, are big Elvis fans. Their home in

Wasaga Beach, Ontario, Canada, is just a stone's throw from Collingwood, Ontario, Canada. Collingwood hosts the annual **Collingwood Elvis Festival** where I first saw Aaron perform. Sitting with his parents waiting to go on stage, Aaron was autographing a stack of his Elvis promotional photos. He is well-mannered, quiet and very shy.

His father looked over at Aaron and said, *"It's time to put your white jumpsuit on."* With a big, adorable smile, Aaron eagerly stands up and takes his father's hand to the dressing room. His mother and father take turns throughout the day, assisting Aaron with his costume changes. Aaron performs several eras of Elvis music. At this point in time, Aaron can sing 25 different Elvis songs by heart...and memory.

Aaron hits the stage, his father starts the backup track music and Aaron become Elvis. He belts out **If I Can Dream** with such passion that you are easily entertained by his sincerity. Aaron sang his three-song set to an enthusiastic crowd of Elvis fans. When he finished singing, he stepped off the stage and quietly went back to autographing his photos.

JACK SMINK

Jack Smink entered the **Business of Being Elvis** in October, 1977. He sang at a church festival in a jumpsuit that his then soon-to-be wife, Karen, made for him. They are both huge Elvis fans so it was easy for Karen to support Jack's activities as an Elvis entertainer. The couple recently celebrated their 24th wedding anniversary and as Karen puts it, *"We've been dating for 30 years now."* Rockledge, Florida is home for Jack, Karen and their two children. Currently, Jack performs three nights a week at the **Nikki Bird Holiday Inn Resort** near **Disney World.**

"I love performing there for a variety of reasons, but the best part is that I meet so many different people from all over the world...especially Elvis fans from the U.K. that come to my shows.

In fact, at press time, Jack left Florida for a two-week tour of England. It is a dream fulfilled.

I've been performing full-time as an Elvis tribute artist for 25 years now. It is nice to be working close to home. I've done a lot of traveling, so it is a welcome benefit to be able to spend more time with my family."

Jack is one of the more thoughtful and caring individuals that I have had the pleasure to meet. He loves to share some of his many stories he has heard from those who knew Elvis Presley. When Jack performs his tribute to Elvis, you are immediately aware of his deep respect for Elvis. Jack is also a great listener. Many times, I have walked down a hotel corridor only to discover Jack's room door wide open and find him with a fellow ETA who, for whatever reason, needs a friendly shoulder to lean on. It is late at night, yet Jack calls out: "*Come on in.*"

A few of us gathered in Jack's room, as Jack listens to the ETA talk about the fact that today was the anniversary of his father's death. Jack offers his thoughts and advice, while at the same time waiting for a telephone call from his wife before she goes to work at 5:00 AM. That is Jack! He is always willing to give his time to anyone who seems to need him. In fact, I have dubbed him the "guru" of Elvis because it seems that the spirit of Elvis is truly with him. Although he doesn't expect anything in return, Jack has received a variety of humanitarian awards for his numerous charitable contributions. Most recently, he was the recipient of the **National Leadership Award** from the **Florida Republican Committee**. Along with other business leaders, Jack will represent the State of Florida in a series of round table discussions with President Bush and other Republican leaders regarding issues that directly affect the state.

"*There are a lot of guys out there, but only a handful that really represent and are involved with the mainstream of the* **Business of Being Elvis**. *It makes me feel good to see the young guys getting in this business. I'm here to do a tribute show. I consider myself a tribute artist. There was only one Elvis and there will never be another Elvis. Up until a year or so ago, I had never entered a contest. I decided to take some time to get involved with some contests. I wanted to get a feel for what that world out there was like. It's like a piece of the puzzle that was missing there for me. It was expensive, but I made the right decision. The contest to win, of course, is Memphis. You win that and you're off to the races. Most of the contests, in themselves, are alright, but if you are going there just to win, you are setting yourself up for a lot of heartaches and disappointment. If you are going to be there, you should have other motives as well. I did a few* **People's Choice Awards**, *which was a great experience because it is endorsed by* **Elvis Presley Enterprises** *and the audience is the judge.*"

One of the bigger highlights in Jack's career was one that he was able to experience twice, well almost! Although I heard the story from Jack initially, I convinced Karen to tell me her side of the story. It all began one night in March of 1999.

"*I persuaded Jack to watch* **This is Elvis** *with me. I told him to pay close attention to the opening scenes. It showed the crew gearing up for the show…at the hotel and around town…then at the* **Cumberland County Civic Center** *in Portland, Maine. The movie showed the stage being set, the jumpsuits arriving at the hotel and a movie version of the Colonel getting the call about Elvis' death. This was also where Elvis was to begin his next tour. Then, I told Jack that he was going to that show. He thought I was kidding, but I was serious. He asked me why and I asked him how old was he. He laughed out loud on that one. Of course I knew how old he was…42. I then asked him how old Elvis was when he died…42. You're doing the show! A few phone calls and a few days later, the* **Cumberland County Civic Center** *was booked. All we had to do was complete the band and buy our airplane tickets. Oh, and then there was the advertising, a new jumpsuit and a few thousand other important details. We had five months to make this happen.*"

On August 18, 1999, **The Unfinished Business Concert** was born. Jack Smink, a virtually unknown ETA in Maine, walked out on the stage to over 2000 screaming Elvis fans. The next day, the headlines in the local paper read **Elvis CAPTIVATES Audience!** Jack's production company is called **Lightning Strikes Twice** and, just as the show started, lightning almost did strike twice. Not in the way of Elvis' tragic death, but a near tragedy all the same. The stage was set up with special lighting and included a fog machine to enhance the illusion of Jack's entrance on the stage. Walking through the dense fog, Jack missed the steps coming in from backstage by the drum set. Falling face down on the wooden floor, Jack's cape and belt flew off. Jack took several minutes to catch his breath and regain his composure, and after assuring himself that he had no broken bones, came out on the stage belting out his powerful rendition of **CC Rider.** Enduring the pain, Jack continued with a host of other great Elvis songs in his two-hour concert and then after the show, graciously went to the lobby to sign autographs and pose for pictures.

Fast forward to three years later during the spring of 2002 and Karen continues her story: "*We got a call one day from a reporter in*

Portland, Maine. The **Cumberland County Civic Center** *would soon be celebrating their 25th anniversary. What a coincidence. It is also the 25th anniversary of Elvis' death. The reporter had talked to Steve Crane, the general manager of the* **Cumberland County Civic Center**, *who, in his opinion, was the most colorful performer he had ever seen at the civic center. Without hesitation, Steve said, 'Jack Smink'... 'Who?' the reporter asked. Steve then told him the whole story about Jack's show in 1999. The reporter went on to interview Jack for inclusion in a newspaper article about the upcoming celebration. Before you knew it, we were headed back to Maine to perform for the* **Cumberland County Civic Center 25th Anniversary Celebration.**"

Jack agreed to do the show on the condition that his performance would be a benefit for **Camp Sunshine**, a local camp for children with terminal illnesses. Jack took a 12-piece band complete with back up singers and a crew that ultimately included 30 people involved in putting the whole show together. This time, however, Jack made his entrance without tripping and was greeted by a sell-out audience of 6000 fans, including Donna Presley Early and her husband, Buddy. The audience also included Dick Grob, Elvis' head of security, and Jim Mydlach, assistant to the Colonel and who was with the Colonel the day that Elvis died. At the time of Jack's second performance in Portland, he was still wearing a back brace and recovering from a near fatal fall he incurred while assisting a friend in a construction project.

"*Eventually,*" according to Jack, "*I'm going to settle in to doing promotions. When I step down from performing as an Elvis tribute artist and let the younger guys take over, I will concentrate more on the producing end of the entertainment business. I also just recorded a single country record written by Razzy Bailey, a top country artist from the 70s and a big Elvis fan. He gave me a stack of songs to work on. The first is ready to be released in Nashville. I hope to continue on with that avenue as well.*"

I thoroughly enjoyed Jack's video, **An Elvis Tribute: Live at The King Center For the Performing Arts** taped on August 4, 2001. I look forward to hearing his new songs. With all the love that radiates around Jack and his family, I know there are many more dreams for Jack and his family to fulfill and memories to be made. Hopefully, one of those memories does not include another tripping incident!

JOHNNY THOMPSON

Johnny started his entertainment career about 11 years ago singing telegrams in the Chicago area. Hired by a Chicago business man, Johnny earned $400 to do a walk-around show and sing to his employer's guests for two hours. Johnny, in recalling his first ETA job, is quick to admit, *"I was hooked after that."*

The road to becoming an Elvis tribute artist has been a long and winding one for Johnny. Young Johnny grew up in Longview, Texas with a family of Elvis fans and today Johnny credits his father for his entrepreneurship and the drive he relies on in his ongoing ETA quest. As a youngster, Johnny accompanied his father to various country clubs to watch Elvis impersonators. Johnny was intrigued with them from the very beginning. Johnny started Karate lessons in high school, later earning a second level black belt in Tai Kwon Do as well as numerous other achievements and honors in a wide range of martial arts. For a while, Johnny taught martial arts—guiding six of his students to the black belt level. Tai Kwon Do is an art form that Johnny claims is a tremendous asset in his performances as Elvis. According to Johnny, after college he did some acting in a series of plays, television commercials and some low budget films. During his acting period, he met ETA Jerome Marion and Jerome encouraged Johnny to become more involved as an Elvis entertainer. Together, they attended a few Elvis conventions and performed in a few shows. Nance Fox, attending one of their shows, was impressed with Johnny's performance and hired him to sing for her son's wedding.

*"From then on, she started coming to my shows and began to take a professional interest in me. I trained her to become my manager, as my career was taking off and I needed someone to handle the organizational things. We were booking more jobs and began producing shows at the **Sabre Room** in the Chicago area...made famous because Frank Sinatra used to perform there. I was surfing the Internet one day and realized that there was no central agency to assist the Elvis impersonators in getting work. That's when I had the idea to form the **Elvis Entertainers Network**. It grew into a full-blown agency, which I ran for a couple of years until I sold the name to Nance Fox in June, 2000. Since that time, I have been building a bigger and better organization*

called **Professional Elvis Impersonator Association (PEIA),** *appointing Doug Church as my first president for one short term. This actually evolved from an organization called* **Elvis Presley International Impersonator Association (EPIIA)** *that was started by Sandy and Ron Bassett. Rick Marino was their first president. I'm not sure what exactly happened with Sandy and Ron, but I eventually turned it over to Jerome Marion who was instrumental in getting me into the* **Business of Being Elvis.***"*

According to the **PEIA** website, the organization offers professional and fraternal services for **PEIA** members. **PEIA** does not charge any agency fees, but does charge fees for an ETA to be represented on their website. The **PEIA** includes a board of directors representing a variety of professional backgrounds.

Johnny's first Las Vegas experience was considerably less successful than he expected it to be. Not giving up on his ETA dream however, Johnny took over his personal marketing and researched a variety of opportunities, including contests.

*"Like most people who are new to the business, I thought I was the best too. Then, I started doing the competitions in the Midwest. I met a lot of great performers and they kicked my butt. It took a couple of years before I started winning them. My problem in the beginning was not practicing. I was still teaching Karate and I didn't have time to practice. It took me a while to realize that you have to sing at least a few days a week, really working on it. It requires a tremendous amount of dedication if you want to be out there with the best of them. I was ready to return to Las Vegas. That's when **9/11** hit; it was a difficult time for everyone and Las Vegas went into a huge slump. People were afraid to travel and the casinos didn't know what was going to happen with the economy. I was lucky to get a job at the* **Elvis-A-Rama Museum** *to do 20 to 30 shows a week, which is like six or seven shows a day. Eventually, I started to get burned out."*

Johnny's entrepreneurial drive, not deterred by an economic slump, materialized in his annual Elvis convention in Las Vegas. In June, 2001, Johnny gathered twenty ETAs from all over the globe to perform in his new event. Currently, Johnny's **Annual International Convention & Showcase** continues to accept only twenty impersonators along with their $100 registration fee, but Johnny's production efforts have proven worthwhile. Over time, he acquired several new sponsors and also met Greg Thompson who is no relation to Johnny but is the owner of **Greg Thompson Productions**. Greg Thompson is highly respected in the entertainment world as a first class producer of stage shows. Johnny recently joined Greg Thompson's show, ***Greased Lightning,*** at the **Casino Magic** in Biloxi, Mississippi for two months. Following his Mississippi engagement, Johnny went on to Canyonville, Oregon for another Greg Thompson production, **Tribute To The King** in the **Seven Feather's Casino**. He performs in **Tribute To The King** as Elvis along with ETAs Donny Edwards and Reggie Randolph but due to his standing commitment in Biloxi, ETA Garry Wesley replaced him on stage for three weeks. With a résumé that began with ringing doorbells and singing telegrams, Johnny's ETA quest is an interesting account of his adventure in the **Business of Being Elvis** and his future continues to look very bright.

JOE TIRRITO

Joe Tirrito may well remind you of James Dean—you know—the rebel-without-a-cause James Dean. Joe is Sicilian with absolutely natural black hair and complimentary dark features. Joe's father was enormously influential in Joe's decision to become an Elvis entertainer. Coincidentally, both project the image of Elvis and both have tremendous admiration for Elvis Presley.

"Being with my father and growing up with a big Elvis fan such as him, I was aware of all of Elvis' music. Just being around it all of the time, I subconsciously learned all of the words and evolved into an Elvis fan myself at a very early age. I started out when I was 16 years old in the era of hard rock music. I was the lead singer in a band called **No Discipline***...with long hair down to the middle of my butt. About six months later, the band broke up and the lead guitar player started his own 50s and 60s style band. He called me up and asked me to sing with them. Gradually we started incorporating Elvis' music into our show. One day, a female fan approached me at a gig we were doing and asked me about doing an Elvis show for her...strictly Elvis music. So I went out and rented my first Elvis jumpsuit from a costume shop in Chicago...cost me twenty dollars. It was the funniest thing I'd ever seen, but to me it was an Elvis jumpsuit all the same."*

Somewhere in the middle of his musical aspirations, Joe took a side trip into the rodeo circuit. Joe had a great time and stayed on the circuit for about seven years before he decided that the rodeo business was too dangerous for him. *After some close calls with the bull riding thing, I decided that was enough craziness,* Joe laughingly told me. Joe then focused on his Elvis tribute artist career and for the past 20 years, the **Business of Being Elvis** has become Joe's best ride. Joe's career ride felt like a roller coaster trip at times, but a trip that Joe believes was well worth it. When not engaged as an Elvis tribute artist, Joe is also a full-time semi-truck driver.

*"Fortunately, I have a great relationship with my employer. They are very reasonable with my schedule at times. I drive a local route around the Chicago area, which allows me the time and flexibility to perform Elvis on weekends with some occasional traveling now. I really enjoy what I'm doing and I thank God I can do both. It is also important to me to have the great benefits...medical, pension and other perks. When you travel as much as I have, it is easy to get caught up in Elvis...talking like Elvis, living like Elvis. In the beginning of this business, I developed such a big head. I thought I was the King himself. I even had my own bodyguards. You fall into that because the people put you into that. You just have to realize it and get back into reality. My life even seemed to be like Elvis'. I married a 15 year old girl, I was a truck driver...but none of that was planned, it just happened that way. I went through two divorces in my journey to understanding the difficulties and successes of the Elvis business. The best agent in this business is yourself. There is so much going on...there is not a day that goes by that I'm not doing something that has to do with my shows. I'm very lucky now to have recently acquired a manager, Monica. I've known her for many years when she managed her husband's musical career. She is an Elvis fan and has attended many of my shows. She is well versed in the entertainment business. She brings everything to me and I still make all of the final decisions. This is the most important aspect of the **Business of Being Elvis**."*

Joe's ride as an Elvis tribute artist includes performances in a variety of venues including both live bands and tracks. Traveling all over the United States, including a tour to Australia and Japan, Joe's professional accomplishments also include working with entertainers who knew Elvis, like **The Jordanaires.** His appearance in Japan left a permanent and favorable impression with Joe.

"*I was hired to do the* **Aloha From Hawaii** *show with a cast of about 15 people. When I walked off the plane in Japan, it was like Elvis himself had arrived with his band. They treated us like the King. They had the press there and the television cameras. The Japanese are very nice people. They gave us everything we wanted and they loved our music. They didn't understand any of the words I was singing, but they were rockin' and having the best time. It was amazing to me to discover how expensive everything is in Japan. A steak dinner was like $80 American money, a* **Happy Meal** *at* **McDonald's** *was $13. When I returned to Vegas, I did a show at the* **Imperial Palace** *for* **Legends in Concert**. *John Stewart is an interesting guy. He's tough though. It's like his way or the highway. Sometimes they want you to have plastic surgery, but if you are under contract with them you have to pay it back. I actually considered that once, but I never did.*"

Joe also designs his own clothing line, beautiful designer t-shirts called **Artistic Integrity Designs**. If you are not able to locate a nearby venue featuring Joe, you may catch his beautiful voice on his Christmas CD, his Las Vegas CD or my favorite CD, **Joe "Elvis" Tirrito – A Tribute To The King**. To date, Joe has not recorded any original music but his current CD does include his beautiful poem, written and narrated by Joe. Sounding like Elvis with a background eloquently enhanced with music, Joe's poem is sure to awaken one more memory of Elvis Presley. Joe and I would like to take this opportunity to share his tribute with you:

Now that he has said goodbye
Lord take him in your arms
The memories he left behind
Will linger for all times
That southern style
That half a smile
That shiny jet-black hair
The way he moved in the early days
When no one else would dare
The happiness he gave to us
Take good care of him Dear Lord
My friend I never knew

His music brightened up our day
And touched our very soul
And to us he'll always be
The king of rock and roll
So sing it tender, and sing it loud
And sing it oh so true
For now you'll sing
For the greatest King
Oh Elvis we'll miss you
There will never be another performer
That's quite as great as you
But I'll carry on your legacy
My friend I never knew

MY FRIEND I NEVER KNEW
Joe Tirrito

JONATHON VON BRANA

A California native, Jonathon Von Brana's eventful ETA saga includes the California discothèques and, for a while, Las Vegas' **Legends in Concert** number one Elvis. Today, Jonathan is probably best known as Hawaii's very own Elvis. Sporting an engaging smile, Jonathan's physical presence is enhanced with his distinctive German and Latin dark features. Jonathan is very adamant that he does not impersonate Elvis, adding *"I talk about Elvis in my shows, about particular songs that he sang and I sing Elvis' music. I don't try to copy Elvis exactly. I don't think I ever looked like Elvis. I do my impression. I am an impressionist, an entertainer giving the audience memories of Elvis."* For the majority of Jonathan's 23 years in the **Business of Being Elvis**, his journey has been very eventful, to say the least.

Lip-syncing to records at a variety of San Diego, California discothèques in the 80s, Jonathan loved to dance and sing along with the music of the 50s and 60s. Dancing and singing was just a natural outlet for him.

"I dressed a little like Elvis, not to be like him, but just because I liked him. I would go to the clubs and dance. One night, I decided to get up in

front of the crowd and dance while singing with an Elvis record. The first time was just for a joke, but the crowd and the DJ liked it so well that he started to offer me and my friends drinks if I would come up and dance a couple of songs each night. A few weeks later, the owner came in and offered me $50, then it became $75 and then it was $100. All of a sudden, in a few months, I was working at three different clubs making $150 -$200 per place. Eventually, I was earning $300 - $600 a week for only dancing to two or three songs. About six months into this, a DJ at one of the clubs told me he thought I was too good to be doing this and suggested that I put a live band together. I told him that I had never sung before, other than to records. He told me that he could still hear my voice with the records because there was a microphone set up. With records, if I stopped singing, the record would still be playing and I had a safety net…it wasn't so fearful."

Jonathon thought the DJ's idea made sense and believed that the discothèque fad was starting to fade. The time might be right to learn to sing with a band. He was living with a gentleman at the time that he considered his stepfather. With his encouragement, Jonathon started rehearsing day and night for three months in his stepfather's garage. His stepfather previously owned several restaurants and hotels in the area and offered to help Jonathon arrange his first show. He eventually became Jonathon's manager and negotiated all of his contracts.

"He invited several of his old friends and some of the most influential people around town, including people that were in a position to hire entertainment. So we got them all liquored up, performed a 45 minute show and managed to get our first booking for a two-week deal. We were there for a month and they wanted to keep us longer, but they already had some contracts with other bands. Then, we managed to hook up with a big hotel in Mission Bay, which also booked us for two weeks, but we ended up staying there for almost a year. The band had evolved into three sets of oldies up to top 40 hits music and two sets of an Elvis show. We basically acted more like a band that had an Elvis show. That is how we sold ourselves. By the time we finished that gig, we were the highest paid band in San Diego…pulling in a little over $2200 a week. That was big money back in 1980."

I started thinking a lot about the Elvis acts that were out there and where the business was headed. There was Johnny Harra who was in the movie **This Is Elvis**. He played an older, heavier Elvis. He had a really good look…nowhere near as good looking as Elvis, but then I've never seen anyone *as good looking as Elvis. He was performing at the* **Thunderbird***, which later become the* **Silver Bird Hotel and Casino** *in Las Vegas. It's torn down now. He ended up getting really bloated and they had to let him go. It was too bad. There was another guy named Alan, out of Canada, who opened up at* **The Dunes***. He didn't look anything like Elvis, but he had a good voice. I believe he came out right after Elvis passed away. He played there for three or four years and became the number one Elvis in Las Vegas. He was making the most money until he had a falling out, lost his job and then toured around to various shopping malls performing as Elvis. I was very impressed with his voice, but very unimpressed with his attitude... extremely self-centered. I guess he got that way from doing so well in Las Vegas all those years."*

Jonathon took a trip to Hawaii in late 1980. He fell in love with the beautiful, tropical islands. In fact, Jonathan was so impressed that he decided to make Hawaii his professional home base but he needed to figure out how to make it happen. Returning to San Diego, Jonathon and his band signed a six-week contract to perform at an Italian restaurant in Encino, California, not far from Los Angeles. The new contract seemed to indicate a considerably longer engagement than six weeks so the entire band moved to Los Angeles. The Encino engagement went extremely well for about nine months when, without any advance warning, the restaurant was sold and closed.

"They stiffed us for about four weeks of pay and there we were. This was about the time that **Legends in Concert** *opened in Las Vegas. I decided to go to Las Vegas and see the show on my birthday May 4th, 1983. I was not impressed at all. The showroom was huge. There was no band on the stage as they had it up where the orchestras usually play. There was no lighting on the stage and the cast of performers...just kids...I mean I was young, but I already had 2-1/2 years under my belt of working 5 and 6 nights a week. They were walking out on stage all by themselves. You can't get in that theater and just stand there by yourself unless you have a lot of talent and charisma. There was no 'umph' in the show. There were some great cast members, especially the gal that did Janis Joplin. She looked exactly like Janis and had a really good voice. In fact, she was so strong she used to close the show instead of the Elvis. But, can you imagine Marilyn Monroe out there all by herself? Dana McKay performed as the first Elvis. He was 6'2" or so and a very good-looking man, but not a good voice and he was a horrible dancer. Dana told John about a guy named J.J.Wiggins who developed the*

*original concept for the **Legends In Concert**. Dana arranged for the room at the **Imperial Palace Hotel and Casino** and showed John Stuart and his investors the concept of a legends type show. J.J. had already mounted a show with something like eight people in the cast, including a **Beatles** act. This was around the time when the hit **Broadway** production of **BeatleMania** came out. John's first show had laser lights and robots in it...like a **Starwars** effect. They put the whole concept together and John ran with it. Though the idea wasn't totally new, it was J.J. who brought it to the forefront. John basically stole the idea from J.J. and even when J.J. became part of the show, John never paid him anything. J.J. and his wife did not have much money, working out of their apartment in Hollywood, making all of the original costumes. I bought my first 15 Elvis costumes from J.J. J.J. also tried to get John to hire me before Pete Wilcox, but he had to go with Dana anyway because he had got John into the **Imperial Palace**. Even though Dana took singing and dance lessons, he just wasn't any good and John finally had to let him go. In fact, about five years later, Dana and his girlfriend were shot execution style in Las Vegas. It was rumored that Dana owed people some money out there. Anyway, the **Legends** show started getting bad reviews and I continued on with my plans to move to Hawaii."*

By now, Jonathon knew a lot of people who believed in his talent as an entertainer and they began to search for investors and available showrooms in Hawaii. Everything seemed to be falling into place and Jonathon was excited with the possibilities. But by the time the new **Legends In Concert** in Las Vegas finished its third week, *"the hotel gave them a two week notice...improve the show or you're out of here,"* according to Jonathon's version. John Stuart, the producer of **Legends In Concert** needed to do something quickly and he phoned Jonathon.

*"John and his wife had attended one of my shows in San Diego. His wife thought I was great, but John thought I was too sexual. Actually, I was far more sexual in my lounge acts. It turns out that John had already tried to hire Pete Wilcox. He performed as Elvis and could imitate several different voices, which he worked into his show. In fact, he did the voice over in the show **Happy Days**. Whenever you heard Elvis' voice on there, it was Pete. He didn't look anything like Elvis, but he was an extremely talented man. Pete wanted to bring his own band and John Stewart already had a band. Then I guess Pete wanted too much money. I think John's wife actually con-*

vinced him to call me. Well, I told him no because I was planning to make
the move to Hawaii. John promised me it would only be for a couple of
weeks. I talked to my manager and he thought it might be a good promotional idea for Hawaii. You know...direct from Las Vegas...Jonathon Von
Brana performing Elvis. I told John I would come under one condition. I
wanted the band and the back up singers on the stage behind me and I wanted to pick my own songs. I want to be in charge of my end of the show. John
agreed. Vegas was never a big turn on for me and yet as much as I loved
Hawaii, I also realized that Hawaii was a gamble. I also saw this as an
opportunity to improve the **Legends** show.

"At the end of my first show, I got a standing ovation. By the end of the
two weeks, John had to admit that I knew my craft and I knew how to handle
audiences. My manager had some showrooms lined up in Hawaii, so we
started making serious plans to move. That's when John offered me a guaran-
teed $1000 a week to stay. It was not only good money, but it was a locked
in amount and that is something I wasn't used to so I accepted his offer.

"The whole cast was tickled pink to know that they weren't going to be
out of a job...it was like I had hit a touchdown or something. I'm not saying
it was just me that improved the show. I loved Elvis Presley and I loved the
audience. By the second year, the show was sold out almost every night. The
showroom seated 900 legally, but we were packing in 1100 people in there. I
negotiated more money for myself and for the cast. It was a shame what they
were getting paid, especially when you realize that John was making $15,000
to $30,000 profit a week. Then in 1984 or so, the actors' and musicians'
union went on strike in Las Vegas. We were not union, so we stayed open
seven nights a week for 4-1/2 months. I was the only Elvis in the
show...John still didn't have a replacement for me. I would get ill on occasion and had to perform anyway. There were times that I would sing in spite
of feeling nauseous. It was 3-1/2 years into the show before John finally
brought Pete Wilcox into the show as an alternate Elvis. I got a week off for
the first time."

Jonathon was now a known star in Las Vegas. The **Legends In
Concert** show received rave reviews and write-ups from the media.
Eventually, Jonathan earned $3200 a week, bought his first new
Cadillac when he was 21 years old and spent money like it was going
out of style. He hired agents and managers, and bought additional
expensive cars, almost as if he was imitating the life of Elvis Presley.

Jonathon was once engaged to the **Legend's** Marilyn Monroe impersonator, Susan Griffiths. It appeared that the infamous city was good to
him and Jonathan and the **Legends In Concert** show continued to
gain international attention. In 1985 and 1987, Jonathan was chosen
as the **Entertainer of the Year** with *Legends in Concert* in Las Vegas.
He loved the glitz of the entertainment capital of the world, but the
24/7 Las Vegas lifestyle began to take its toll. Jonathan started to dab-
ble in drugs, drank heavily and the arguments with John Stuart became
their normal way of communicating. His rigorous show schedule started to affect his voice and Jonathan, obviously, wasn't very happy. Yet,
it would take another year and a half before Jonathan would meet his
Las Vegas demise.

   *"I started doing a lot of stupid things. Everyone in the show was partying
a lot, too. We used to go out into the desert and target shoot with our pistols
when we were drunk. Had a couple of close calls there. I had to run two
humidifiers in my room all the time because the air in Vegas was so dry. John
was constantly bringing in new cast members, changing the production. A lot
of the cast members were doing drugs and stealing things from the hotel. One
cast member stole $11,000 from me. Johnny picked up some contracts for
shows on* **Cruiseliners***, of which I was the first one to perform Elvis. One
of the Elvis guys he put in the show was David Scott from Canada, who
spent thousands on plastic surgery. Johnny would often recommend plastic
surgery to the various performers.* **Legends** *would pay for the investment
only to reimburse themselves from the ETA's paycheck. He got into some
trouble with some females on the ship, which ended up costing John the contract. David was fired and a couple of years later, he committed suicide. I
was getting worse and worse…Johnny was pulling more and more crap. He
was putting up with me because he didn't want to lose me. John only knows
how to put glitz in a show, instead of quality sometimes. I was letting him get
away with less and less too. Then it all came down to the 1987* **Legends**
*New Year's Eve show. We had an excellent crowd. Just the kind you like for
the countdown on New Year's Eve…all excited. Well, the producers of*
Legends *were so cheap, they only allowed me to give away five $1.50
scarves to 1100 people at a show. I'm on stage, the women are screaming
for a scarf and I had already given away all of my scarves. One lady just
wouldn't give up, begging for a scarf. I kept saying 'I'm sorry sweetheart, I
don't have any more scarves' and finally I said, 'I can't give you any more*

scarves because the producer of the show is such a cheap...' Well, the audience slowly erupted, the band started laughing and the spotlight guy was shaking the light from laughing. Then someone in crowd asked me for my sweaty towel and I said, 'I can't give you the towel because the towel belongs to the hotel and they are even cheaper than the producer.' It turns out that the hotel owner's son was sitting in the audience with a bunch of VIPs and the next thing you know that whole table had left. I did the second show and went back to my room. About 2:00 a.m., my manager called to asked me what happened. I told him about it and then he tells me I'm fired. I was surprised because I knew that the audience had a good time with it. Looking back, I realize that Johnny did try to save me. He offered me the chance to perform at the **Legends** that was just opening in Reno. I might have taken it, but he only wanted to pay me $2000 a week. He thought he had me in a position to break me, but I learned a long time ago that you have to claim your self worth. Rarely does Johnny do a show without the Elvis, but he has done it. He almost has to because he's trying to keep all of these Elvis.' He works them for a month or two and then he expects them so sit around the rest of the year waiting for him to call. He's always threatening that if they go to work for the competition, they will never work for him again. Now, of course, if you are talented enough, John will always use you again. He would even hire me again, if he came here to Hawaii."

Jonathon made his long dreamed of move to Hawaii and worked in the **Legends** show in Hawaii until it closed. Jonathon additionally performed at conventions and made a tour in Japan. He went on to produce and perform Elvis in his own show **Blue Hawaii** for several years and currently performs on the **Navatec1 Cruiseliner**. He is also involved with a new show production and his first CD. Jonathon and his wife, Ilene Fairbanks, a **Madonna** impersonator, recently divorced after 15 years of marriage. Jonathon quickly points out that "We are still very good friends.

"I want to have children at some point. I would really like a family. I love Hawaii...the ocean, the dolphins, the flowers everywhere. I believe that Hawaii saved my life. It is so refreshing here. The weather is perfect everyday and I think I have added ten years to my life. I don't think I will ever go back to Las Vegas to perform. It is like an ant hill of Elvi there. Las Vegas is so corporate driven now. A corporation owns John Stewart now as well, so he is just a figurehead. No one dresses up any more. Las Vegas has lost its *class. In the big picture in the* **Business of Being Elvis,** *I have really been blessed."*

Unfortunately, you will have to travel to Hawaii if you want to see Jonathon Von Brana as an Elvis tribute artist. A vacation to the Island sounds like a good idea to me, especially in the middle of a cold and snowy winter. I am told that if you know some locals, known as Kamaaina, you are able to buy tickets at a discounted price. Jonathon's career history reads like a fabulous book, a book with no immediate end in sight. It is interesting to note that Jonathon's Dana McKay's murder story and David Scott's suicide are available on the Internet. The movie, **This Is Elvis**, was the only movie made about Elvis that was authorized by both Elvis' estate and Priscilla Presley. Many of the scenes were filmed at Graceland. Johnny Harra, who performed the latter years of Elvis in the movie, including the re-enactment of his death, is the only surviving Elvis actor from that movie today. All of the other actors who portrayed Elvis died in tragic deaths. Paul Boensch, the child Elvis, died shortly after the film concluded in an automobile accident, David Scott, playing the young Elvis, committed suicide in 1993, Ral Donner, the narrator Elvis, died of a heart attack, and Dana McKay, who played the hospital scenes of Elvis, was gunned down mob style in Las Vegas after his show. Yes, this is the same Dana McKay. You can purchase an autographed copy of the video from Johnny Harra through his website at: http://www.geocites.com/jharra2000/movies.htm

ROBERT WASHINGTON

ETA Robert Washington, born in St. Louis in 1958 and raised in Cape Gerardeau, Missouri, performs all of the Elvis eras. My favorite, however, is Robert's rendition of the **'68 Comeback Special.** He is disciplined in his daily physical workouts that help him maintain both his shape and his stamina. Now a resident of Maine, Robert also paints huge merchant ships full-time. He is well-versed in his Elvisology, studying Elvis so well that he has perfected many of Elvis' Karate moves. Any doubt in the depth of Robert's Elvis research quickly disappears when he hits the stage because he convincingly brings Elvis to life. When Robert sings Elvis' music, he sings from the depth of his soul demonstrating both his love and respect for Elvis Presley.

"My love for Elvis began when I was a child watching all of Elvis' movies. I was instantly hooked. Then I started to listen to all of his records. I am always reading books and biographies about Elvis. I enjoy the many interesting stories people tell about him. In fact, I am currently reading **Careless Love***, the second part. Some of the things I've read about Elvis remind me of me. I have an absolute respect for Elvis."*

Like Elvis, Robert is soft-spoken, always polite and consciously aware of just who he is as a person. When he is not on stage as Elvis, he is definitely Robert Washington and does not allow the **Business of Being Elvis** consume him. Some controversy seems to come with the appropriateness of Robert's portrayal of Elvis because he is Afro-American. Robert is absolutely dedicated to being the best Elvis performer that he is capable of, perhaps in part to discourage some of the disapproving remarks directed his way. Participating in the **Images Of The King** contest in Memphis, Tennessee, ten times since 1987, Robert placed in the top three for the past three consecutive years. Almost universal agreement exists among both participants and audiences alike at the **Images Of The King** contest that Robert has more than earned, and deserves, a first place **Images** win. In John Paget's documentary, **Almost Elvis,** Robert is featured with ETAs Irv Cass and Doug Church in their quest for the crown in the **Images Of The King** contest. The portrayal of their quest includes discussions concerning the possibility of a man of color winning an Elvis contest. Some firmly believe that there is clearly a level of prejudice directed toward Robert. Is it possible that old racist values and beliefs continue to roar their ugly heads in the contest judging? Should the contest be moved to another city? Does the contest itself need to be changed? The contest has positioned two Canadian Elvis impersonators and one Japanese impersonator in the winner's circle. Clearly, Elvis was not a Canadian, an Asian or an Afro-American, but should an individual's ethnic identity or skin pigmentation be of significance in an industry that is theoretically based in the love and adoration of Elvis? Personally, I believe that contestants should be judged solely on their costuming, their moves and their ability to replicate the voice of Elvis. Fellow ETAs and fans alike admire Robert and Robert pays his audiences back with stunning performances as

Elvis, but the first place **Images** trophy continues to elude Robert Washington. Elvis Presley was often ridiculed because he did not believe that a fellow human being should be judged by the color of their skin, so where do you think Elvis would stand on this particular controversy? I also wonder how many great Elvis songs we would not have the privilege of listening to if Elvis believed that skin color was important and as a consequence, simply dismissed the old spiritual and gospel music that he grew up with. The old spiritual and gospel music substantially influenced both Elvis' style and his music and it seems to me that as **Almost Elvis** suggests, *"Elvis is a name for something that we have in us, or we don't,"* and I would like to believe that equality is the major component for both fans and contest judges alike.

"In 1977, when I was in the United States Marine Corp, Elvis died on my 19th birthday. I felt an even stronger connection to Elvis after that. When I got out of the service, my wife and I added a microphone to our stereo system and I started singing Elvis' songs for our close friends. In 1983, I performed for the first time on stage in Waukegan, Illinois. I am so inspired by Elvis' music and that is really why I love singing it.

*The biggest thing with the Memphis contest is that you don't get to see your scores from the judges. You get so many points based on your look, voice, moves, and performance. If you don't get to see those points, you don't know what your strengths or weaknesses are. This is very important in determining what part of the Elvis performance needs more polish. Some of the other contests allow you to view the judging sheets. There are also too many contestants in the **Images** contest in Memphis. They have the luck of the draw to determine when you perform. I do enjoy going to Memphis, especially getting downtown on **Beale Street** to see the other acts."*

Robert recently participated in **The Faithful**, a feature length documentary film exploring some of the better-known cultural icons of our time—Elvis Presley, Pope John Paul II and Princess Diana. **The Faithful** is presented through the eyes of individuals who cherish/idolize these figures the most—their admirers and the media and entrepreneurs who capitalize on their fame. **The Faithful**, produced by **Fish in the Hand Productions** in association with the non-profit **Center of Independent Documentary (CID)** (htttp://documentaries.org/), examines the complex of contemporary social forces involved in elevating ordinary men and women into large-than-life images. According to *The Faithful,* the phenomenon of elevating cultural icons permeates popular culture worldwide.

GARRY AND ELAINE WESLEY

From a child growing up in the small, small town of Willard, Wisconsin, Garry Wesley never would have dreamed that he would become a successful Elvis Tribute Artist. In the **Business of Being Elvis** Garry is, indeed, the best kept secret.

*"It's a classic story of being persuaded by my two best friends to do Elvis for Halloween. They were going as **The Blues Brothers**. I lived in Milwaukee at the time and an old girlfriend convinced me to go all out. She dyed my dishwater blond hair to black, made me a suit and everything. We all laughed so hard at ourselves and decided to go out to **Nick's Nic-a-Bob's,** a nightclub on **State Street.**"*

As it turns out, no one recognized him. Not even Nick himself knew it was Garry. **Jerry Allan and the Rockin' Robins** came on stage to perform and Jerry said: *"Elvis is in the building"* while looking right at Garry. The band talked him into getting up on stage and singing a few Elvis medleys of the 50s.

"I was scared to death. I sang in church, but that's different because you can blend right in. Even though I sang to many of Elvis' 45s as a young kid. I studied and studied Elvis' music…listening to the records over and over to make sure I listened and did everything Elvis did. I still had never sung in public like that before. I was amazed when I saw the reaction of the audience."

Without realizing that history was in the making, Garry eventually put a band together, learning a lot more Elvis songs. This being in the early 1980s, numerous nightclubs were hiring bands, but not too many Elvis impersonators. Garry continued performing while holding down a variety of day jobs ranging from being a certified welder to working in fast food chains and even an investment company.

"It really took a lot of convincing by others for me to go for it. At that time it was estimated that there were 8000 Elvis impersonators, so this was really a big step to take. We eventually learned about making tracks, before there was Karaoke really. It was basically a tape deck and it worked well for auditions."

After returning to Willard as the performer, friends that Garry had grown up with and gone to school with didn't recognize him at all.

Then, in 1981, a pretty and talented young gal from Racine, Wisconsin by the name of Elaine Grant performed with her band **West Wind** at **Nick's Nic-a-Bobs** nightclub on **State Street**. It was a benefit for orphaned children. Garry Wesley was also performing there. They occasionally worked together until the late 1980s when they started dating. They finally settled down, married and put their talents together into one show.

Added Elaine, *"It was really difficult back then. I had young children from a previous marriage and I had to be home with them. During the summers though, we brought them with us on the road and Garry and I could perform together."*

By the late 80s, Elaine and Garry were performing rock and roll, top cover country, and Elvis Tribute Shows. Thus, they decided to add a second tribute, **Patsy Cline**. Elaine has a paralleled and equally powerful voice to Garry's. Each could perform individual shows, but the combination adds an overwhelming style of entertainment.

Elaine is gifted with the look of **Patsy Cline** in a wonderful, natural way. You will even recognize her when she is strictly working back-up vocals for Garry. It is obvious when they perform that they are having a good time together, exchanging wisps of humor with lots of love goin' on. Garry and Elaine traveled with their band, **Memories**, performing throughout the Midwest states.

For last 14 years now, they have performed at **Alfred's** on **Beale Street** in Memphis, Tennessee, in August during the Elvis Anniversary Week. Fourteen years ago, their official fan club was founded there too. A gal by the name of Jane Brom walked into **Alfred's** to get out of the heat. She asked the cocktail waitress if they were having any entertainment that night. The waitress then proceeded to tell her about a gentleman all the way from Wisconsin that would be doing an Elvis show. Jane didn't want anything to do with that… *"I don't care if he's good or not, he's not Elvis so I don't have time for it."* About that time, Garry started in with his rehearsal and Jane was quickly smitten. She asked the cocktail waitress if she could speak with Garry for a few minutes. The waitress went up to Garry and politely relayed the request. Jane asked Garry what time he would be performing.

Garry said, *"10 until 2...are you going to be able to come and see the show?"*

Jane responded, *"I'm not sure. Give me a smile. Did you have your teeth fixed to look like Elvis'?"*

"No ma'am," said Garry.

Jane was so impressed with his politeness and sincerity, rather than the arrogance that she expected, she thought to herself that maybe there is one Elvis impersonator that's not so bad. Jane and her friends ended up staying at **Alfred's** from three in the afternoon until show time. And they have been coming back ever since.

"She became our Fan Club president for the southern region, for 14 years now. The club started with those eight members and has grown to well over 100. They literally set their schedules and vacations around our shows. They really are terrific and unbelievably loyal," Garry summarized.

For fan club information, you can e-mail Jane Brom at disasterkat@aol.com.

In 1994, Garry got a call to go out to Laughlin, Nevada to perform at the **Hilton Hotel and Casino** with the **American Superstars Show** where he first met **The Jordanaires**. A year later, the show was transferred to the **Palace Hotel and Casino** where Garry performed for three years. The show was then moved again to the **Gulfport Grand Hotel and Casino** in Biloxi, Mississippi, until the show pulled out and left the area, leaving the remaining **American Superstars Show** in Las Vegas, Nevada. The Wesley family currently resides near Biloxi, which is where I interviewed with them in February, 2000. I was also there to see Martin Fontaine in **The Elvis Story** production show. Elaine and Garry had begun working with Dan Lentino Management. The best-kept secret in the **Business of Being Elvis** would soon no longer be a secret.

Upon returning home from another week and another year at **Alfred's,** one of the first most exciting opportunities was just about to happen.

Excitedly, Elaine e-mailed me: *"...we just got home from Memphis and received a call from Dan. We have been invited to perform an Elvis Tribute Show with Travis LeDoyt in Chile, South America."*

It was great to hear from her, as we all were still recovering from the great week in Memphis, 2002. Garry and Elaine performed at **Alfred's** with their terrific show. My husband and I, of course, were all over Memphis with a variety of venues. We interviewed lots of Elvi.

We were exhausted. Can you just imagine how tired all of these performers must have been?

Well, it was off to Chile, South America for Garry and Elaine Wesley along with their band, D.J.Fontana, Joe Esposito, Dan Lentino and promoter Mario Giordani. The photos of the **Estacíon Mapocho** in Chile depict an image of the **Cystene Chapel**. Hand painted figurines are emanating the spirituality of an apostolic church.

*"We started out performing on a large network TV program that reaches over 5 million people, then we performed outside a casino in Santiago, Chile. Ultimately, we did the concert at **Estacíon Mapocho** in front of over 5000 people who could not speak English, but knew the words to all of Elvis' songs. It filled me with an almost spiritual feeling,"* described Garry.

"It was viewed by 8 million people. In fact, we recently found out from the producer that the show aired throughout Europe via satellite, therefore it was actually viewed by millions more."

In January, 2003, Garry took first place in the **Isle of Capri, Tribute To The King Contest** in Lula, Mississippi, winning the highest purse awarded to an Elvis Tribute Artist. Prior to entering this contest the year before, he had no contest experience, so to speak.

"I was so excited. I can't explain it. The other Elvis competitors were really good. They were incredible. The prize money is going help escalate some plans we were already making. The first order of business is to move back to Wisconsin to be closer to our parents and extended families. Maybe I will buy another new jumpsuit though,"

Garry recently completed a show for **Greg Thompson Productions** in Oregon along with ETA Don Edwards, who performs a young Elvis. Garry believes that Edwards has tremendous potential as a performer and looks for him to be a rising star in the **Business of Being Elvis.**

The list of accomplishments is long. They continue to do an annual tribute show to Elvis during Elvis week in Memphis in August. They have done a host of productions shows and venues all over the country. In the fall of 2003, they will be heading to Canada to work with the **Legends Alive** production of **Elvis-Elvis-Elvis..** They have produced a variety of CDs and, yet I think the best is still yet to come.

The schedule and information about the show in Canada can be obtained on the Legends Alive.com site. In addition, tune in to Lady Luck Music.com to hear Garry sing. You can e-mail Elaine and Garry

at Garry Wesley@aol.com or check the Garry Wesley.net site.
Garry and Elaine Wesley are reminded that **Elvis Lives** and is *"still the greatest entertainer. It is an honor to pay tribute to his memory worldwide."*

BOB WEST

Bob West, in the Business of Being Elvis for 27 years, maintains his full-time job with the Public Works Department in a suburb of Chicago. He is an Elvis tribute artist and concentrates on Elvis' gospel music. Bob loves the gospel music and uses his vocal talents to support charities and benefits.

*"I started in 1975 doing some shows for a couple of years. Then I gave it up for a while to concentrate on my marriage…too much social life was interfering. I've had quite a few opportunities to travel and move up in this business, but I didn't take them because of my job and my family. I'm just Elvis part-time. I am fortunate…I have always been able to provide for my family. My favorite Elvis songs are **How Great Thou Art** and **Hurt** because I love spiritual…gospel music. Elvis put so much passion into Hurt every single time he sang it. Elvis would say 'Do you want to hear it again?' And he would go through the whole song again. I really became an Elvis impersonator because of the charities. When I started out, I didn't have the money to give to benefits like the **Jerry Lewis Telethon.** I realized that I could give my talent as a donation. I continue to feel very strong about that. This is probably how I am most similar to Elvis. Elvis was very humble. My feet are planted on the ground. I don't go to work dressed like Elvis…although I did become obsessed with it over the years…but when I pull into my driveway, my neighbors know who I am."*

Bob recently joined the **Elvis Entertainers Network (EEN)** and is a previous member of the **PEIA.** If an Elvis contest is not associated with a charity, Bob is most likely not involved with the contest. Bob and Joe Tirrito have performed in numerous benefits together. Bob especially enjoys Ronny Craig's **Elvis Explosion** because it raises money for the **Children's Miracle Network.** Bob added, *"the only other reason I will do a contest is to fulfill a commitment. If I told someone I would be there, then I will be there. When I'm gone from this earth, if the only thing people remember about me is that Bob West always kept his word…and had an amazing talent, I would feel really good about my life."*

On Friday, July 13th, 2001, Bob's 65-year-old mother was diagnosed with lung cancer. Unaware of his mother's news, Bob performed at a festival that evening and the audience included both his mother and father.

*"I knew my parents were out there. Midway through my performance, I played a couple of songs on the guitar and then I said, 'My mom and dad are here tonight and I would like to dedicate this song to my mom. It's **Young and Beautiful** from Elvis' **G.I. Blues**'. Afterwards, people came up to me and told me that my mother was really crying. Well, I found out about three weeks later that on that very morning of the festival, she had gotten the bad news from her doctor. She later told me, 'When you dedicated that song to me at the festival, it could not have come at a better time.'"*

Bob's mother recently passed away at the age of 66.

"I am still trying to deal with it. She came to all of my shows and was always very proud of me."

Although Bob has never been to Memphis, Tennessee, or even to **Graceland,** he did see Elvis perform in October, 1976 at the **Chicago Stadium.** He also very proud of an oil he painted of Elvis.

*"In **Aloha From Hawaii,** there is a surfer and I did an 18 x 24 oil painting of that with Elvis. I gave the painting to some people I knew that had a connection to Elvis Presley. She and her husband took it to **Graceland** where it was hanging in the basement for a while. It is still there some place. I don't know because I've never been there. It went down there in June and Elvis had some concerts in October…I always think in my mind that was Elvis' way of thanking me. I don't have a picture of it and I have always wished that I did. My father was a police officer so I always collected police badges…long before I knew that Elvis collected them. I also have a twin brother named Bill who is about 40 pounds heavier than me. He cannot sing a note. Bill and Bob…my parents had a lot of imagination didn't they? I have to work at keeping my weight down. I always starve myself the day of the show. If I ate a hamburger in a jumpsuit, you would be able to see it sitting right in the middle. That's one of the benefits of the Elvis shows. I drink coffee in the morning for my voice, then I do a **SlimFast** and just before the show I drink a **Red Bull.** I am sure all of the guys have some regimen they follow."*

One of the biggest highlights of Bob's career in the **Business of Being Elvis** includes his tour in Japan.

"It's amazing...a totally different culture. The Japanese clap very softly, which is like a standing ovation over there. They are very reserved. After a month of being there, I found out that if you go into the audience and approach a table full of people, you always went to the head of the table first. It is being respectful. The food is interesting, but we did finally discover some restaurants that offered American food. The first week I was there, I couldn't get through to an overseas operator so I had to go through the switchboard. It cost me 4700 Yen, which is $470 American dollars so I cooled it on the calling back."

Thank you sincerely, Bob West, for your active participation in your many worthwhile charity causes and sharing with your fans, your musical gift as an Elvis tribute artist.

Chapter 8

The Business of Being Elvis

The date of Elvis' death on the 16th of August, 1977, was a day that changed the world for literally millions of people. Over a quarter of a century later, many Elvis fans are still able to recall vividly and exactly where and what they were doing when they received the awful news that their 42-year-old idol was indeed, dead. For some, it was a personal nightmare, but their loss fueled a major new industry and signaled the beginning of a new chapter in the magic of Elvis. On the 25th anniversary of Elvis' death, at least thirteen stocks continued to trade publicly on Wall Street that somehow persistently claimed a connection to perhaps the single most important musical figure in the field of 20th century popular music.

The "King of Rock and Roll" is indeed dead, or at least I believe that he is, but his financial world and the individuals associated with his world—even remotely—continue to roll in colossal amounts of money. In 1977, perhaps 150 entertainers used the stage to emulate the voice and classic images of Elvis. Today, the estimate exceeds 35,000 impersonators and those are only the ones that we are aware of. The number of individuals associated with the magic of Elvis, including those behind the scenes, defies accurate calculations. I know from my personal experience that the world of Elvis and his impersonators persistently multiplies and continues to generate impressive financial spreadsheets. It was into this fascinating world that I took my first step into the **Business of Being Elvis**.

I never doubted that Elvis was the King and I continue to recognize him as the King. I was fascinated however, by an industry whose cornerstone was built on Elvis' death. I was initiated into the Elvis impersonator world during my first trip to Memphis, Tennessee in August, 2000, the anniversary week of Elvis' death. My husband and I played the typical tourists and we enjoyed every Elvis sighting from **Graceland** to **Beale Street**. The highlight of our trip included the renowned *Images Of The King* contest. I was literally overwhelmed by the assortment of available Elvi. I was even more amazed by the dedication of the impersonator fans—often paying as much as $150 for front row seats—and their considerable expenditures for impersonator memorabilia. Even as a rookie, it seemed clear to me that the Elvis wheel received substantial financial grease from the contest and that the entire concept of re-creating the image of Elvis was, indeed, big business.

As of press time, the original owners of the *Images Of The King* contest acknowledged two new partner/investors, both entertainment professionals, into their organization. Industry observers and most ETAs are hopeful that the infusion of new blood and resources into the *Images Of The King* contest structure will provide a window of opportunity that will set the standard for fairness in the entire contest industry. Ultimately, the general consensus is for all of the contests to adhere to the same rules and guidelines, and contestants will be judged in the future solely on their era-correct costuming, moves and ability to replicate the voice of Elvis.

Since I started my journey, I have interviewed over 150 people worldwide, from the members of the scarf cottage industry to some individuals associated with the publicly traded entertainment venue, **Legends in Concert**. I learned that *The Business of Being Elvis* includes numerous entrepreneurs, many who never see the stage lights or are visible to the dedicated fans, but their work is instrumental nonetheless in supporting the illusion of Elvis. After nearly three years of research, I appreciate and respect Elvis Presley more than I did when I started my investigative journey. It is conceivable that there is room for a sequel because I have learned many new things and the Elvis phenomenon continues to expand and improve. I am convinced that the ongoing process of elevation from Elvis impersonator to Elvis tribute artist is a positive step for the industry. I know that no one can, or ever will be, ELVIS, but the dedicated ETA is committed to achieving the total "Elvis package."

The cost of achieving the total Elvis package often carries a price tag that is significantly higher than a simple financial investment.

Many ETAs have submitted to one or more painful cosmetic surgeries to permanently transform themselves visually into Elvis. As the world recently witnessed with Michael Jackson, the ultimate outcome is not always a healthy one, either emotionally or physically. Some ETAs have chosen a less drastic method by enduring the application of permanent make-up, a procedure similar to tattooing. Nearly all of the ETA's packages includes some form of over-the-counter cosmetics; some claiming it is necessary because of the intense heat generated by stage lighting. For others, I would suggest enrolling in the "Elvis Make-up 101" course, which is not yet available. The folks at **MaryKay** or **Avon** might consider investigating the idea of providing an Elvis make-up program.

The total package for some might also include the alternative avenues for achieving the Elvis eyes and the Elvis smile, but the necessity for tanning is an industry requirement to achieve that "extra" Elvis glow. Perhaps one of the more positive and healthier aspects of the **Business of Being Elvis** is the required regimen of diet and exercise. It seems clear that most ETAs truly respect Elvis because they have no desire to portray Elvis in his latter and failing years. Likewise, the majority of ETAs are very careful about projecting any kind of message that might be interpreted as promoting or emphasizing the use of drugs and alcohol.

Other than their presence on stage, the vast majority of ETAs no longer rely on the wigs or the pasted on sideburns. They have also concluded that Elvis sunglasses should be worn in the sun and not on the stage. After all, Elvis didn't do that. The industry as a whole seems to be more focused now on the re-recreation of Elvis, not a re-invention of the man. In fact, there are many ETAs who accept their God-given looks, thereby placing a greater emphasis on their voice, moves and entertainment skills, and, from my perspective, as they should be. Last, but not least, is the financial investment of the Elvis attire.

Although many Elvis tailors flourish in the business today, **B & K Costumes** is still considered the ultimate tailoring enterprise because of the firm's original Elvis connection. A minimum investment of $10,000 is typical for three jumpsuits. If there are 35,000 Elvis impersonators in the world and they each purchase one **B & K** jumpsuit at a cost of $3000, their jumpsuit purchases alone generate $105 million dollars. If the same 35,000 Elvis impersonators additionally purchase five scarves at fifty cents each, assuming they perform only one night a week, their scarf expenditures generate $4.5 million dollars. The deluxe scarves, which average $1.50 each, would generate $13.1 million dollars. Jumpsuits and scarves are just a fraction of the financial picture in the **Business of Being Elvis.**

In addition to an ETA jumpsuit, knowing Elvisology is now considered a pre-requisite in the **Business of Being Elvis**. It is essential that an ETA know the Elvis eras—which song to sing and with which costume. In fact, Elvisology has become one of the more hotly debated issues in the judging of contests. Over time, the contests have developed a rather complex set of rules, regulations and guidelines that qualify an Elvis contestant as a winner or loser. Although rules and regulations are the standard for contestants, no standard seems to exist for evaluating a judge's credentials. I have yet to see the résumé of a contest judge nor am I aware of a process where individuals are deemed qualified to judge a contest because they adhere to a set of rules, regulations and guidelines, and perhaps most importantly, a modicum of professionalism. Unfortunately, I have personally witnessed too many judges who are visibly bored with the entire judging procedure. I do believe that the ETA's fans rather than the ETA's performance is often the critical component of a judge's decision, maybe because the fan applause woke the judges up from their nap. Even the world-renowned beauty pageants introduce their judges by name and reference their professional background but not so in the **Business of Being Elvis.**

The appearance and image of the King is indeed important, but the *business* is equally, if not more, important. The ability to promote and market the total Elvis package requires an investment as well. A worthwhile promotional package includes quality tracks, high-resolution photographs, CDs, or videos that will ultimately convince an agent/client to hire the Elvis to perform. The winning promotional package transforms the bottom line into financial rewards. Agents and managers discard the majority of the "promo packages" they receive because the package is not well done or because the Elvis tribute artist lacks quality. The total package for most of ETAs now includes websites, which is also a very effective sales tool. If considerable time and money is invested developing web sites, it is reasonable to expect a polished promotional package as well.

I was very impressed with the ETAs who sent their promotional material to me. In some cases, the ETAs brought their condensed portfolio to our interview while others sent their promotional package to my hotel prior to our interview. This type of ETA response demonstrates both enthusiasm and interest. Judging a book by its cover has often proven to be a buyer's first and only lasting impression. Hundreds of books, not to mention ETA promotional kits, are sent to agents each day. The competition is fierce for space on a bookshelf just as it is with the ETA striving to be on the main stage. A majority of the people interviewed for this book believe that there are really very few ETAs, but there are a whole lot of Elvis impersonators or "wanna-bes." I believe, however, that the new generation of Elvis performers is dedicated to changing this notion. It is also my hope that **ELVIS LIVES— The Business of Being Elvis** will be a positive factor in revolutionizing the industry.

In the **Business of Being Elvis,** from Las Vegas to Wall Street, from the movies, CDs, books and magazines to the total package and the credibility of the judges, the ultimate control mechanism for the financial rewards generated by the industry is vested in the pocketbooks of the fans. Just how deeply the fans are willing to financially dig to be near, see, hear or read about their favorite ETA member all contribute to the new financial chapter in the magic of Elvis. The consummate ETA has the talent and ability to transform the fans back to "what was," even if only for a fleeting minute and the fans continue to grease the financial Elvis wheel for that moment. As cynical as many may interpret my statement, I would like to add that all of the ETAs and their numerous fans stand as living testimony to Elvis Presley as the single most important musical figure in the field of 20th century popular music. **Elvis Lives!**

It is not the critics that count nor the man who points out how the strong man stumbled or where the doer of deeds could have done better. The credit belongs to the man who is actually in the arena; whose face is marred by dust and sweat and blood; who strives valiantly; who knows the great enthusiasms, the great devotions, and spends himself in a worthy cause; who, at his best, knows the triumph of high achievement; and who, at his worst, if he fails, at least fails while daring greatly, so that his place shall never be with those cold and timid souls who know neither victory nor defeat.

– Theodore Roosevelt
"To the Man in the Arena"

CHAPTER 9

ELVIS TRIBUTE ARTISTS WEB SITES

You may enjoy visiting one of the many WEB sites maintained by the ETAs referenced in Elvis Lives: The Business of Being Elvis or sites hosted by their booking agencies. All of URLs listed below were active as of 01 April 2003 although a few are "under construction."

Jay Allan:
http://www.JayAllanRocks.com

Jesse Aron:
http://www.jessearon.com

Martin Anthony:
http://www.martinanthony.com

Adam Ashcroft:
http://www.ashcroftbryant.freeserve.co.uk/
adam1.htm

Everette "Howie" Atherton:
http://www.onenightwithyou.com

Jim Barone:
http://www.jimbarone.com

Brandon Bennett:
http://www.elvismyway.com

Trent Carlini:
http://www.thedreamking.com/

Paul Casey:
http://www.paulcaseyproductions.com/

Irv Cass:
http://www.elvisentertainersonline.com/

Steve Chuke:
http://www.stevechuke.info

Doug Church:
http://www.dougchurch.dk (Denmark)
http://www.dougchurchusa.com (USA)
http://www.dougchurch.com/mycustom-
page0012.htm (United Kingdom)

Michael Conti:
http://www.elvisentertainersonline.com/

Ronny Craig:
http://www.elvisexplosion.com

Kavan Creamer:
http://www.KavanTCB.com

Leo Days:
http://www.ledpro.homestead.com

Michael Dean:
http://www.michaeldeanandmemphis.com

Butch Dicus:
http://www.butchdicus.com

Lance Dobinson: not currently available

Eric Erickson:
http://www.elvisentertainersonline.com/enter-
tainers/Eric_Erickson/index.html

Martin Fontaine
http://www.elvisstory.com/

Paul Fracassi - KidElvis:
   not currently available

Stephen Freeman:
http://www.echosofalegend.com

Rob Garrett:
http://rnrheaven.net/

Ray Guillemette Jr.:
http://www.arayofelvis.com

Tony Grova:
http://www.tonygrova.com

Paul Halverstadt:
http://www.jim-jacks.com/elvis.htm
http://www.elvisentertainersonline.com/

Keith Henderson:
http://www.keithillusions.com

Robin Kelly:
http://www.robinkelly.net./

Matt King:
http://www.elvisentertainer.com

Shawn Klush:
http://www.shawnklush.com

Kjell Elvis:
http://www.elvis.no/home.htm

Curtis Lechner:
http://www.CurtisElvis.com/

Darren Lee:
http://www.darren-lee.com

David Lee:
http://www.elvismyway.homestead.com/ELVI
SMYWAY.html
http://www.thedavidleeshow.com

Rick Lenzi:
http://www.ricklenzi.rocks.it/

Mark Leen:
http://www.emeraldelvis.com

Johnny Loos:
http://www.johnloos.4mg.com/

Chris MacDonald:
http://www.chrismacdonaldelvis.com

Rick Marino:
http://hometown.aol.com/rickmarinotcb

Jerome Marion:
http://www.elvisentertainersonline.com/enter-
tainers/Jerome_Marion/index.htm

Todd C. Martin:
http://www.toddcmartin.com

Richard Messier:
http://www.thekingsband.com

Eddie Miles:
http://www.eddiemiles.com

David "Jesse" Moore:
http://hometown.aol.com/heartofelvisshow/in
dex.html

Travis Morris:
http://www.elvisentertainersonline.com/

Mike Morrissette:
http://www.elvis-tribute-mikemorrissette.com
http://mywebpage.netscape.com/soloan-
geltcb10/page17.html

Craig Newell:
http://community-
2.webtv.net/CRAIG2001DJ/THE-
CRAIGNEWELLELVIS/

Kraig Parker:
http://www.thekinglives.com

Ed Elvis Parzygnat:
http://www.elvisentertainersonline.com

Ryan Pelton:
http://www.ryanpelton.com

Steve Preston:
http://www.elvistribute.org/
http://mywebpage.netscape.com/soloan-
gel10/page1.html

Aaron Skilton:
   currently not available

Jack Smink:
http://home.cfl.rr.com/aelvistribute/

Joe Tirrito:
http://www.joe-evis-tirrito.com/

Johnny Thompson:
http://www.johnny-thompson.com

Jonathon Von Brana:
currently not available

Robert Washington:
http://www.elvisentertainersonline.com/entertainers/Robert_Washington/index.html

Garry Wesley:
http://www.garrywesley.com/

Bob West:
http://albinjd.freeyellow.com/

ADDITIONAL RESOURCE WEBSITES:

Almost Elvis -John Paget:
http://www.almostelvis.com

American Superstars:
http://www.stratospherehotel.com/entertainment/ent.american_superstars.html

B & K Costumes-Butch Polston:
http://www.b-k-enterprises.com/

Collingwood Elvis Festival:
http://www.collingwoodelvisfestival.com

East-West Entertainment-Dan Lentino:
http://www.east-west-entertainment.com/

E-Impersonators-Big T/Kevin:
http://www.E-impersonators.com

Elvis-A-Rama-Chris Davidson:
http://www.elvisarama.com/

Elvis Collectors Gold-Andylon Lensen:
http://www.epgold.com/

Elvis Entertainers Network-Nance Fox:
http://elvisentertainersonline.com

Elvis Is In The Browser-David Sumpter:
http://www.elvisisinthebrowser.com/

Elvis International Magazine-Darwin Lamm:
http://www.ElvisTheMagazine.com

Elvis Explosion contest-Ronny Craig:
http://www.elvisexplosion.com

Elvis Presley Enterprises:
http://www.elvis.com/

Elvis Wedding Chapel-Oscar:Marino:
http://www.theelvischapel.com/

ETA Hall Of Fame-Jim E. Curtin:
http://elvisempire.com/eejim.html

ETA Wall Of Fame-Bill Bibo:
http://www.biboland.com

E-Tribute-Meikel Jungner:
http://go.to/meikel

Golden Voice-Kjel Elvis:
http://www.elvis.no/

IGCITA-Fil Jesse:
http://igcita.org

Images of the King contest-Jackie/Doc Franklin-Nance Fox-Ronny Craig:
http://imagesofthekingcontest.com/

Isle of Capri Casino contest:
http://www.theislecorp.com

Jump Suits Fit For A King:
http://www.jumpsuitsfitforaking.com/

Kathy Lee Creations:
Currently not available

King Tracks-Ralph:Foster:
http://www.kingtracks.com

Lady Luck Music/showcase-Joanna Johnson:
http://www.ladyluckmusic.com

Legends In Concert:
http://www.imperialpalace.com/legends_main page.html

Music Maestro:
http://www.musicmaestro.com/

Ottawa Elvis Fest:
http://www.ottawaelvisfest.com/

PEIA-Johnny Thompson:
http://www.elvisentertainers.com/

Potowatami Casino contest:
http://www.paysbig.com

Progressive Concerts-John Kondis:
http://www.legendsalive.com

Suite 101-Melody Sanders/June Moore:
http://www.suite101.com

The Entertainment Network-Bea Fogelman:
http://www.entertainment-network.org/

The ExSpence Account Showband:
http://www.exspenceaccount.com/

The Jordanaires-Ray Walker:
http://www.jordanaires.net/

World Wide Elvis-Paul Dowling:
http://www.worldwideelvis.com

Autographs and Memories

Elvis Lives **Order Form**

Order Information: Ship to (if different):

Name _____   _____

Address _____   _____

_____   _____

_____   _____

E-mail address"

_____

Quantity: $_____

@ $21.95 each $_____

$5.00 shipping and handling each $_____

Total amount enclosed: $_____

Send check or money order to:

Books by Pamela, Ltd.
P.O. Box 2091
La Crosse, WI 54602-2091

See us at www.pamelaltd.com for information regarding
volume discounts and other products.

Please allow up to 3 weeks for delivery. We accept major
credit cards ONLY on our website: **www.pamelaltd.com**

Thank you for your order.